TIME TO SA\

How to govern ourselves in the age of anti-politics

Henry Tam

P

First published in Great Britain in 2018 by

Policy Press
University of Bristol
1-9 Old Park Hill
Bristol BS2 8BB
UK
t: +44 (0)117 954 5940
e: pp-info@bristol.ac.uk
www.policypress.co.uk

North American office:
Policy Press
c/o The University of Chicago Press
1427 East 60th Street
Chicago, IL 60637, USA
t: +1 773 702 7700
f: +1 773-702-9756
e:sales@press.uchicago.edu
www.press.uchicago.edu

British Library Cataloguing in Publication Data
A catalogue record for this book is available from the British Library.

Library of Congress Cataloging-in-Publication Data
A catalog record for this book has been requested.

ISBN 978-1-4473-3824-6 (paperback)
ISBN 978-1-4473-3826-0 (ePub)
ISBN 978-1-4473-3827-7 (Kindle)
ISBN 978-1-4473-3825-3 (ePDF)

The right of Henry Tam to be identified as author of this work has been asserted by him in accordance with the 1988 Copyright, Designs and Patents Act.

The statements and opinions contained within this publication are solely those of the author and not of The University of Bristol or Policy Press. The University of Bristol and Policy Press disclaim responsibility for any injury to persons or property resulting from any material published in this publication.

Policy Press works to counter discrimination on grounds of gender, race, disability, age and sexuality.

Cover design by Hayes Design
Front cover: image kindly supplied by Hayes Design

Contents

Acknowledgements

The more time one spends on finding ways to deal with political challenges, the more indebted one becomes to the numerous colleagues who have helped over the years. With the ideas developed in this book, covering the related fields of deliberative democracy, participatory government, civic republicanism, communitarianism, and citizen politics, I have benefited from countless conversations, seminars, and exchanges of writings, involving so many leading social and political thinkers. Long may these stimulating interactions continue, though alas, they will be forthcoming no more with those who have left us – Bernard Crick, Bob Bellah, Philip Selznick, and Ben Barber, to name but four in the last decade.

I have also been most fortunate in having the chance to explore new thinking on democratic governance with others during my time as Visiting Professor of Lifelong Learning at Birkbeck College, London; Director of the Forum for Youth Participation & Democracy at the University of Cambridge; and the lead for classes on politics and government with institutions from the Workers Educational Association to the Civil Service College. For these opportunities, I remain grateful to John Annette, Diane Reay, Hilary Cremin, Phil Coward, Sharon Watson, and Sonny Leong.

One other major source of learning for me has been the experience in heading up a number of government policy divisions – in the Home Office, and in the Department for Communities & Local Government. As the Head of Civil Renewal in particular, with a key remit to improve the engagement with citizens and communities in reviewing and shaping public policies, I gained first-hand knowledge of the practical impact of a variety of ideas for democratic reforms. To my colleagues in Whitehall and the many community and local government partners I had the pleasure of working with, I want to extend my heartfelt thanks.

From exploring the initial concept of this book with Alison Shaw, to taking the project forward with the support of Emily Watt, Jamie Askew, Ruth Wallace, Susannah Emery and others at Policy Press, it was everything a writer could ask for from a top publishing team.

Finally, since any well-observed truth is worth repeating, let it be said, without Celia, none of this, not one word of it, would have been possible.

Introduction:
Democracy in distress

To govern or not to govern ourselves? That is the ultimate political question. Can we afford to risk having no government, thus allowing the unscrupulous to take advantage of others? Or dare we leave our fate in the hands of arbitrary rulers, when so many of them throughout history have turned out to be clueless, capricious, or simply self-serving?

Democracy is supposed to offer us a way out, so we can take charge of our own destiny and govern the institutions, neighbourhoods, cities, and countries to which we belong. Whether we make the decision on any given issue by ourselves directly, delegate it to a subgroup, or elect representatives to deal with it, democracy is meant to give us a framework to shape our own governance.

The symptoms

So why is despair in the air? Amid the widespread talk of our entering the age of anti-politics,[1] is the idea that we can govern ourselves actually a hopeless pipe dream? At one level, the symptoms are indeed worrying. Research published in 2016 found that over 70% of people born in the US and UK in the 1930s believed it was 'essential to live in a democracy', but barely 30% of those born in those countries in the 1980s share that view (Taub, 2016). Previously, from the early 20th century on, when universal suffrage was secured in most Western, developed

---

[1] In 2013, the Political Studies Association set up an 'Anti-Politics Specialist Group'. The sense of crisis has been growing since the turn of the century (Bromley et al, 2004; Leonard, 2014; Diamond & Plattner, 2015).

1

countries, citizens had looked to one or another established political party to take their concerns into account and put forward a programme that could command the majority support of the electorate so as to become the basis of how their country would be run until the next election. But from the late 1970s, four notable trends can be discerned.

First, the extent to which people identify with a major political party has steadily declined. In all European countries (bar Austria, Cyprus, and Finland), the average percentage of the electorate who belong to a political party is just 5%, with both France and the UK under 2% (Van Biezen et al, 2011; Keen & Audickas, 2016). In the US, more Americans now consider themselves 'independent' (42%) than either Democrats (29%) or Republicans (26%) (Jones, 2016). More and more people feel that their views are not necessarily reflected by the outlook of any single party, and they do not feel motivated to support them. While turnout fluctuates over time, the historic high of 84% in the 1950 UK elections is now a distant memory, and in both the UK and the US it is common for around a third of registered voters not to vote at all.[2]

Although it is often suggested that voting should be made easier, or even compulsory, the fact remains that many people do not vote because they have little understanding of the impact of different political parties winning power. Some think that the main parties are so similar that none is worth backing over any other, especially when perception is coloured by news reports about politicians behaving badly (from over-claiming expenses to receiving questionable donations). Even when the evidence would suggest there are important differences in many policy areas, they can be overlooked unless one side is associated with someone with a radical profile. For example, in the UK, although both Ed Miliband and Jeremy Corbyn had put forward policies that were significantly different from those offered by the Conservative Party (Bush, 2017), it was

---

[2] In the UK, voter turnout dropped below 70% after 1997 (even the 'exceptionally high' turnout for the 2017 snap election only reached 68.7%). In the US, turnout for presidential elections last exceeded 80% in 1876, but is now consistently below 65%.

Corbyn, with his rebel persona,[3] who was seen as someone offering a distinct agenda, and he won 40.2% of the votes in the 2017 election, compared with Miliband's 30.4% in 2015. In other cases, warnings about the dire consequences of one party winning are just not taken seriously enough. In the 2016 US elections, despite the Republicans' vow to repeal the Affordable Care Act which could deprive millions of US citizens of access to healthcare,[4] the turnout among Democrat voters actually dropped (Regan, 2016).

Secondly, political iconoclasts who reject the approaches adopted by traditional parties have been embraced by more and more people who see them as champions of the forgotten. For those who want to vent their anger at ethnic minorities and immigrants, the likes of Donald Trump and Nigel Farage help to validate their negative perception of 'others'. Other radical right-wing politicians across Europe have also won growing support by promoting Islamophobia. For those who want to break with the prevailing political traditions, they can turn to parties such as Syriza in Greece, which was formed to challenge the establishment, although soon after it won power and took charge of the country, it broke up into those who would now accommodate establishment policies and those who would leave to protest against them. Or they could embrace Emmanuel Macron's move to set up an entirely new 'neither right nor left' party, *En Marche!*, which in 2017 defeated the Front National in France in the presidential and parliamentary elections.[5]

Thirdly, the control of mainstream media outlets and manipulation of social media content have enabled the backers of certain political agendas to sow confusion and distortion among the wider public. For example, it was not uncommon for people who were badly affected by certain policies – for example, the 'Bedroom Tax', cuts to the police and the NHS, slowdown in

---

[3] Corbyn defied his own party's whip 428 times between 1997 and 2010.

[4] The Congressional Budget Office estimated that 22 million US citizens would lose healthcare coverage under plans put forward by the Republicans after they won control of Congress (Berman, 2017).

[5] But despite Macron's success in galvanising support for his new party, its victory in the 2017 parliamentary elections in France took place with a turnout of just 43%.

building affordable housing – to know little about how these policies should and could be reversed. When some politicians try to explain what should be done to tackle widespread problems, they are branded by their opponents as untrustworthy. When people are urged by some to listen to independent experts, they are told by others that experts are just as remote as professional politicians and cannot be trusted.

Nothing illustrates this quite as sharply as the UK's EU Referendum. If it had been conducted like a jury trial, those making the decision would have been left in no doubt that they must discard the false claims about how much the UK paid towards the EU; how comparably advantageous trade deals could be swiftly negotiated all around the world outside the EU; how vast sums would be injected into the NHS with a Brexit vote; how immigrants were harming the British economy;[6] or how no one would lose from the termination of EU funding. Many of those who voted for Brexit were incredulous when they learnt subsequently that there would be substantial negative consequences for their towns, businesses, and regions. Of course some of the politicians advocating Remain made unwarranted claims too. But the crux of the matter is that when expertise, rational analysis, and facts are jettisoned as part of the prevailing voting culture, then voting is a long way from the role it was meant to play in our collective self-governance.[7]

Fourthly, disengagement from established political parties has led to detachment from holistic democratic governance. Most key issues affecting society are interconnected, and how one is dealt with has implications for the prospects of others being properly addressed. Traditionally, political parties provide a platform for an overall programme to explore, prioritise, and

---

[6] Dean Hochlaf and Ben Franklin, authors of a report for the International Longevity Centre, used the Office for Budget Responsibility projections to calculate that by 2064-2065, the UK's GDP would be 11.4% (£625 billion) larger with high migration than it would be with low migration (Lusher, 2016).

[7] Trump was found to have made far more completely false or groundless claims than any other established national politicians, but his maverick persona enabled him to keep making them and attracting support (Kessler, 2016).

tackle these related issues. But when these were no longer looked to as the focal point for joined-up strategies, people's attention began to be drawn increasingly to single-issue campaigns (Lawson, 2013; Tam, 2015a, pp 167-172).

Since the 1970s, these have proliferated: fighting discrimination based on race, gender, disability, or sexuality; championing consumer rights or animal rights; opposing corporations in their drive to cut jobs and undermine worker unions; stopping pollution and protecting the environment; challenging the decisions to engage in military action across the globe (Vietnam, the Falkland Islands, Grenada, Iraq, Afghanistan); mobilising against state censorship and surveillance. Although these causes are important, their splintering into compartmentalised activities not only deprive them of the chance to realise their latent synergy in securing political power to advance them, but it has often pitted potential allies against each other and set them both back from achieving their goals (for example, Jews against Muslims; secularists against religious groups; trade unions against environmentalists).[8]

Misdiagnosis

Democracy, as a system that is meant to enable people to govern themselves, is clearly in trouble when people increasingly feel they have little control over their lives. In response, the aim of this book is to set out what everyone with governance responsibilities – politicians, senior public officials, community leaders, corporate decision makers, heads of organisations operating at the local, national, or global level – should learn about how democracy ought to work and apply the lessons to the policies and practices that fall within their respective sphere of influence. The prospects for collective self-governance depend on democratic dispositions and aptitudes being nurtured as widely as possible across all forms of human association.

For democratic governance to function effectively, there are a number of underlying vulnerabilities that need to be addressed.

---

[8] The rise of academic interest in intersectionality reflects the growing awareness of the inadequacy of focusing on single-issue problems.

But before we examine how democracy is to be saved from terminal decline, we should look at a number of misdiagnoses that can deflect remedial efforts towards dead-ends, or worse, counterproductive actions. We can group these broadly into five types.

First in line is the familiar complaint that democracy needs too many checks and balances to operate effectively. People are allegedly disillusioned because, unlike regimes abroad that pay scant attention to democratic niceties such as public scrutiny and respect for human rights, their government is held back from doing whatever it takes to protect them (from the usual suspects of criminals, rioters, terrorists, and assorted foreign threats). Essentially this approach views democracy not so much as a patient to be revitalised as a disease to be contained, if not quite eliminated.[9]

Next we have the assessment of democracy as a form of hypersensitivity to what the public want. Democratic responsiveness is regarded almost as an allergic reaction, leading to a constant interventionist tendency to generate endless laws and policies to chase votes. In order to subdue the 'nanny state' (or the proverbial 'big government'), it is claimed that people must take back control themselves and regain their freedom by shrinking government continuously. In practice, market libertarians just want corporations to be left alone, while communal anarchists insist individuals must be trusted to sort problems out by themselves. If people disagree with what certain corporations are up to, or about what are destabilising their communities, no governing body would arbitrate, let alone intervene.

The third diagnosis regards the problem as a kind of political hypochondria. The persistent worry with democracy not being robust enough to bring people together to work out what to do to secure their common good is treated as an unhealthy obsession. Diverse thinkers such as Schumpeter (1976), Dahl (1989), and Fukuyama (1992) have all suggested that so long

---

[9] Witness the surge of anti-human rights stances in political campaigns: Donald Trump's attack on the Geneva Convention as the problem during his successful bid to be the Republican presidential candidate, and Theresa May's stance when she was home secretary on pulling the UK out of the European Convention on Human Rights.

as there are free elections, rival parties, and multiple centres of power we should not be so anxious about improving such arrangements to make them more truly democratic. All three of them believe that we should accept what we have, and it would be misguided to press for more extensive forms of self-governance lest we end up with something much worse than the democratic system that is in operation.[10]

Our next misdiagnosis regards democracy as a malignant growth that has been exported unsuccessfully as part of the West's imperialist adventurism. Every political problem in Asia, Africa, South America, and the Middle East is blamed on attempts to introduce democracy. By contrast, the economic success stories attributed to countries such as Singapore and China are tied to authoritarian aspects of their governance. Although events like the dramatic growth of China's GDP or the disillusionment following the Arab Spring uprisings may lend superficial credence to this, it overlooks the many problems that arise when those who govern cannot be held to account by the governed. Whatever factors lead to the ebb and flow of regional stability, or the rise and fall of economic growth, it is not what some people may claim to do in the name of democracy,[11] but the protection from arbitrary rule that genuine democratic accountability secures which should be the relevant measure. Across the world, where democratic governance is more developed, not merely declared as being in place, the people are less at risk of having their interests brushed aside.[12]

Finally, we come to one of the oldest health warnings against democracy. It is allegedly incurable due to its reliance on what is in short supply: the intelligence and civic-mindedness of ordinary people. Since the 'masses' are deemed ill-informed and easily manipulated, opening up any form of governance to them is to risk mishaps at best and disasters at worst. We are told then that

---

[10] Schumpeter thought societies would vote for socialism; Fukuyama believed the convergence would be towards a fairly homogeneous liberal kind of society; and Dahl was at times too sanguine that diverse power centres would keep oppression at bay.

[11] For example, the invasion of Iraq under George W. Bush.

[12] The annual Democracy Index provides a useful guide (Economist Intelligence Unit, 2016).

democracy is inherently flawed and the power to govern should rest with a suitable elite. But if that is the case, why should anyone believe that the elite who will hold power exclusively will be intelligent and civic-minded enough? And without democratic arrangements in place, how can people stand together to check the unwise and self-serving actions of the ruling elite, short of organising a large-scale uprising?

The key to political health

When people complain that democracy holds back those in power from doing what should be done, or when others criticise democracy for opening the floodgates for those with governing authority to do too much, do they suppose that there is a Goldilocks line which marks out exactly what governments should do – no more, and no less? Or are they just advocating changes that would suit themselves? How are such conflicts to be resolved? And when non-Western critics dismiss democracy as unacceptable simply because it is Western, why then do they embrace Western medicine, engineering, information technology, and so on? As for the gulf between those who reject democracy as fundamentally flawed in having to rely on the 'unreliable masses', and those who assure us that democracy in its prevailing form is as good as it gets, can it not be bridged with what our political experience has actually taught us?

The arrangements for democratic governance that have developed following the American and French revolutions at the end of the 18th century do not adhere to a single blueprint. Instead, throughout the 19th and 20th centuries, there were constant reforms, adjustments, and experimentation in different countries, at different levels of society, leading to a vastly diverse range of systems and procedures. It may be tempting to offer a cure-all prescription with a new kind of constitution, a new electoral process, or a complete renewal of our civic spirit through education and inspirational leadership. But while each of these suggestions may have a role to play, none of them by itself gives us the whole picture. How well we manage to govern ourselves involves a multitude of factors. We need to take a holistic approach to improving our political health so that what is made better in one area is not undermined by something else that has been neglected.

In order to reconnect debates about the future of democracy with why and how it has been seeking to improve itself in the past, we will in this book explore what objectives proponents of democratic governance have sought to achieve, how they have responded to the obstacles encountered, and what challenges remained each time the latest struggle for progress was over. From the ideas of these civic-communitarian reformists, we can develop a comprehensive conception of how democracy is to be improved. Progress will be neither smooth nor certain. History is punctuated by progressive efforts to bring us closer together to rule ourselves, and regressive countermoves by some to divide and rule over us.

In Chapter One, we will look at how past endeavours to govern human interactions led to challenges that democratic ideas and practices evolved to meet. In Chapter Two, we will consider how the development towards universal adult suffrage from the late 19th to the early 20th century engendered, in the decades that followed, diverse intellectual currents preoccupied with democratic renewal. A core theme to emerge is the need to keep watch on the extent to which democracy is being truly advanced, and how its shortfalls should be rectified.

By learning from the insights of past thinkers and the findings of more recent civic experiments, such as innovations in deliberative engagement around the world and the wide range of action learning promoted by the UK government's Civil Renewal Programme (2003-2010),[13] we get a better understanding of nine key factors for sustaining our political health:

- Shared mission
- Mutual respect
- Coherent membership
- Collaborative learning

---

[13] I was in charge of the programme as the government's Head of Civil Renewal in the Home Office, and later in the Department for Communities and Local Government (Tam, 2015b). More about the programme will be covered by the book, *Whose Government is it? The renewal of state-citizen cooperation* (Tam, forthcoming).

- Critical re-examination
- Responsible communication
- Participatory decision making
- Civic parity
- Public accountability

After giving an outline of how these nine factors relate to the improvement of democratic governance, we will explore each of them in detail in Chapters Three to Eleven. In each chapter, we will explain why they are needed, how to guard against misinterpretations, and what recommendations we should consider for advancing them. The lessons we draw from our examination can then be applied not only to the governance of society at the national level, but also to governance at the subnational and transnational level, and to institutions that are independent from the state but must comply with statutory requirements and government policies.

After setting out in total 40 recommended improvements for reviving democracy, we will conclude by reflecting on the prospects for our learning to govern ourselves more effectively. In an age when rapid technological innovations are the norm, it is not surprising that many feel that governance arrangements should also be swiftly replaced. But mere change is not synonymous with better outcomes. Not only are many suggestions for 'new' ways to run our lives little more than a return to a variety of old approaches that have failed us in the past, the future of human coexistence is too important for our governance to be thrown into turmoil just to see what may turn up. If we are serious about improving the health of our body politic, we must recognise that the prescription of democracy has too often been administered in a haphazard manner. Only by identifying and clarifying the remedies that will enable us to govern ourselves well can the proper treatment of our political ills commence.

PART ONE

Has democracy a future?

ONE

Why we need democracy

Civic amnesia has left too many people thinking democracy is something they can do without. Even with the relatively high turnout for the snap 2017 election in the UK, 15% of those entitled to be a registered voter did not register; of those who were registered to vote, nearly 32% did not turn out to vote; which means that across the UK, 42% of those who could have had a vote stayed away from the ballot box.[1]

If we are to revive democratic governance, we need to make sure everyone understands its critical role in solving problems inescapably rooted in human coexistence. Whenever a group of people, stationed across however large or small an area, sense that the rules and arrangements they have been living by are not securing for them the support and stability they are counting on, discontent will spread. For centuries, regimes across the world thought that the answer rested with holding firm to one or another of what may be termed the 'four classic governance strategies'. Even now, detractors of democracy are disposed to picking one out of these as their favoured alternative to collective self-governance. By examining the nature of these strategies, and how they generate challenges that only democracy can meet, we can begin to set out anew the case for deliberative citizens' rule.

For any group of people to be governed to their satisfaction, at least three conditions have to be met. First, the arrangements

---

should secure sufficient togetherness that the group is not at risk of polarising into irreconcilable enemies or breaking up completely. Secondly, there needs to be an accepted source of objectivity in resolving conflicting judgements so there are real prospects of agreement being reached as to what members of the group should accept as correct. Thirdly, power balance is required to prevent any individual or some subgroup from overriding the concerns of others and trampling on those who cannot stand up for themselves. We will look at how each of the four classic strategies deals with these requirements.

Four classic governance strategies

Long before democracy became widely adopted, four basic strategies for governing human interactions were generally in use. When people today suggest that democracy is more of a hindrance than a help to how society should be organised, implicitly or explicitly it is supposed that some variant of one or another or these four strategies would do a better job. Although they have been deployed in different parts of the world, they were first articulated formally in the classic texts of a country with the oldest tradition in political analysis. That country was China. And it happened during a prolonged period of civil disintegration.

After the Zhou Dynasty established itself in China around 1046 BC, scholars and administrators under the new regime were preoccupied with documenting what led to the decline and fall of the previous Shang Dynasty (which had lasted around 700 years), and what was being done by the new political masters to secure greater longevity for their rule. But within 300 years, the Zhou regime itself was already coming under severe pressures that were undermining its hold over its territories. Lords and princelings carved out their own states and referred to themselves as 'kings'. By the dawn of the 5th century BC, over a hundred years before Plato's *Republic* was written, the world's first critical governance debate was in full swing.

The hierarchical strategy, developed by Confucius and his followers, was the first to be set out (Yao, 2000). It aims to hold society together by convincing people that each of them has a designated role to play. The roles are different and while the subordinates should obey and serve as required, those with higher responsibilities should command and care for those under their jurisdiction. As to how those roles are defined and what actions people are expected to carry out, agreement is to be reached with reference to past traditions. And power balance is to be maintained by the acceptance of the supremacy of those higher up in the hierarchy, and unanimous rejection of any move to depart from the established power relations.

While the Confucians used the writings attributed to Confucius and their own commentaries as the definitive basis for interpreting the wisdom of past traditions, the hierarchical strategy can be deployed with other interpretations of any venerated tradition. For example, under theocratic regimes, from medieval Europe to contemporary Islamic countries, the tradition in question would involve the invocation of 'God' at the apex of the hierarchy. Edmund Burke spoke for the conservative-minded when he criticised radicals who sought to depart from the tradition of how Britain had been governed. And since the hierarchy rests on an interpretation of what some perceived tradition enjoins, others from Plato to Leo Strauss have even argued that the 'tradition' in question can be based on some useful myth that will lead people into accepting their assigned role in life (Drury, 2005). A common feature of the hierarchical strategy is therefore a web of ritual practices, conventional ceremonies, and reinforced expectations of how people should behave in the presence of their superiors/inferiors as traditionally conceived.

In sharp contrast, the minimalist strategy was not keen on hierarchical controls at all. It was put forward by Daoist thinkers such as Laozi, who promoted the idea of light-touch governance, whereby those entrusted with watching over groups would do as little as possible so individuals could flourish without intervention from others (Cleary, 1993). Zhuang Zi took this even further and celebrated the prospect of total anarchic abandon where everyone would be able to act as they pleased. Togetherness, for them, is not to be organised from above, but best left to human beings' natural sociability to generate from below. Without any artificial doctrines to force beliefs on the populace, people will either agree or agree to disagree in the light of their experiences. As for the danger of power imbalance, that is to be overcome by everyone appreciating that it is wiser to let go of power than to seek it.

Aside from the Daoists, the Epicureans later offered similar advice – human collaboration was best kept away from large collective institutions, and left instead to individuals to conduct as they saw fit. The same thinking surfaces in the anarchist ideas of William Godwin and Pierre-Joseph Proudhon, and the market libertarianism of Herbert Spencer and Robert Nozick. Although they may differ over how much residual authority is tolerable, or whether communal spirit or business deals will suffice in holding off exploitation and discontent, they all favour the minimalist strategy because they are far more concerned with the problems that can be caused by the misuse of a central power than the difficulties that may persist without the proper application of such power.

The third classic strategy was championed by Mo Zi, respected by his contemporaries as the chief rival of Confucius, but largely forgotten during more recent times, even in China (Mei, 1929). Building on his ideas, the Mohists developed the egalitarian strategy for governance, which is focused on how to sustain mutually supportive human relations where people will not be asked to contribute anything they do not expect others to contribute similarly in return. The sense of fairness, or the golden rule of reciprocity enshrined in every civilisation, will unite people in keeping at bay any attempt to sacrifice the wellbeing of some of them for the benefit of a few. When it comes to resolving differences about how unequal conditions and treatment are to be curtailed, the Mohists maintained that people could refer to past records, the testimony of anyone with the relevant experience, and the eventual outcomes of present initiatives to ascertain what would or would not work. As for the threat of power imbalance, they came up with the distinctive approach of organising themselves as a vanguard force that would defend any town or state from an invading army. For example, when a militant lord refused to listen to Mo Zi's advice to refrain from attacking a neighbouring town, Mo Zi's followers were sent to that town and swiftly fortified it for the ensuing battle.

Philosophers from Rousseau to Marx share an affinity with the Mohists in targeting the rise of divisive inequalities for their impact on the breaking down of human cooperation. They too reject any minimalist stance that idealistically (or cynically in some cases) supposes all will somehow turn out fine when people are left to their own devices. It is no coincidence that the Mohists and the followers of Rousseau and Marx resorted to the establishment of a strong counterforce in the hope of creating and maintaining more equal conditions. In their respective attempts to rectify the unfair advantages and exploitative manoeuvres of the aggressive kings and princelings of late Zhou Dynasty China, the aristocrats of France's *Ancien Régime*, and unrelenting capitalists across the world, they all concluded that they needed a bulldozer to bring about a level playing field. But if the counterforce unleashed by the egalitarian strategy is too weak, one could end up being wiped out like the Mohists;[2] if it's too strong, it either provokes a reaction to bring it down, as the fate of the Jacobins bore witness, or it ushers in other forms of oppressive inequality resembling those that prevailed through the Soviet Union's seven decades. Getting it just right remains perennially elusive.

We then come to the disciplinarian strategy, summed up by Han Feizi and the Legalists, around the time the ruler of Qin was about to defeat all other rival states in China and impose a unified regime (Watson, 1996). Faced with dissent and chaos, the Qin emperor was advised by the Legalists to set out clearly what was expected from his subjects, codify these as strict legal requirements, and enforce them rigorously. Infamously, and ominously, the disciplinary tools included the burning of books not approved by the state and the burying alive of scholars who were critical of the laws. Togetherness was imposed in accordance with state laws. There would be no room for disagreement with what had been laid out in the rules and regulations, and interpretations of their applications would rest with those given the authority to do so by the state. Stability of the power structure

---

[2]   The Mohists' readiness to defend any city or state from attack might be noble, but too many were killed in battle, and by around 100 BC, 300 years after Mo Zi's death, the Mohist School had virtually disappeared.

would be guaranteed by the undisputed supremacy of the ruler, and no one would dare disrupt the social, economic, and political arrangements the ruler had proclaimed.

The leading Legalist, Han Feizi, died in 233 BC, and 1,884 years later his disciplinarian strategy found new expression in Thomas Hobbes' *Leviathan*. The Hobbesian formulation is seductively simple: without a powerful enough authority to set out and enforce strict rules, there will be internecine conflicts and people's lives will end up 'brutish, nasty and short'. A flipside of this is that only a strong, unquestioned leader can deliver the total unity that will secure greater success and glory for the people. That in essence was the message from the fascist philosopher Giovanni Gentile. The nightmare of the English Civil War drove Hobbes into the arms (in both senses) of an absolute ruler. The promise of national greatness enticed Gentile into collaborating with Mussolini. And the 9/11 attack in the US swung the country behind a government that castigated as unpatriotic any opposition to its invasion of foreign countries, surveillance of its own citizens, and torture of suspects.

These four governance strategies have been adopted by countless regimes ruling over localities and corporations, as well as kingdoms and empires. It is understandable why, under certain circumstances, people may deem it appropriate, even necessary, to have a well-preserved hierarchy, more freedom to live and let live, firm curtailment of inequalities, or strictly enforced discipline to tackle imminent dangers. But regimes that define themselves by a single strategy lack adaptability. Not being informed by other factors, they cannot refer to wider criteria to check what variations should be adopted even within their own preferred strategy.[3]

For example, when should any hierarchy be considered as having become so vast or rigid that it must be loosened? What

---

[3] Of the four classic strategies, the Mohist Egalitarian approach was potentially the one most receptive to being developed into the meta-strategy of democracy. The notion that everyone should be respected equally fitted well with the process of democratisation. When Chinese reformists in the early 20th century promoted the adoption of democracy, they were generally sympathetic to Mohist ideas, but critical of Confucian, Daoist, and Legalist doctrines.

are the warning signs for detecting that minimising intervention has gone too far? What if the arrangements to reduce one type of inequality is exacerbating other inequalities that can lead to even worse outcomes? How drastically must the disciplinarian cure be pulled back when it appears to be hurting the patients more than the feared ailment of insecurity?

To answer these questions responsively, we need a meta-strategy to help us navigate our way forward without being tied exclusively to one or another of the four archetypal governance strategies. This is where democracy comes in. It functions not as a replacement for the other approaches we have looked at, but as a guide to applying them in the light of changing circumstances, and revising them with reference to all relevant factors, not just the dispositional preferences of those in charge.

Democracy as a meta-strategy

History has shown that leaving one individual (a family, a clique, a party) to govern with a fixed strategy, or with the option of changing strategies at will, is high risk in the short term, and wholly unreliable in the long term. The fewer people there are who can determine what will happen to everyone else without having to give due consideration to what others have to say, the more likely those few will think only of their own interests, overlook errors that others may have spotted, or persist with harmful policies simply because no one can hold them to account. The antidote is to share power so that everyone affected by governance decisions can play a part in shaping those decisions.

The Athenian experiment in democratic decision making, while it remained in place for barely two centuries,[4] had a lasting effect in leaving us with two vital lessons. First, it demonstrated that enabling the governed to share their views and concerns in shaping the governing process could be highly beneficial in uniting people to achieve far more than they could otherwise. The cultural, intellectual, and economic flourishing of Athens

---

[4] Cleisthenes' reforms came into effect from around 510 BC, and Athens' democratic system was finally terminated by the Macedonians in 322 BC.

during its democratic heyday testifies to the success of the experiment. However, the second lesson passed down to us warns against complacency in thinking the experimentation can stop. The broad aspiration to involve the governed in their own governing does not bring with it a detailed blueprint, and the ancient Athenians' failure to keep testing what further alterations were required to stay true to that aspiration led to their downfall.

As Athens became more prosperous, the wealthier citizens not only continued to be content that a section of their fellow residents was confined to the class of slaves, they were also increasingly relaxed about the poorer members of society becoming less influential as the gulf widened between top and bottom. In parallel with its solidarity weakening internally, Athens' relationship with its neighbours was also deteriorating as it treated them with the kind of tyrannical arrogance it had declared intolerable within Athens itself. By the time Athens was tangled up in one battle after another with other Greek states or with Persia, its limited form of democracy was no longer helping it find the right direction. For example, in 411 BC a group of oligarchs managed to 'persuade' the Athenian Assembly into voting to abandon the city's democratic system.[5]

It was not until the 13th century that democratic experimentation re-emerged as a means of guiding adaptive governance. In 1291, three Swiss cantons joined forces to strengthen their collective defence in the uncertain times following the death of the King of the Romans, Rudolph of Habsburg. To convince the people of each canton that they would not be ruled according to some arbitrarily adopted strategy, a commitment was given to put all major issues to a direct vote by the people. And in 1294, the first *Landsgemeinde* – cantonal assembly – took place, establishing a tradition of direct democracy that continues to this day.

A political experiment with even greater long-term impact was instigated by Simon De Montfort when in 1265 he summoned the first democratic parliament in England. His aim was to

---

[5] It involved bribery, intimidation, and assassination of prominent democratic leaders. Eight years later, democratic rule was restored, but the decline of Athenian democracy could not by then be reversed.

involve the people through their own representatives in putting a permanent end to arbitrary rule by the monarch. Henry III, like his father John before him, had turned his back on the terms of Magna Carta, sealed only 50 years before in 1215. De Montfort believed that he could challenge the king without being accused of trying to become an arbitrary ruler himself, if he shifted the power base of national governance to an elected parliament. And he might well have halted monarchical oppression if only he had had sufficient time to consolidate his innovative system of democratic rule before the king's army caught up with him in his final battle.

Despite De Montfort's death, the democratic experiment would go on to gain wider support in England. As a meta-strategy capable of selecting different strategies for changing conditions, it would surpass any reliance on a single individual or exclusive group of individuals. Neither the city-state of Athens nor the federated cantons of Switzerland had found all the answers, but their readiness to enable more people to play a meaningful part in shaping how they would be governed improved their chances of being governed well. The key was to keep learning about what could be done better with more inclusive arrangements and wider support.

A turning point came when, four centuries after Henry III crushed the De Montfort experiment, Charles I tried to tell Parliament that he alone had the ultimate power to rule. But Parliament, now with broader democratic backing, turned the tables on the king. Charles was defeated, tried for treason, and executed. The English Revolution (1642-1651) and its aftermath encapsulated why the meta-strategy of democracy would come to be seen as preferable to getting stuck with any single governance strategy.

To begin with, Charles I has shown how the hierarchical strategy could be taken too far when he pushed forward policies irrespective of vocal objections simply because he was by tradition the supreme head of the country. During the battle to end his rule, the Levellers proposed that Parliament should take over the ruling powers but only on the basis of every adult (male) being given a vote to elect those who would sit in the legislature. But their advocacy for greater democratisation was rejected by Cromwell, who feared that it would lead to the levelling of economic as well as political status. Around that time, the Diggers, or True Levellers as they preferred to call themselves, did advance an egalitarian strategy that they implemented by proclaiming land as belonging equally to all. After Cromwell and his supporters halted the activities of the Levellers and True Levellers alike, he took charge as the Protector, and revealed just what a disciplinarian strategy could mean through his personal rule without Parliament and his puritanical demands on people's everyday life. Following Cromwell's death, Charles II regained the throne and his minimalist strategy of live and let live seemed tolerable until it became clear it might let his brother, James, succeed him as a Catholic monarch. What happened next was a pivotal moment in the development of democratic governance.

With the so-called Glorious Revolution of 1688, powerful members in Parliament hatched a deal with William of Orange, Stadtholder of the Dutch Republic, and husband of James II's daughter Mary. William would invade England with his army, force James II to give up his throne, and he and Mary would then rule the country on terms set out by Parliament to ensure that no one could henceforth pursue any governance strategy without discussing it with and getting the support of the representatives elected by the people. The democratic arrangements put in place were not to displace all previous strategies, but to steer their future adoption and revision in accordance with those who would be governed by them.

From that moment on, the problem of governance acquired a meta-strategic dimension. The key question is how to ensure that those who are being governed can experiment with different governing strategies over time and amend their choices in the light of subsequent experiences. The 1689 Bill of Rights, which helped define the framework of how views should be sought from whom on what policy matters, became an inspiration to English settlers in the American colonies who were beginning to question their own governance, and to reformists in France looking to match their country's chief rival in attaining more effective political management. In its centenary year of 1789, the first elected president of the United States of America took office after the former colonists had thrown off British rule, while revolution broke out in France that would lead to all male adults being granted the right to vote without any property requirement. The Levellers' case for strengthening democracy, previously ignored, was far from forgotten.

Nine challenges for democratic governance

Throughout the 19th century, America, France, and Britain led the way in advancing democratic governance and became overall more successful compared with other countries. The right to vote was guaranteed to ever more previously excluded groups. Organisations with power, state controlled or privately run, would be limited by law as to how they could use their power over the people affected by their decisions. Education was extended to enable a growing number of people to understand what was going on around them. During the 20th century, disciplinarian regimes in Italy, Germany, and Japan embarked on an aggressive, anti-democratic path, but those countries only became more stable and prosperous after they embraced democracy themselves. Meanwhile, Scandinavian nations, which applied the democratic approach to governance even more extensively than the US, the UK, and France came to feature regularly at the top of global assessments of good places to live.[6] On every continent, democratic arrangements became more prevalent as the new millennium approached.

But in the early 21st century, questions are increasingly raised about whether democracy has run its course. From the symptoms we looked at in the Introduction, there are indisputable strains in contemporary governance. However, it is just as clear that there is no turning back from the meta-strategic approach of democracy. This does not mean that the democratic arrangements in place at any given time should be treated as a take-it-or-leave-it package. Democratic experimentation by its very nature is about providing a non-violent platform for trying out different ways to enable people to steer their own governance. There are inevitably difficulties to overcome, and so long as the focus is kept on finding effective responses to them, improvements are possible.

[6] See, for example, the UN's Human Development Index.

Before we look in the next chapter at how since the late 19th/early 20th century a succession of social and political thinkers with a shared civic-communitarian perspective have put forward ideas for improving democracy, let us identify the key problems we are facing. These can be set out with reference to the three conditions for effective governance we outlined before: togetherness; objectivity; and power balance.

We will take togetherness first as no attempt to govern any social entity can be deemed successful if it results in the constituent parts splintering in conflicting directions. In relation to democratic governance, there are three notable challenges:

1 Loss of common objectives

One of the biggest mistakes made by Western powers in managing the transition of their former colonies was to impose an electoral system on people who were arbitrarily brought together by boundaries which took no account of their diverse backgrounds and traditions.[7] Without cultivating an identifiable set of common objectives, the electoral mechanism merely drove rival factions to vote for their 'own' and cast doubt on the legitimacy of the other side. Ironically, the religions and customs that once defined individual Western countries have themselves ceased to have a monolithic hold on them. To paraphrase Dostoevsky, when the 'god' of a unifying tradition is dead, people are beginning to wonder if anything goes. Polarising views on what really matters are now increasingly threatening to shrink the common ground on which democratic politics depends. The UK's Brexit vote, for example, left the country more divided than ever.

---

[7] From the rushed partition of India and Pakistan, to the imposition of national boundaries in Africa and the Middle East, based on previous colonial arrangements set up by France and Britain, polarisation of interests was almost cemented into the foundation of those countries.

2 Support for discriminatory behaviour

Societies are held together by a nexus of rewards and penalties reinforcing helpful actions and deterring harmful behaviour. But the more rewards and penalties are dished out in a discriminatory manner, the less confident will people be that their readiness to support others will be reciprocated by those who are negatively predisposed towards them. From the mid-19th century to the late 20th century, both the law and general customs moved in the direction of curbing discrimination. The electoral franchise was expanded until every adult was given the vote. Prejudices expressed by the state, private businesses, or individuals were increasingly subject to legal restraint. But from the 1990s on, those who had for a long time been unhappy about having to be tolerant and inclusive began to attack 'political correctness'. Sensitivity towards vulnerable groups and concerns about verbal abuse of minorities, for example, became targets of the media and provocative political campaigns. After the 9/11 attacks in 2001, intolerance went beyond words to the ill-treatment of people on the grounds of geography, professed religion, and cultural background. The 'War on Terror' paved the way for Islamophobia, which fuelled far right extremism and the consequent rise of anti-Semitism and anti-migrant hostility. In the US, torture of Middle Eastern suspects came to be sanctioned by presidential edicts under George W. Bush; and the denigration of Mexican migrants as rapists became a part of Trump's campaign platform in his successful bid to become US president. And in the UK, the Conservative government openly proclaimed its intention to abolish the Human Rights Act;[8] and dismissed as 'offensive' the UN report criticising its discriminatory policies towards disabled people (Sims, 2016).

---

[8] Ironically it was a UK Conservative MP and jurist, David Maxwell-Fyfe, who helped to draft the European Convention on Human Rights, which in turn provided the basis for the UK's own Human Rights Act.

3 Uncertainty over belonging

People's readiness to cooperate with others in working out joint solutions is inseparable from their sense of belonging to something that binds them together. Globalisation, alas, has not led to everyone feeling they are an integral part of a world community (Walby, 2009). Many have ended up feeling they do not belong anywhere at all. Transnational corporations may make a lot of money out of ordinary people, but ordinary people count for little in their eyes except as variables on the balance sheet. Meanwhile, those who are moving up in the world seem to be able to escape to some paradise abroad, while foreigners who will take local jobs for less pay appear to 'overrun' every local neighbourhood. Beneath the resentment against other people's freedom to move around (especially when one has nowhere to go oneself), there is the deeper anxiety that one is increasingly alone in a globalised society, and no promise of collective action will get one back to the imaginary golden age that flourished not so long ago.

The next set of issues revolves around objectivity, since without it there can be no non-arbitrary way of resolving contested claims about what people ought to believe. These take us to three further challenges:

4 The cult of scepticism

Democratic governance is dependent on people finding out what would work best for them. Education has always been vital in enabling people to learn about how to enrich their own understanding and distinguish credible expertise from unsubstantiated claims. Unfortunately, in recent decades academic doubt under the guise of postmodernism has fused with the fetishisation of 'inner belief' in popular culture to promote a solipsistic mindset (Kumar, 1996). When people think they alone can establish what is to be believed, irrespective of the findings by others who have investigated the matter much more thoroughly, we have a growing cult of scepticism, proudly dismissing objectively validated claims in favour of nothing more than '*I* am not convinced'. One's 'inner' mind does not have to engage with rational arguments or verifiable evidence, because everything can be doubted except one's own judgement. The path to objective deliberations thus faces a major roadblock. Examples from the MMR vaccine scare to widespread climate change denial show that this problem can often be compounded by scoundrels seeking to take advantage of suspended rationality and manipulate public beliefs for their own gains.

5 Yearning for the unquestionable

While many have come to take pride in disbelieving what others, backed by a consensus of experts, may believe, there are also a lot of people who are fed up with there not being enough certainty in their lives. With ever faster and more complex changes around them, they yearn for doctrines and declarations that they can hang on to no matter what else is said. So if teaching creationism in schools, declaring same-sex marriage immoral, or denouncing multiculturalism gives them a sense that there is still some form of unquestionable guidance they can live by, they will stand by such guidance regardless of how it will get in the way of finding mutually acceptable ways to coexist with others in society. The resurgence of fundamentalist craving for absolute certainty is constantly raising more barriers to an objective meeting of minds.[9]

6 Misinformation flow

Without the free flow of information that makes objective discussions possible, democratic deliberations cannot hope to guide collective actions intelligently. For a long time, the main issue was simply to secure freedom of the press so government and businesses cannot stop people knowing what they are really up to. But the rapid advancement of information technology has

---

[9] It is not just confined to fundamentalists who profess faith in Christianity, Islam, Judaism, or Hinduism, but among self-proclaimed Buddhists who are quite prepared to use violence against those they view as enemies (for example in Myanmar and Sri Lanka), and race-myth supremacists are not shy of resorting to intimidation or force.

created many more opportunities to turn things on their head (Morozov, 2011). 'Paper' trails have been replaced by encrypted ones and zeroes in cyberspace. Both government institutions and large corporations have at their disposal a growing arsenal to amass information about where we go, what we do, and what we say. At the same time, in the name of national security or commercial confidentiality, the public is denied access to information about what is going on behind doors that are firmly closed to them. The demand for freedom of communication is then all too often diverted to support abusive and hate speech, or flagrant acts of media irresponsibility in spreading misleading stories.[10] Over time, people are either overloaded with distorted views or left not knowing what to believe.

Finally, we turn our attention to power balance, an essential ingredient of societal cooperation, which plays a key role in ensuring none is ever too strong to intimidate others into submission, and all can count on sufficient support in having their interests taken into account. This brings us to the last three of the nine underlying challenges to democratic governance:

7 The risk of personality contest

Instead of allowing power to be seized by force or bought by wealth, democratic governance is premised on the pooling of individual assessments of the arguments put forward by aspiring representatives. By keeping any undue external influence at bay, choices for policies and candidates would then be made on their actual merits. But the perceived personality of a politician may have a strong influence on how people vote, though it may not be a good reflection of whether that person deserves public support at all. Athenian democracy had to face this problem from the beginning. In 482 BC, for example, Aristides the Just proposed that the silver found in a colony should be shared out among all Athenians, but others were not so keen and proposed to have him ostracised and removed from Athens. Before the

---

[10] See, for example, how the dominant forces in the UK media distort coverage of key political issues (Watson & Hickman, 2012; Ponsford, 2017).

vote, one person who did not know Aristides by sight told him that he was voting to ostracise Aristides simply because he was fed up with hearing him being lauded as 'Just'. In 1848, Louis Napoleon made the most of his relation to his uncle, Napoleon Bonaparte, to present himself as the saviour of France. He won the vote to become president of France's Second Republic, and followed that up three years later with a plebiscite victory that made him emperor for life. In 1933, Adolf Hitler led the Nazi Party to win the largest share of the popular vote and used the powers he gained to put an end to democracy. And demagogues whose personalities appeal to large enough numbers among the voting public continue to pose a threat to democratic politics, in terms of how they can dismantle democratic arrangements when they do win power, and the conundrum of how democracy can ever be protected from them without ceasing to be democratic.[11]

8 Widening inequalities

One of the most notable observations by Alexis de Tocqueville (1981) on democracy in America in the early 19th century was the sense of equality that prevailed. There was no glaring gap between the rich and the rest, and citizens exchanged views about their towns or their country with neither condescension nor diffidence on display. But de Tocqueville could not be so sanguine about the rest of the world. And by late 19th century socioeconomic inequalities were rapidly increasing in America too. Although between the 1920s and the 1970s income inequalities fell to an all-time low in the UK and the US, since Thatcher and Reagan came to power (in 1979 and 1981 respectively), the gap has been on the rise again back towards

---

[11] In the US, the Trump presidency became a test case of whether there were enough constitutional checks and balance to rein in arbitrary rule.

the levels in the early 20th century.[12] Now not only have pay differentials continued to widen between a small minority in the financial sector and everyone else, but many of the public mechanisms to create a more level civic playing field – such as free education, adequate social security, legal aid – have been cut back after billions of pounds and dollars were spent to bail out those in the financial sector. The democratic aspiration of all citizens being treated as equals is supplanted by the plutocratic tendency that enables the rich to live longer, get better education for their children, exploit tax loopholes, win court cases that the poor would almost certainly lose, sue governments, and buy enough influence to change laws to suit them.

9 The deregulation mantra

A key development of late 19th century politics flows from the recognition that once the danger of an overbearing state has been nullified by democratic controls, the state should be steered towards dealing with other institutions that may be too powerful and liable to mistreat people under their control. Factories, prisons, mental asylums, monopoly suppliers, plantation owners, private lenders, among others, needed to be regulated so they were less likely to abuse their power. But by the late 20th century, the rise of what has been termed the New Right had resurrected the pre-18th century image of the domineering ruler and warned that 'big government' must be shrunk to preserve 'freedom' (Marquand, 2004). Scrutiny of public bodies is deplored as bureaucracy. Regulation of private organisations is castigated as red tape. Yet when any of these institutions acts without due probity or consideration, it is taken as a further illustration of the state being incapable of overseeing

---

[12] In the UK, the top 0.1% had over 11% of the gross national income in 1913. It declined to just above 1% in 1978, then from 1979 on it rose again unremittingly to around 6% in 2009. The top 10% had around 39% of the gross national income in 1919. And after a similar drop in the years leading to 1978 (staying below 30% for much of the 1960s and 1970s), it rose after 1979 and had by 2011 reached 39% again (Jenkins, 2015, Figure 7.6).

what is beyond its competence.[13] In their determination to block the Obama presidency with legislative inertia, for example, the Republican-dominated Congress dedicated itself each year during Obama's second term (2013-2016) to become the most unproductive Congress ever.[14] When disillusioned voters feel that the government is not responding to their concerns, they are told that the problem is that the government is too big to be responsive. And the deregulation mantra continues unabated.

The nine challenges to democratic governance outlined above would suggest that the currents of anti-politics have never run far below the surface of society. When their harmful influence is confined to a negligible minority, it is tempting to overlook them. But when their contagious effects spread to the extent that sufficiently large numbers may tip the balance in critical referenda or lend support to candidates for high office who only a decade or two previously would be dismissed as totally unfit for such office, the problem must be urgently tackled.

The complexity of the challenges means that there is no easy fix to reconnect the governed satisfactorily with the key governing decisions that affect them. But as we will go on to see, these challenges are not insurmountable, and they flow from causes that can be identified and rectified. In the next chapter, we will explore the ideas and experiences we can draw on to develop an overall approach to revive our democratic health, before going on to look at each of the key components of this approach in detail in the remaining chapters.

---

[13] Although privatisation, deregulation, and cuts to inspection and enforcement support for tenants were issues that surfaced in the aftermath of the tragic fire at Grenfell Tower (Heathcote, 2017), it was notable that the Conservative government focused on the suspected failings of the local authority and its chief executive.

[14] The jury is still out as to which out of 113th-116th Congress during those four years would qualify, in terms of the paucity of laws enacted, as the most 'Do Nothing' Congress ever.

TWO

Rethinking how we govern

Having identified the key challenges for democratic governance, let us consider how they should be tackled. We can see that these are not problems that have suddenly appeared. They are core vulnerabilities that, whenever left exposed, will undermine any attempt by us to govern ourselves.

Many friends as well as foes of democracy assume that it is fully in place as soon as all adults are given the formal right to speak out, vote, and stand for office. Those who wish it well sometimes think that that is as good as it gets. Its antagonists reject it as inherently flawed and want it displaced with the imposition of whichever happens to be their favoured governance strategy.

By contrast, there are political thinkers who have been pointing out the need for continuous improvement to democracy. They appreciate that activists throughout the 19th century had to focus on breaking down the establishment's resistance to giving every adult male and female the vote in electing their representatives in government, but they knew that it would not be enough. Although their writings deal with different aspects of the problem, they share what may be termed a civic-communitarian perspective that treats democratic governance as an organic process to be nurtured over time, and not as some mechanical contraption that can be assembled once and for all.

Among these thinkers are those who took forward the Owenite cooperative-communitarian tradition in championing workplace democracy and the management of common resources through diverse forms of cooperative enterprise (Pateman, 1970; Claeys, 1989; Harrison, 2010; Lewis & Conaty, 2012); theorists such as John Dewey (1991), L. T. Hobhouse

(1994), and Emile Durkheim (Cladis, 1992), who injected the communitarian dimension into the development of democracy beyond its limited role for much of the 19th century;[1] civic republicans from Hannah Arendt (Canovan, 1992) to Michael Sandel (1996), who drew attention to the attitudes and mutually supporting relationships that must be cultivated to sustain self-governance; civic advocates for democratic practices that are more participatory, deliberative, associative, or strengthened by community organising;[2] and progressive communitarians who opposed both New Right and Third Way politics by setting out the case for democratic solidarity based on a deeper sense of responsibility among citizens and more effective state-community partnerships.[3]

While academic studies often compartmentalise these thinkers' ideas, a holistic approach to improving democratic governance should draw on them as complementary elements. Through building on their insights and criticisms, we can develop a more comprehensive understanding of what needs to be done.

Towards a holistic approach

Although the spread of anti-political sentiments is viewed as a problematic feature of contemporary society, the danger of democratic politics failing to engage citizens properly in their own governance was anticipated well over a century ago.

From the late 1860s to the early decades of the 20th century, there was a clear trajectory pointing towards universal suffrage. After staunchly opposing the Whigs/Liberals in giving the vote to more people beyond property owners, the Conservatives conceded that the tide was against them and brought in the 1867 Reform Act. That was soon overtaken by the Liberals'

---

[1]   Other important contributors include Mary Parker Follett (1998), Herbert Croly (1998), John Hobson (1996), and Jane Addams (1960).

[2]   Key figures include Benjamin Barber (1984), Paul Hirst (1994), James Fishkin (Fishkin & Laslett, 2003), Amy Gutmann (Gutmann & Thompson, 2004), and Saul Alinsky (2013).

[3]   The leading communitarians include Philip Selznick (1992), Robert Bellah (Bellah et al, 1992), Jonathan Boswell (1994), Amitai Etzioni (1997), and Henry Tam (1998).

1884 Reform Act which extended the franchise to 60% of adult males in Britain. Everyone knew by then that more reforms would follow. Following the American Civil War, the denial of the vote to blacks was ended by the 15th Amendment to the Constitution in 1870.[4] The resistance to granting the vote to women also began to crumble. New Zealand (then a self-governing British colony) led the way by giving all women the vote in 1893. The US followed with the 19th Amendment to guarantee women's right to vote. And the UK, after a half-hearted attempt to concede the vote to women aged 30+ with property in 1918, also granted full voting rights to all adults, female as well as male, in 1928.

It was during those decades that far-sighted reformists foresaw that people would not necessarily govern themselves well just by virtue of having a vote on some policy issues or on choosing who would represent them in public office. They were all too aware of how voters could be manipulated. In France, Napoleon III had finally been deposed after he managed to use universal male suffrage as a tool to amass vast personal powers and make himself Emperor. In Britain and the US, it was hard to ignore how owners of factories, railways, and banks were as capable as any unaccountable ruler in taking unfair advantage of those over whom they had power. Democratic control of the government alone would not protect the people unless that control could lead to state actions against those who threatened the wellbeing of individual citizens.

The civic-communitarian themes to emerge around this time would be echoed in the subsequent course of democratic development. There was the notable concern with education because without an adequate understanding of social issues, political arrangements, historical lessons, or what would constitute sound reasoning, people would not develop informed opinions. At a time when many parents could not afford to get a good education for their children, and some felt that their children were better off working in a factory than going to school, free access to quality education was a difficult goal

---

[4]   Though it took almost another 100 years before its intent was effectively enforced as a result of the Voting Rights Act of 1965.

to attain for most people. Higher education was reserved for the privileged few and opened the door for them to the most prominent positions in society. In parallel with the campaigns to widen educational access, activists succeeded in setting up learning institutions designed to help people on low incomes to acquire the knowledge, skills, and confidence to play a more influential role in society.[5]

The determination to promote outreach to the marginalised majority to help them learn, led to the recognition that those who were fortunate enough to be higher up in the social hierarchy had much to learn themselves. Samuel and Henrietta Barnet, for example, set up Toynbee Hall in England in 1884, to enable university students to meet low-income residents in the locality, live and learn together the difficulties poor families faced, and what could be done to improve the situation. Jane Addams, inspired by her experience of Toynbee Hall, set up Hull House in the USA in 1889 in pursuit of similar objectives. Mutual learning evolved into neighbourhood problem solving, which Addams encouraged visitors and residents of Hull House to engage in as an instructive experience in the exercise of collective power (Mattson, 1998).

Another pioneering activist in expanding the work of social centres, Mary Parker Follett, argued that in addition to local neighbourhoods deliberating together on what should be done, they should join forces to explore what a whole city should do, and beyond that, cities and regions should collaborate in working out what their respective state, the entire USA, and indeed different countries should do to advance their common wellbeing. Follett's advocacy for citizens' engagement in exploring and articulating what the instruments of collective power at all levels should do, put the spotlight on the question of what role government should play in a changing world.

The late 19th/early 20th century was a time when big business corporations emerged, exerting greater control over most

---

[5]   For example, the Working Men's College (founded 1854), Cooperative Women's Guild (1883), Ruskin College (1899), Workers' Educational Association (1903), Cooperative College (1919), and the National Council of Labour Colleges (1921).

people's lives than monarchs of the past could even dream of. What food they could eat; what to wear to keep warm; what shelter they could rent to keep their families safe; what energy, means of transport, and communication they could access; and what work they could get to earn money to pay for any of these – this was all increasingly determined by the decisions made by a rich minority. Some felt that if anyone was fortunate enough to inherit vast wealth or have built up a business empire, nobody, least of all the government, should interfere. But others could see that the reason why governments should be held in check was because, without adequate democratic control, they could amass and misuse power against ordinary people. The same applied to powerful businesses.

Under the influence of the New Liberals in Britain, advocates of Solidarity politics in France, and Progressive thinkers in the US, a new conception of government as the tool wielded democratically by the people to protect themselves against any kind of excessive power came into being.[6] This was reflected, for example, by the subsequent actions of Theodore Roosevelt's presidency in the US (1901-1909), the Radicals and their allies in charge of France (1902-1909), and the Liberal government of Britain (1905-1915). Policies such as sick pay for workers, old age pensions, compensation for injuries at work, indemnity for trade unions from being sued for strike action, progressive income tax, arbitration to resolve disputes between workers and employers, criminalising the selling of impure food and drugs, and the tackling of monopolies, all helped to reduce the power gap between the business elite and ordinary citizens.

Despite those reforms, however, people were still not exactly equal as citizens in terms of the influence they could bring to bear on their government. Economic inequalities meant that some could wine and dine powerful politicians, while others could barely feed their own children. The democratisation of economic life became a key reform issue. In 1870, the Co-

[6]   Hobhouse (1994) was a key influence on the Liberal Party; Croly (1998) was held in the highest regard by Theodore Roosevelt; and Leon Bourgeois (1902) would become prime minister of France himself in the period 1895-1896. The political label of 'progressive' originated with the London Progressives in 1889 (Rodgers, D. T., 1998, p 52).

operative Central Board was founded in Britain to promote the development of cooperatives, which gave their stakeholders a democratic say in their policies.[7] By 1917, the cooperative movement was convinced that it must seek political power to advance its agenda, and set up the Co-operative Party to champion its views in Parliament.

As influential thinkers such as G. D. H. Cole (1917, 1920) made the case for industrial democracy and a pluralist, cooperative approach to managing the production of nationally vital goods and services, sympathetic business leaders took their own initiative to bridge the gap between themselves and their workers. For example, Joseph Rowntree provided his employees with a library, free education, a social welfare officer, a doctor, a dentist, and a pension fund. It was the prototype of a 'welfare state' within a corporation. In 1929, Spedan Lewis went even further when he initiated the process of transferring the ownership of the retail businesses he had inherited to trustees who would hold them on behalf of all who worked in what became the John Lewis Partnership. All profits would be distributed to its employees, either as cash or as fixed-interest stock in the new company. And all employees, as Partners, could discuss company issues at local forums, and elect their representatives onto the Partnership Council, which would oversee the activities of the Board.

Democracy subverted

The wide range of civic-communitarian ideas for improving democracy were having a tangible impact on the lives of citizens by the early 20th century. So why were those improvements not sustained? One factor was Germany's disdain for democracy under Wilhelm II, and his bellicose attitude that led to the First World War. The large-scale slaughter with the use of machine guns and chemical weapons stunned many and drove erstwhile optimists into paralysing despair. But others concluded that such conflicts made democratic improvements even more urgent, and

[7]   One of its co-founders was George Holyoake. It soon changed its name to the Co-operative Union, before finally becoming Co-operatives UK, as it is known today.

that they must be advanced not just within any single nation, but across the world.

Unfortunately, there is never any guarantee that the advice of democratic reformists can win over more support than those who want to subvert democracy for their own ends. In fact, the contest can be loaded in favour of those with enough money to buy far greater influence through campaign finance. For example, US Senator B. Penrose (Republican) told his wealthy business supporters his vision of politics: 'I believe in the division of labor. You send us to Congress; we pass laws under which you make money ... and out of your profits, you further contribute to our campaign funds to send us back again to pass more laws to enable you to make more money.'[8]

In the run-up to the US presidential election of 1920, Penrose discovered that the candidate in the lead to secure the Republican Party's nomination was Leonard Wood, an advocate for profit sharing and employee share ownership, and a supporter of Theodore Roosevelt's trust-busting policies.[9] So Penrose sent a message to Wood, offering to swing the remaining delegates behind him, provided Wood would in return give Penrose and his oil interest friends control of three business-related posts in his cabinet. Wood refused. So Penrose used his connections in the party to push enough votes in the direction of Warren G. Harding to get him the nomination.

Harding went on to win the 1920 election, and led a presidential administration mired in scandals and corruption. Just as Penrose had hoped, taxes were cut for the rich, businesses were free to shed their social obligations, and workers became more precariously dependent on their bosses as wages were repeatedly reduced (Goldberg, 1999). Harding was followed as US president by Calvin Coolidge, and then Herbert Hoover. Together their 12 years of plutocratic Republican presidency brought not only the US, but the world, to unprecedented calamities (Richardson, 2014, pp 171–192). As the gap between

[8]   Penrose made that statement in 1896 (see also Koven, 2008, pp 47–48).
[9]   Although Theodore Roosevelt became US president as a member of the Republican Party, his progressive policies proved too much for the party and when he sought re-election, he stood as the candidate for the Progressive Party.

the rich and poor widened, many were encouraged by financiers to borrow and gamble on shares irresponsibly in the hope of making up lost ground. But when workers were too poor to buy the products they had helped their companies make, sales stalled and declined, and share prices dropped. More and more people lost vast sums on their stock speculation and could not pay back their loans. Banks reined in their lending, and as many businesses could not take the strain, closures led to escalating unemployment. The Great Depression swept across the Atlantic and bred social discontent that was exploited by far right leaders who rallied mass support for their oppression at home and military expansion abroad.

The battered political system of the US at least allowed the public to back someone who was willing to switch governance strategy to deal with the twin economic and military threats. President F. D. Roosevelt, with the support of his fellow Democrats in Congress, brought in legislation to curb business irresponsibility in the face of the most hostile opposition from corporate powers. The New Deal policies helped those at the powerless end of society to rebuild their lives and confidence. The lesson was not lost on the UK. At the conclusion of the Second World War, the British people thanked Winston Churchill for his wartime leadership but voted in Clement Attlee's Labour government on the understanding that it would build the foundations of a society in which resources, sacrifices, and protection would be shared out fairly, not just in times of war, but also in an era of peace (Bew, 2016).

The convergence of US and UK thinking on strengthening democracy (so it would not give way to fascist dictatorship or communist totalitarianism) through on-going support for citizens and the development of safe and vibrant communities was signalled by the two countries' commitment to the Atlantic Charter. The vision was that of a world made conducive to democratic governance. The Charter took a firm stance against territorial gains, while any territorial adjustments must be made in accord with the wishes of the people affected. It called for economic cooperation between nations to advance social welfare for all so that no one needed to fear not being able to make a living.

A small but important step in facilitating global cooperation was taken with the establishment of the United Nations.[10] In addition to the setting up of the Security Council, the General Assembly, and the Universal Declaration of Human Rights, the UN was instrumental in establishing a number of international organisations, such as the Food and Agriculture Organization (to provide a global overview on problems of malnutrition and food supply); the International Labour Organization (to involve workers' representatives in improving job security and working conditions); UNICEF (to give ongoing support as well as emergency relief to children caught up in disasters, wars, or abject poverty); and the World Health Organization (to coordinate responses to public health challenges).

From the end of the Second World War to the early 1970s, the improvement of democratic governance appeared to be back on track, not just in the US and the UK, but seemed set to spread internationally with the support of the UN, despite Soviet resistance. But by the end of the 1970s, progress was once again derailed. It turned out that the Penrose doctrine of plutocracy would be given a new lease of life once it was fused with the myth of the 'free' market, the revival of 'traditional' values, and a heavy dose of 'patriotic' militarism.

The ideas for such a fusion first emerged in the 1950s. Opinion formers such as William F. Buckley and Frank Meyer set out how big corporations (wanting the freedom to act with little government regulation), anti-progressive traditionalists (wanting the freedom to promote their long-held views about non-whites, the place of women in society, homosexuality, people with the wrong or no religion, and the evil of abortion), and military hawks (wanting the freedom to deploy arms against anyone in whatever manner they deemed fit) should join forces under the banner of 'freedom'. Such a composite agenda, for what came to be known as the 'New Right' (King, 1987; Lowndes, 2008), would enable its backers to take control of government powers

---

[10] As Mary Parker Follett had advocated, democracy needed to be nurtured at an international level as well.

and reverse the trend towards equal citizenship for all.[11] Buckley founded the *National Review* to champion these ideas and set up in 1960 the Young Americans for Freedom to develop a new generation of activists who would take the agenda forward. Ronald Reagan served as the national chairman of the Young Americans for Freedom (1962–2004) and cited Meyer as a key inspiration for his own vision. New Right thinking soon spread to the UK, and in 1974 Margaret Thatcher and her ideological mentor, Keith Joseph, set up the Centre for Policy Studies to advance a similar political agenda.[12]

And just as the dire economic problems of the 1920s/1930s paved the way for the rise of fascism, the turmoil of global finances in the 1970s opened the door to forces inimical to democratic self-governance. As the 1960s drew to a close, the dwindling purchasing power of the marginalised non-developed countries of the world was dragging the West towards recession. In 1971, all the major industrial countries began to experience a slowdown in their economic growth, and with supply running ahead of demand, unemployment also started to rise. Instead of addressing the poverty and underdevelopment in most parts of the world, the West decided to reflate their own economies. In 1973, the artificial boom pushed up demand for raw materials to such an extent that their prices began to rise steeply. This led to rising costs of the manufactured products and constant inflationary pressure. Workers demanded wage increases to keep pace with anticipated price rises and made inflation even more difficult to control. At that juncture, the Arab nations at war with Israel put oil prices up as well as cutting production to put pressure on the West to get Israel to withdraw from the former Arab territories it was occupying.[13]

---

[11] For grassroots development in support of this new political approach, see McGirr (2002).

[12] A third co-founder was Alfred Sherman, and like their American counterparts, they drew on the works of thinkers such as Friedrich Hayek and Milton Friedman.

[13] The Organization of Petroleum Exporting Countries (OPEC), dominated by the Arab nations, announced two days after the Arab-Israeli War broke out (in 1973) a rise of 70% in the price of oil. Not long after, they announced a further price increase of 130%.

In the wake of what came to be known as the Second Great Crash (Cairncross & McRae, 1975) – bringing in its wake high inflation, workers' unrest in the face of wage restraints to combat inflation, more expensive imported goods, high energy costs, economic slowdown, and declining levels of employment – the New Right seized their moment. Thatcher became Prime Minster of the UK in 1979, and Regan won the US presidential race in 1980. Income inequalities, which had fallen to a historical low towards the end of the 1970s, began to rise and have been on the increase ever since.[14] Public institutions concerned with the pursuit of the common good came to be presented as a drain on national resources, and cutting their budgets promoted as a means to secure tax cuts. Their powers would be reduced to give corporations more freedom (but increased to undertake military or covert security activities). Where possible, they would be disbanded altogether, or privatised so businesses could profit from a quasi-monopoly position or large public subsidies.

Many bought into the New Right mantra that private actions by individuals and corporations were inherently better than the initiatives of public bodies. And when the Third Way approach devised by the New Democrats and New Labour in the US and UK respectively proved in the 1990s/2000s to be essentially an attempt to moderate the New Right rather than displace it, a growing number of people began to think that no real alternative was available from any of the established political parties (Tam, 2001b).

The readiness of Third Way politics to accommodate the powerful financial sector, wage wars without evidence of genuine threats, acquiesce in tax loopholes for the rich, join in the rhetorical attacks on benefit claimants, and expand the involvement of for-profit organisations in delivering public services or sell off public assets altogether means that the seeds of anti-politics were widely sown. If success (or failure) in life was to be measured by one's private actions alone, and the

---

[14] The impact of inequality on democracy will be examined in Chapter Ten, 'Civic Parity'. For a detailed account of the rise of income and wealth inequalities in Britain and the US after Thatcher and Reagan won power, see Irvin (2008).

public domain was to be constantly denigrated and shrunk at every opportunity, then it was only to be expected that more and more people would come to see engagement with public policies as a waste of time.

Towards nine remedies for democratic governance

History has shown that the need to develop democracy beyond a mere voting system was not unanticipated. It was being addressed from the early 20th century on, until the plutocratic misadventure promoted by the likes of Penrose led to the Great Depression, the rise of fascism, and the Second World War. Reforms were back on track in the post-war years when the foundation was being laid for more effective self-governance on not only the national, but also the international level. But then came the rise of the New Right, financial deregulation, socioeconomic polarisation, and the banking crisis which left many deeply sceptical about whether the politics of collective action could offer any real hope at all.

Since the 1990s, diverse currents in aid of democratic renewal have been surfacing again. For example, Michael Sandel (1996) and Charles Derber (1998) have exposed the erosion of democratic collaboration by the widening gap between private corporate powers and the general citizenry. Benjamin Barber (1995) contrasted the escalating problems caused by social discord with the improvements secured through systematic support for democratic dialogues and joint working. Bernard Crick (2001) championed citizenship education to improve democratic participation. John Stewart (Ranson & Stewart, 1994; Clarke & Stewart, 1999) pointed to the advantages of enabling more decisions to be made at the community level. Phillip Selznick (1992) and Amitai Etzioni (1997) warned of the disorientation arising from social values becoming detached from a sense of shared community experience. Michael Lewis and Pat Conaty (2012) advocated the development of fully democratic cooperatives. Paul Hirst (1994) and Jonathan Boswell (1994) explored associative and collaborative approaches to reach collective decisions without relying solely on a centralised state.

By the 2000s, these ideas were increasingly promoted by scholars and policy experts (Tam, 2001a; Brennan et al, 2007; White & Leighton, 2008; Crick & Lockyer, 2010). Democratic activists put forward a variety of civic innovations. David Blunkett, as home secretary in the UK government, set up the Civil Renewal Unit to improve state-citizen cooperation (Tam, 2015b). And community organising came to be a core feature of Barack Obama's two successful presidential campaigns.

However, many initiatives, due to budgetary constraints, were only carried forward as one-off projects. The ideas behind them were often seen more as standalone cures, rather than as a set of complementary proposals that can together enable citizens to govern themselves more effectively. In the absence of a concerted response to strengthen democracy, those who seek to subvert collective governance for their personal ambitions or plutocratic gains have in the 2010s won even more victories as they rally support for causes and candidates inimical to inclusive democratic cooperation.

In addition to the encroachment on democracy by unscrupulous corporate interests, there is the growing problem of extremist rejection of democracy altogether. Barber has long warned that between the mind-numbing consumerism of McWorld and the fundamentalist obsessions of any form of 'Jihad',[15] there would be ever less space for civic cooperation. His advice on dealing with the threats to democracy remain pertinent today – we must redouble our efforts to extend the depth and breadth of democratic institutions (Barber, 2001).

We need to synthesise the wide range of civic-communitarian ideas[16] into a holistic set of analyses and recommendations that can be applied to the systematic improvement of democratic governance. The structure for such a synthesis would correspond to the three areas we have identified as critical to any form of reliable governance: the togetherness of those involved; the objectivity that can underpin the resolution of conflicting claims;

---

[15] Barber's notion of 'Jihad' in this context referred not exclusively to militant or extremist Islamic tendencies, but to the fundamentalist tendencies in all religions and cultures that do not tolerate consensus building or pluralist cooperation (Barber, 1995).

[16] An examination of some of these ideas can be found in Tam (1998).

and the extent to which power balance can be maintained to avoid arbitrary rule.[17] By applying the relevant civic-communitarian ideas to these areas, we can formulate an overall guide to what should be done to support their development, and how each of the underlying challenges identified in the previous chapter is to be dealt with.

First, let us look at the need for togetherness. People require a shared sense of mutual responsibility if they are to trust that their commitment to work for the common good will be reciprocated by others. Simply telling people that there is a greater purpose they must serve, or urging them to remain united, will have little impact if the forces dividing them are stronger than what has kept them together so far. In relation to the three challenges to sustaining democratic cohesion, there are three corresponding remedies to be explored:

- Shared mission: to prevent the loss of common objectives, and engender real solidarity, people should be supported in developing a shared commitment to attaining a set of goals they recognise as important for all of them, and which are more achievable if they join forces.
- Mutual respect: to tackle the spread of discriminatory behaviour, and ensure people are disposed to view each other with equal respect, the parameters for such respect should be set out, inculcated through appropriate socialisation, and sustained by enforceable rules.
- Coherent membership: to ease the destabilising uncertainty over people's sense of belonging, and enable them to adapt as a group/community to changing circumstances, there needs to be a membership system that is transparent and flexible enough to retain people's confidence in working together.

---

[17] Philosophically, these can be compared with Habermas' three dimensions in his concept of communicative rationality: (1) the relation of a suffering and passionate subject to its own subjectivity and the subjectivity of others; (2) the relation of a knowing subject to a world of events; and (3) the relation of an acting, practical subject to a social world of others (Habermas, 1992, p 109).

Secondly, we turn to the need for objectivity. Without a proper understanding of what is in fact happening, the problems being encountered, or how they can be dealt with, people cannot reach an informed agreement over what constitutes an accurate assessment, let alone what is likely to be the most appropriate response. Neither dogmatic assertions nor pervasive scepticism would help to end the impasse. In relation to the three challenges to maintaining objectivity in democratic deliberations, there are three corresponding remedies to be explored:

- Collaborative learning: to combat the cult of scepticism, and make it possible for people to learn through shared evidence and critical exchanges, it is essential for learning support to be of a sufficiently high quality, and made universally available to all on a lifelong basis.
- Critical re-examination: to counter the yearning for the unquestionable, and ensure that vital claims and assumptions are subject to scrutiny and revision, there must be no permanent exclusion from re-examination, especially when new ideas and evidence undermine previous assertions.
- Responsible communication: to stem the misinformation flow, and facilitate the exchange of relevant details to guide discussions and judgements, the people must have a reliable system to access relevant information, protect legitimate secrets, and differentiate factual communication from provocative distortions.

Finally, we must consider the need for power balance. So long as some can, by superior force or with greater wealth, secure the adoption of their own agenda at the expense of others, there is little prospect for people's common wellbeing to be prioritised. The rhetoric of demagogues would only breed further disillusionment. In relation to the three challenges to securing the power balance necessary for democratic collaboration, there are three corresponding remedies to be explored:

- Participatory decision making: to minimise the risk of personality contests deflecting attention from the real issues, and empower people to be genuinely involved in shaping the decisions that affect them, we need decision-making arrangements that facilitate engagement and deliberations.

- Civic parity: to curb widening inequalities, and help those less favoured by good fortune to obtain equal treatment before the law and protection from being exploited or marginalised by others, it is necessary to redistribute power and resources to create a level playing field for democratic cooperation.
- Public accountability: to debunk the deregulation mantra, and ensure that people with power over others can be held to account for their actions, we must have a system that is robust enough in setting out the rules, investigating compliance with them, adjudicating disputes, and enforcing due rewards and penalties.

The next nine chapters of this book will be devoted to an exposition of the nine proposed remedies respectively. In each chapter, the remedy in question will first be examined in terms of why it is important and how its neglect can seriously undermine democratic governance. Secondly, the potential misunderstanding or distortion of what the identified remedy should entail will be critically examined and clarification offered. Thirdly, suggestions for making improvements will be considered, along with examples to show how difficulties can be overcome. Together they provide a basis for understanding what is preventing democracy from fully functioning as the most effective form of governance, and a guide to reviewing and improving current practices to overcome the key obstacles.[18]

---

[18] In Chapters Three to Eleven, at the end of each of chapter there is a short section called 'Remedial checklist' with a series of questions that anyone with governance responsibility at any level can go through to assess the relative strengths and weaknesses of their current governance arrangements, and identify the priority areas for improvement.

PART TWO

How to sustain democratic togetherness

THREE

Shared mission

Democracy can only be sustained through the pursuit of common objectives shared by those involved. Otherwise, it can be subverted to serve the interests of an elite or merely gratify the impulse of a mob. In order to work out cooperatively what collective action is to be taken forward, people need to have a sense of what they seek together. A shared mission may cover the pursuit of security, the development of learning, the improvement of living conditions, or other objectives that matter to everyone. In this chapter, we will look at why democratic endeavours need to be guided by some form of shared mission, what misinterpretations of 'shared mission' must be guarded against, and how shared missions at different levels of society can be more effectively developed.

Why we need a shared mission

The symptom of non-voting is often thought of as the core problem of democracy. Correspondingly, it is suggested that, with the stick of compulsory voting, or the carrot of an electronic voting app, the voting figures can be pushed up and democracy will be in a healthier state. But when a third of even those who have registered to vote tend not to cast their ballot, and many others vote without much due diligence at all in considering what they are actually voting for, the problem lies at a much deeper level.

No meta-strategy for selecting governance strategies can work if it does not ultimately have the confidence of the governed that it is better than other alternatives in picking out what, over time, will enhance their wellbeing. This in turn depends on there being sufficient common appreciation of what constitutes shared goals among those involved. But attempts to build civic solidarity have to overcome the barriers erected by those inimical to collective arrangements. And there is no shortage of such barriers.

For example, New Right advocates, invoking Adam Smith's notion of the 'Invisible Hand', have argued that leaving individuals to think only about their own interests and not some amorphous 'common good' will achieve more than any other approach. This libertarian contention has become central to diminishing the role of democratic government (MacLean, 2017). Setting aside what Smith really intended to convey (Smith, A., 1976; Griswold, 1999), the claim that interactions of atomised selves will lead to the best of all promised lands without any unifying objectives overlooks two crucial aspects of social reality. One is that individuals who fail to see potential common interests with others, and thus neglect to join forces with them, are the ones most likely to fall prey to exploiters and oppressors. The other is that one of the most important things people discover when they do reflect on the interests of themselves and others is that new group interests emerge to widen their perception of what matters in life.

The thinker who in fact stands far closer to the New Right's 'leave individuals alone' philosophy is Bernard Mandeville, whose *The Fable of the Bees* (1970) argues that instead of telling people they should follow any moral plan or engage in any public project, we should leave them to their own individual inclinations. Like bees, they would then do what is natural for them to do, and all would work out for the best. At first glance, bees do appear to act on their own impulse without reference to any commands that have been issued to them. Provided no outside forces intervene, they will succeed in ensuring the needs of every member of the hive are met. But on closer inspection, it can be seen that different types of bees have been biologically given a set of abilities and a corresponding role, and each will unquestionably carry out their assigned role. As the queen, the foragers, and the soldiers never waver from their genetically fixed assignments, a rigid hierarchy is preserved.

From a New Right perspective, if people were left alone with their inherited wealth and aptitudes for the prized skills of buying cheap and selling dear, then society would function as well as it could.[1] Unlike bees, however, human beings do not hesitate to go beyond what they are expected to do. Some would lie or intimidate to take unfair advantage of others. Some would react against the conditions they have been told to accept. The resolution of these conflicts requires a governance structure to assess impartially and intervene competently.[2]

Once the romanticised fantasy of bee-like harmony prevailing in a marketised society is exposed, the unavoidable question of what should be the deciding factors that hold people together returns. Thinkers such as John Rawls have tried to uncover a set of principles that can serve to establish the necessary common ground. The principles he proposes are derived from a series of counterfactual arguments that he thought would demonstrate their general acceptability (Rawls, 1973, 2005; Daniels, 1975).

Unfortunately, Rawls' assumption that people would sign up to some form of egalitarian strategy that would prioritise helping those most in need, so long as they did not know what their own socioeconomic position would be, is flawed for two reasons. First, there are the risk takers who enjoy gambling above all else. Far from wanting to avoid any system that would take from the many and hand it over to a lucky few, they crave it. If they turn out to be among the lucky few, they celebrate. If they end up on the losing side, they can live with it. At every casino, every stock exchange, there are people like that, and they would find Rawls quite presumptuous in thinking they would rather play it safe. Secondly, there are the realists who would argue that political intelligence is based precisely on acting on the facts. If they were hampered by uncertainty, they might hedge their bets and go along provisionally with an egalitarian approach. But if they knew they had various advantages over others, some of them

[1] Mandeville's ideas were repackaged by Matt Ridley (1996) along with references to bees and ants. A critique of Ridley can be found in Monbiot (2010).

[2] Even bees encounter conflicting views. For a study of how they resolve differences over where they should move to when an old hive has to be abandoned, see Seeley (2010).

might want to exploit those advantages to the full, and would consider anyone insisting they do otherwise as sanctimoniously meddlesome – which is exactly how pro-welfare liberals have been portrayed in US politics.

In the absence of a shared mission that people can relate to, abstract principles based on contested philosophical assumptions are not sufficient to draw people together to cultivate a sense of common concerns (Walzer, 1994; Sandel, 1996). Common purpose has to emerge from experiences of joint deliberations and shared narratives. Otherwise, they either fade like memories of wartime solidarity, or never take hold in the first place.

The individualist outlook promoted by the New Right through the deregulated market system and anti-collective rhetoric has eroded social bonds that are indispensable for democratic cooperation (Bellah et al, 1996; Putnam, 2011, 2015). When people focus more on how they will have to manage on their own, and spend less and less time on activities that bring out and reinforce the value of group pursuits, their familiarity with the necessity of give-and-take compromises dwindles, while their appreciation of the fruit of joint efforts declines.

It is no accident that decades of New Right dominance have brought anti-politics to the boil. If success and failure in life are ultimately all about what individuals chalk up by themselves, why waste time on getting involved with groups that may not deliver substantial gains for oneself. If one feels unhappy about how one's life is turning out, and a lot of people are saying the European Union and the migrant workers from other EU countries are to blame, then why not tell the EU where to go with a vote for Brexit. If one is fed up with the deteriorating prospects facing many US citizens, why not declare one's support for a presidential candidate who has no track record in public office or the slightest capacity for diplomacy, just because he makes many people feel able to give vent to their anger and prejudices. While large numbers of Britons feel the separatist urge in relation to the EU, there are Scots who want to break away from the UK. And social fragmentation continues to gather pace in different spheres of life. Business owners feel perfectly entitled to give workers zero-hour contracts or move jobs abroad with no alternative offer for those made redundant

(Standing, 2014). Workers are demoralised, with little sense of loyalty to their employers. The old blame the young for not being sufficiently committed to finding work, while the young are encouraged to resent the old for getting more than their fair share. At the same time, religions, places of birth, and skin tones are used to define hermetically sealed identities.

To counter these trends, democratic governance requires every institution to reach out to and engage its members in identifying their common concerns and articulating a shared mission they will take ownership of. This cannot be done by someone simply stating what their goals ought to be, but must involve people exchanging their views and feelings, and drawing on their own felt experiences in gradually forming a shared understanding of what they value and seek together (Bellah & Sullivan, 2001).

Sceptics about there being any kind of shared mission beyond the coincidence of individual interests may cast doubt on the prospect of anything meaningful emerging from interpersonal dialogues. For them, individuals have a fixed set of interests, and they will pursue as many of them as possible, dropping some if necessary, and putting up with others' pursuits if that would be helpful to oneself, or at least not prove to be a hindrance. They do not recognise that interests can qualitatively change when people get to know each other and come to appreciate new perspectives. Authentic engagement with other people is a potentially transformative experience, with those involved reshaping their sense of what is important to them (Macmurray, 1995). This does not mean that people will give up all their personal goals and devote themselves solely to some 'greater good'. What happens is that a broader conception of what one cares about is formed out of integrating one's own objectives with those of others, and in so doing, some of one's objectives may change, not because the change serves an instrumental purpose in relation to some of the things one originally wanted, but because one has come to care about other things beyond one's initial emotional boundaries.

This social development is integral to healthy human interactions. It has been found in research relating to evolutionary studies (Bowles & Gintis, 2011), developmental psychology (Tomasello, 2009), and behavioural psychology (Axelrod, 1984).

When people have the opportunity to cooperate with one another, they form a shared understanding of what they should do above all to maximise the chances of attaining the goals of the group and its members, as these have evolved in the light of their ongoing relationships.

What emerges is not a single mission for everyone at all times. People can be involved in different groups. Different groups may find themselves interacting with each other in a larger group. And just as individuals change their personal objectives and priorities in the context of the respective group deliberations, so different groups, from the local or national, to the global level, will also adjust and form their own conception of what they ought to pursue. At each juncture, there is a risk that the constituent members and the wider group may come into conflict, and the extent to which it can be minimised depends on their ability to review their current preferences and formulate a new shared mission around which they can rally.

For the government of any country, this points to a three-fold challenge. It needs to improve the conditions for individuals to develop a shared mission within each of the diverse groups they belong to. A worker cooperative or a John Lewis Partnership may give their members a chance to do that, but many organisations still operate like a mini-monarchy (and some are de facto empires). A government also has to enable citizens and their different groups to develop a shared mission for the whole country. And last but not least, it has to consider how its own country and other countries may reach an agreement about the shared mission to guide corresponding transnational activities.

Before we go on to look at how shared missions can be engendered, we must tackle in the next section the problem of misleading conceptions of 'shared mission', which can pose as great a threat to democratic governance as having no shared mission at all.

The problem of pseudo-shared missions

The development of a genuinely shared mission can be blocked off either by those who want to obtain political power through some unifying call that only serves their own ends, or by well-meaning but misguided advocates who push forward allegedly common goals that are in fact quite divisive. To guard against such moves is an important part of keeping the civic space clear for the cultivation of democratic solidarity. A set of goals can only come to be shared if they are capable of engaging the interests of different people with diverse perspectives. Attempts to impose commonality or erect ill-considered barriers will fuel resentment beneath a shaky foundation.

While the libertarian wing of the New Right eulogises the minimalist ideal of the unencumbered individuals, its neoconservative wing favours deploying concepts of absolute hierarchical unity (Thompson, M. J., 2007). The basic idea is that whether people know it or not (and those on the lower rungs of any given hierarchy are presumed to be largely ignorant of these matters), there is a higher purpose or mission they should all strive to fulfil by playing their part. For example, neoconservatives often declare that a patriotic nation must unite against some designated enemy, and everyone must do what is expected of them without questioning those in charge of the country's security. But their vision is not of citizens fighting as one, but of those on low incomes being given financial incentives to join the armed forces and fight whoever they are commanded to, while those on the highest incomes prosper from investing in corporations that profit from military interventions abroad (Klein, 2007).

Of course the trumpeting of patriotic unity may sound as though there is a common cause that people ought to rally around. But all too often behind the hollow cries of 'let's take back control' or 'make our country great again' there is no tangible goal that actually serves the people. The agenda of the demagogues is ultimately formulated by a few for their own benefit with little consideration for the vast majority of the people concerned.

Although in the distant past it might have once made sense for individuals to follow their chieftain or king unreservedly and accept their assigned roles, modern societies can only function if people learn to question assumptions, and explore new opportunities to contribute to diverse projects. As Durkheim remarked, mechanical forms of solidarity must give way to organic forms of solidarity because, as groups become more complex and their functions grow more sophisticated, the ability of individual members to think for themselves becomes more important (Lukes, 1973; Durkheim, 1984). Setting a blueprint that treats everyone like a mere cog in the machine would only hamper the workings of the group. Improvements come from adjustments that people on their own cognisance can put forward.

However, a shared mission that is highly adaptable may for that reason be considered too 'thin' to direct an organisation, let alone a country. The aim of making sure that everyone is protected from harm, for example, may only secure universal assent by leaving the contestable details unspecified. But adaptability does not have to entail vagueness. It can be based on responsive interactions that operate in line with subsidiarity. The mission to secure protection for all in a local town or district can be spelt out through the interactions of local people, their elected representatives and local state institutions. Even more detailed objectives may be defined by a neighbourhood group, which can set its own priorities in the light of what the members of the group have experienced together. The missions of diverse districts and neighbourhoods to protect themselves will in turn have to be reviewed to ensure they can cohere with each other and with what will constitute the national mission, so any local prejudice or oversight can be dealt with.

How relatively thinly formulated aims should be thickened into more detailed objectives at different levels is a contested issue (Tam, 2011a). Some may want to take it as predominantly a matter of customs, so that how people in an area have always felt about something or acted to counter it is regarded as the main basis for spelling out what a protective mission should mean in practice in that area. By contrast, it can be more constructively treated as a matter of experimental learning, so that the experiences, research, and customs of the whole country are to be considered along with those of particular neighbourhoods and districts in order to discover what lessons they hold for people's security.

For example, a town may claim that it has never had more than a handful of migrant families, and it would feel unsafe if more were allowed to move into the town. Based on its own customs, which have evolved with little interaction with people from other cultures, it treats any new arrival from a different national, ethnic, or religious background with deep suspicion. However, the experiences of other towns that have over time developed with a much higher number and mix of foreigners, as well as the interactions the town in question has had with the few migrant families settled there, show that with time, openness, and the suspension of prejudices, people can grow to not merely tolerate, but appreciate each other's diverse backgrounds, and attain wider friendships and a richer form of life.[3]

And the reason why any given town cannot legitimately insist that it should be left to its own ways irrespective of the impact of its own behaviour is no different from that which rejects the attempt of any individual person to act as though everyone else is of no consequence. As we all live in a highly interconnected world, if anyone is granted the absolute licence to behave regardless of what it may mean for others, everyone's safety will diminish.

How well we navigate from the conflicting interpretations of what any broad mission consensus may mean to setting out specific aims and requirements will depend on the extent to which we steer away from exclusionary declarations toward inclusive deliberations. Exclusionary declarations consist of words that no one is supposed to doubt and all must obey. Papal edicts in medieval times, commands from tribal warlords, and the outpourings of political extremists all fall into this category. To people who are gripped by low self-esteem, deep despair, and rising anger, such declarations can superficially provide a focus for their lives. But the coming together in these cases is achieved not only at the expense of excluding others whose views and concerns are relevant, but at the cost of missing out on better outcomes for those involved.

[3]   The contrast outlined here reflects observations on how areas with different levels of ethnic diversity reacted to newcomers over time, referred to in internal documents of the Home Office that I discussed with Robert Putnam and David Blunkett when the latter was home secretary. For the possible correlation between high levels of anti-immigrant sentiments and low levels of encountering immigrants, see Dodds and Akkoc (2015).

Fundamentalist leaders and manipulative demagogues are adept at seizing on some religious texts, past customs, or concocted symbols of glory to dress up their preferred vision of life as the ultimate goal for all faithful followers. But their approach deliberately takes no account of what others have found, and ignores the suffering thus caused to those they dismiss as irrelevant as well as their own followers. Unfortunately, instead of guarding against this kind of group mission formation, some politicians seek to facilitate it with religious segregation and faith-based education.

For example, while professing to recognise the danger of religious extremism and how it can be fuelled by exclusive absorption in one set of 'unquestionable' doctrines, the Conservative government during the 2010s actively promoted the development of faith-based schools. Humanists UK (formerly the British Humanist Association) has found that figures contained in the government's own research show that allowing schools to choose all pupils on religious grounds will lead to increased ethnic segregation across England. Christian schools with 100% religious selection are less diverse and admit a far higher proportion of children classified as 'of white origin' than schools which cap religious selection to 50% or do not select on religious grounds at all. Yet the government insisted that it would remove the 50% cap.[4]

Faith in any doctrine, which without any objective evidence or deliberative engagement with others declares people who disagree with it irredeemably wrong, can never be the basis of any sustainable shared mission. This is not about opposing faith with secular assumptions. It is about whether we are dealing with people who believe they have access to infallible truths and hence never need to revise their views in the light of what others may put to them, or with people who appreciate they

---

[4]   In existing Church of England free schools that are bound by the 50% cap, 63% of pupils are classified as 'of white origin', but in Church of England secondaries that religiously select all of their places, 78% are white. In 'other Christian' free schools opened under the cap, 55% of pupils are white, but in fully religiously selective 'other Christian' secondaries, 85% of pupils are white (British Humanist Association, 2016).

should keep an open mind and be ready to learn from anyone who may have something instructive to say.

A shared mission, by definition, has to go beyond a single individual. And since the group mission that brings its members together has to adapt if it is not to be pushed aside by other groups, the interactions of groups at different levels necessitate missions that can transform themselves through inclusive discussions with other groups with diverse characteristics. A closed mission that implacably considers any other mission as absolutely wrong must either retreat from every point of contact with others, or constantly threaten to take an offensive stance against them.

It does not follow that one must concede to whatever others regard as the priority objectives, only that one should be genuinely prepared to exchange ideas, share experiences, and be open to learn from what others have discovered. This is precisely what ecumenical explorations, faith-humanist dialogues, community consensus-building, and truth and reconciliation commissions all strive to do. And despite sceptics' dismissal of them as futile gestures, they have often succeeded in bringing people together to deal with substantial disagreement and develop important common ground (Kurtz & Dondeyne, 1972; Chapman & Van Der Merwe, 2008).

John Dewey (1962) wrote of the prospect of a common faith arising from people's readiness to learn from each other's deepest concerns and values. But he was aware of how the sharing of our highest aspirations could be halted by the basest of negative emotions. And hatred and prejudices do not just grow in the dark corners of organised religions. The space for secularism might also have its own fringes where thoughtless intolerance sprouts. For example, in France in 2016 there was much clamouring that in accordance with the ethos of Laïcité (secularism), anything associated with religious symbolism, such as female swimwear that covered the whole body on the alleged basis of Islamic customs, should be banned. But what anyone wears in an open, secular society is no business of the state. What Laïcité calls for is the keeping out of religious influence in the determination of public policies, *and* the keeping out of government influence in the determination of religious practices. It is one thing to prohibit the wearing of the burqa in public places where security and identification needs might be unduly undermined. But to use state power to forbid something just because it is an expression of one's religion (or, as many have argued, a cultural tradition) would be a perversion of the secularist accommodation between state and religion.

The issues that can cause citizens to break into factions (workers versus bosses; the indigenous versus the 'foreign'; traditionalists versus progressives) at the intra-national level pose even more problems at the international level. With fewer opportunities for people in different countries to learn from each other's experiences, it is more likely that insular views would persist and dialogues with others to explore shared missions are shut out by presumptions about inherent incompatibilities. Alas, it is not uncommon to come across suggestions that national or civilisational dividing lines are so entrenched that policy makers should accept them rather than attempt to bridge them (Huntington, 2002). Instead of collaborating to formulate shared missions, we would be told to focus on minimising provocations to others and deterring transgressions by them.

There should of course be ready tactics to prevent disputes from breaking out or escalating. But a Huntington-type conception of shielded civilisations resembles the myopic conception of atomised individuals (Nozick, 1977) in that it fails to recognise wider patterns of human interactions, cross-fertilisation, and cultural symbiosis. People, even total strangers, are not necessarily locked in a state of mutual suspicion, relieved only by some kind of policing function to keep them from doing harm to others. People are capable of getting to know each other, developing new group objectives (city-wide, nationwide, worldwide) in addition to those they previously held.

At the most basic level, there are many challenges that people from diverse national, cultural, civilisational (however these are defined) backgrounds can only meet if they learn from each other, adjust their understanding in the light of others' experiences, and set new collective priorities. From threats such as economic insecurity, environmental degradation, military aggression, to opportunities such as space exploration, medical advancement, and artistic development, individuals, groups, and nations that work as a team with shared goals are better equipped to succeed.

There are many complementary approaches we can adopt: grassroots movements with learning shared across borders (Ekins, 1992); federal systems that facilitate deliberations and revisions conducted at the interface of different levels of governance (Kinsky, 2001); collaboration between mayors/leaders of cities from around the world (Barber, 2013); and foreign policies that build global coalitions with shared goals and pooled resources (Gvosdev, 2016). The key is to reject the false premise that groups beyond a small organisation, a neighbourhood, a country, or a civilisation cannot develop a shared mission.

The claim that human differences will always keep solidarity at bay is at best a misguided distraction, and at worst a highly damaging self-fulfilling prophecy. People's capacity for learning through interactions with people from other countries is influenced, for example, by at least two factors: their educational attainment as an indicator of their ability to learn and reason; and the opportunities they have for meeting other nationals under peacetime conditions. When applied to the high-profile case of Brexit, YouGov (2016) found that among those aged 18-24 (that is, those who have by and large mixed with other Europeans as a routine part of their lives), 71% backed Remain and just 29% backed Leave. The reverse was true of those aged 65 or over (that is, the generation who have had relatively the least contact with non-British people given the lower levels of migration and visits abroad prior to recent decades), with 36% backing Remain and 64% backing Leave. There is a similar contrast with education as a comparative factor. Among those educated to degree level, 68% backed Remain and 32% backed Leave. But of those educated to GCSE or below, 30% backed Remain and 70% backed Leave.[5]

Instead of declaring that people of different nations (religions or ethnic backgrounds) cannot possibly form shared missions, experience would suggest that if better education and more

---

[5] For an exploration of the links between low levels of experience of immigrants, higher levels of prejudice, and the propensity to favour Brexit, see Meleady et al, (2017).

extensive opportunities for people to interact in a non-hostile environment are provided, the dispositions to cultivate shared missions will correspondingly increase.

How to cultivate shared missions

Between those who think citizens can govern themselves with no sense of shared mission and those who try to fill the civic void with some chimera of pseudo-unity, democracy has been stumbling through one bout of malaise after another. As a meta-strategy, its role is not to impose a mission on those seeking to govern themselves, but to ensure the people concerned can come together to work out what that mission should be. And once we have removed the conceptual barrier that falsely presents individuals and groups as psychologically sealed with their own immutable inclinations, we can move on to the practical task of enabling people to nurture mutual understanding and develop shared missions that will anchor their democratic collaboration.

The key is to enable people to engage with others with the understanding that constructive interactions may lead not only to the greater satisfaction of many of their own demands if they are willing to support others in pursuit of theirs (Axelrod, 1984), but they may come to rethink their initial demands so that their priorities in life take into account more relevant factors, and thus become more coherent in a wider social context.[6] For those with governance responsibility at any level in society, they should ensure that those within their sphere of governance recognise that the development of a shared mission is about maximising synergy, rather than playing out some zero-sum game. And they should take on board five approaches in their efforts to advance solidarity among their members:

- developing familiarisation arrangements;

[6] For example, they may come to see some of their demands as outmoded or misguided, and adopt new ones that fit better with their broadened experience; they may come to understand some of the demands made by others and attach value to their fulfilment even though it would have no bearing on any of their own demands; and they may form new demands in partnership with others as a result of the emergence of shared concerns.

- ensuring planning processes are structured for co-designing;
- giving collective endeavours a clarity of purpose;
- building in sustained engagement; and
- strengthening support through mission-forming intermediaries.

First, far from breeding contempt, arrangements to promote familiarity can actually engender better understanding between people who may otherwise view each other as strangers with little in common. It is encounters with others' life stories and experiences that frequently change people's views about the fears and hopes of others.[7] From office away-days to national events such as the Paralympics, it is widely acknowledged that getting to know others with whom one was barely acquainted before can help to develop a sense of togetherness. The challenge is to set up such arrangements whenever there is a need for them. They are generally low cost but high impact. For example, some professionals in healthcare and policing have facilitated informal gatherings between themselves and the communities they serve to promote a relaxed atmosphere in which they can together talk about the priorities they wish to set and what commitments everyone will then have to make, resulting in higher satisfaction with and greater confidence in the collective solutions to public problems.[8]

Another factor commonly cited as a key social dividing line is age, but it can be transcended with the help of familiarisation events. The National Institute of Adult Continuing Education (NIACE), for example, has documented many cases where the supposed antagonism the media frequently focus on between the young and the elderly is displaced by activities that successfully draw them into common endeavours (Thomas, 2009). The First Taste charity enabled groups of young people aged 8-17 to meet residents in care homes, and develop together a

---

[7] In his essay on Heidegger, Rorty asked his readers to imagine how Heidegger might not have been so supportive of the Nazis if he had fallen in love with a Jewish woman (Rorty, 1990).

[8] Examples can be found in the reports relating to the Together We Can programme (Tam, 2015b). More detailed consideration of approaches to cooperative problem solving is set out in Chapter Nine, 'Participatory decision making'.

range of projects that included film shows, staging a play, and photography exhibitions that raised their mutual understanding and appreciation. Age Concern facilitated discussion groups that brought young and elderly people together, with the former learning about preparing for the world of work and the latter coming to feel valued and no longer isolated. In one community safety project, the older residents of a neighbourhood and the young people they felt threatened by when they were 'hanging around street corners' were introduced to each other through a series of tea and cake events, and the older residents came to feel safer because they began to perceive the youngsters as their potential protectors out in the open, and the youngsters felt valued as they were seen in a positive light rather than being treated with constant suspicion.

People from different cultural and ethnic backgrounds are sometimes subject to conceptual polarisation as though they could never form any shared mission. But community outreach that facilitates cross-cultural engagement shows that any divisions can not only be bridged, but can in practice be relegated to insignificant levels when new bonds are formed (Mayo et al, 2013). Sporting events, open concerts, art projects, and community meals are just some of the vehicles that have helped to bring people together to broaden and deepen their understanding of those who would otherwise simply be perceived as 'others'. Food has become a particularly popular means of facilitating mix and meet, with initiatives such as the Refugees Food Festival in Paris, Eat Offbeat, which delivers ethnic meals prepared by refugees settled in New York City, and the UK's Upbeat Communities, which organises community meals to bring residents from varied backgrounds together to sample diverse home-prepared cuisines. Furthermore, housing design such as that pioneered through the development of garden cities can play a major role in enabling residents to meet in open and relaxed surroundings that are conducive to the formation of cordial relationships (Howard, 2010).

Next we should make sure planning processes for collective action are structured for co-designing. While familiarisation paves the way for the exploration of shared priorities, people need organised support to engage in co-designing objectives and planning for their achievement. The Guide Neighbourhood programme,[9] for example, facilitated diverse community groups in learning from communities where effective organising had been put in place to aid the development of shared views among local people and connecting these to government agencies (McCabe et al, 2007). Residents and public officials applied what they had learnt to set up their own ways of option exploration and consensus building. Housing, environmental quality, security, and regeneration issues were all addressed with democratic input, not in terms of who happened to outnumber whom in a simple majority vote, but on the basis of what people had learnt together as a community.[10]

Worker cooperatives provide another model of how people with broadly shared aims can build up organisations to define and pursue more detailed goals and expand to bring in more people to support the objectives they will continue to develop collectively. From groceries, accessible transport, to telephone services, childcare, and training consultancy, the model exemplifies how a shared mission can be formulated in any social and economic endeavour (Co-operatives UK, 2008). Where finance proves difficult to raise, there is the option of community shares, which is frequently an effective means to test out the extent to which a group of people really want to see certain services or practices put in place. Furthermore, it can help to translate what can sometimes be a vague sense of support into specific investment commitment to make the provision happen (Brown, J., 2010).

Thirdly, attempts at mission forming should be guided with a clarity of purpose. All too often vague rhetoric obscures what joint response should be made to a common problem, when a clear focus is needed to devise an effective solution. Take, for example, two very different approaches to engaging citizens in dealing with a nationwide problem. Road safety was once an internal issue for those in charge of traffic management. But since

---

[9] The Guide Neighbourhood initiative was part of the last Labour government's Together We Can programme to improve state-citizen cooperation.

[10] We will examine collaborative learning more closely in Chapter Six.

the 1970s local communities across Britain have been engaged by government, local authorities, charitable organisations, and residents' associations in cutting down preventable road injuries. The shared focus on discouraging any behaviour that may endanger lives on the road (for example, drunk driving, driving without wearing a seatbelt, crossing roads without due care) channelled efforts into speed and alcohol checking, peer pressure against dangerous driving, police visits to schools, and neighbourhood-led traffic calming measures. People at every level embraced the priority of targeting risky behaviour and proposing appropriate traffic controls, with legal penalties if necessary. Fatalities from road accidents dropped steadily from 7,499 (in 1970) to 1,857 (in 2010).[11]

By contrast, despite decades of concern with teenagers resorting to abortion after becoming pregnant, there is no clarity of purpose in discussions about what should be done. Some want to focus on changing the sexual behaviour of teenagers; some want to concentrate on the provision of contraception; some are involved in the debate between adoption or abortion to deal with unwanted pregnancies; some want to put economic pressures on young single mothers; and others see the key issue as the social marginalisation and related low self-esteem in deprived areas. But these different advocates are not brought together to consider the underlying shared aims of reducing teenage pregnancies, while the government could not make up its mind about how to ensure education in sexual matters and birth control is provided in every school. During the period when road fatalities fell by 75%, abortions among 13-15-year-olds rose by 65% from 2,300 (1971) to 3,800 (2009).[12] Although in Western Europe the UK has the safest roads after only Sweden, it has the highest figures for teenage pregnancies. How different things might have been if public health concerns were focused on helping teenagers

[11] The figures are for Great Britain, excluding Northern Ireland, available from the Department for Transport: www.gov.uk/government/collections/road-accidents-and-safety-statistics

[12] These figures are for England and Wales, available from archived data at the Department of Health: http://webarchive.nationalarchives.gov.uk/20130123231223/http://www.dh.gov.uk/en/Publicationsandstatistics/Statistics/StatisticalWorkAreas/Statisticalpublichealth/index.htm

realise they have a better future without risking getting pregnant as systematically as road safety campaigns have been on opening everyone's eyes to potential traffic dangers.

Checking for clarity of purpose is also a handy way to separate out the development of missions that have genuine contents that relate to solving problems all concerned would recognise, from rhetorical posturing that presses the emotional buttons of the unsuspecting (and often gives dog-whistle signals to those harbouring deep prejudices) but in fact offers nothing to improve people's quality of life.

Fourthly, if a shared mission is not to drop out of sight, we need sustained engagement. When people first come to understand why they should adopt a particular form of mutual support, they are generally willing to run with it. But in time, if they or later generations forget its importance and, critically, the likely consequences of not having it around, it may decline or end up being dismantled altogether. Mutual building societies once provided affordable mortgages for their savers. But once economic policies opened the door to their demutualisation, their members were tempted by short-term gains and consented to their transformation into profit-chasing banking organisations which played a large part in the financial crash in 2008 (Mullineux, 2014).

On an even larger scale, the post-war shared mission in developing a welfare state for the benefit of all has run into a fog of amnesia. While its architects reached out to the wider public to discuss with them the value of such arrangements, those who came to take on the day-to-day running neglected to sustain the mutual understanding that was vital to its long-term efficacy (Timmins, 1996). People who claim benefits are now alienated by a system that is remote and which routinely treats them as unwelcome supplicants. Meanwhile, many of those who are not drawing benefits but are paying into the system have lost sight of the nightmare of poverty and squalor disfiguring society before the system was put in place, and is already showing signs of returning as the system is weakened by relentless cuts. Thus the quest for communal wellbeing loses its momentum as it becomes more and more of a disengaged bureaucracy steered by remote administrators (Duffy, 2016).

To maximise the chance of engagement being maintained, it should be built into a system's operational routines. For example, the world's largest cooperative institution, the Mondragon Corporation, has grown since 1965 from its base in the Basque region in Spain into a global enterprise with €12 billion in revenue, generated by over 74,000 workers in 261 businesses based in 41 countries around the world (2015 figures). It is unwavering in its commitment to maintaining the shared understanding with its members so that everyone is aware of why they are stronger as a cooperative group and it does not splinter into self-interested segments that undermine the viability of the overall organisation. Of course it has its share of problems, having to operate in a global economy dominated by non-cooperative businesses (Kasmir, 2016), but it has kept its members together far better than most (Ayo, 2016).

Finally, we need better support through mission-forming intermediaries. Cooperatives with the reach commanded by the likes of the Mondragon Corporation are rare, but every country has a wide network of local government, and local democratic councils can provide a permanent base to bring people together to consider, prioritise, and keep under review shared objectives. Subnational public bodies can reach out to people at the regional, city, and neighbourhood levels, and help them develop informed views on what most needs to be addressed at each level. Experts on local government have long argued that it is best placed to offer a democratic platform for setting collective direction (Jones & Stewart, 1985; Quirk, 2011). With tools such as community planning, regular local forums, and ongoing community development outreach (Bowles, 2008), citizens will be able to exchange ideas under open and courteous conditions before they reach a wider consensus.

Beyond the core structure of local authorities, attention should be given to other mission-forming intermediaries horizontally and vertically. Horizontally, there are matters which may relate in part to local government's jurisdiction but are otherwise mainly non-statutory issues. There is a growth of commons organisations that provide an inclusive focal point for people to come together to determine how common environmental or technological resources can be managed for the wellbeing of everyone (Kuhne, 2015; Ostrom, 2015). Working in partnership with such organisations, local government can enrich its own engagement with citizens and help civil society cultivate shared missions, without having to expand its role into areas where community-based groups can adequately deal with the issues that arise.

Vertically, local statutory bodies need to join up with national governments, which in turn should collaborate with other states to provide mission-forming intermediaries to address transnational concerns. The Brexit campaigns, building on decades of misinformation about the role of the European Union, have shown how easy it is for large numbers of people to come to overlook the critical need for cross-border government institutions, and how difficult it is to rescue shared missions – on security, economic, environmental, scientific research, and so on – once these intermediaries are removed.

Antipathy to transnational and subnational state organisations poses threats to democratic governance in general. Whatever their rhetoric may say about reclaiming democratic powers, all too many politicians who have for decades been undermining the roles of the European Union (or in the case of the US, the federal government) and local authorities just want citizens to have less power to shape policies that affect them. Democratic governance can only function well when, instead of having a monolithic command structure that sets objectives for everyone, there is a commitment to enable a mosaic of shared goals to be formulated by different groups at their respective levels, which together form a coherent picture of what the overall mission should be.

Remedial checklist: shared mission

With reference to any group[13] the governance of which you are concerned about, you can use the checklist below to assess what may require the most improvement in relation to the need for a shared mission:

☐ Is there a shared mission known and accepted by all members as important? Is there enough sustained engagement with members to prevent the ideas behind the mission from becoming misunderstood or outmoded?

☐ Are members convinced that the mission will be continuously taken forward? Or do many of them regard it as a hollow commitment? Is the pursuit of the mission guided by a clarity of purpose so that members grasp what in practice they should be doing to support it?

☐ Is the shared mission periodically reviewed and readily adapted to changing circumstances? Are members able to raise the issue of a review when they perceive circumstances as necessitating revisions? How far can they rely on planning processes that are structured for co-designing solutions to resolve contested views? How effective are the intermediary organisations in place at facilitating mission development and revision?

☐ Are there signs that the shared mission is being overtaken by incompatible concerns? Can emerging mutual suspicion be healed with the help of familiarisation arrangements so that people are not alienated from each other? Are there legitimate and feasible routes for some members to form their own smaller and more agile entities, or should a wider mission be established in partnership with others to deal with challenges the current setup cannot cope with?

---

[13] For example, an organisation, a city, a country, or a transnational body.

FOUR

Mutual respect

Many people think of democracy simply as a majoritarian mechanism that favours any decision backed by most of the people asked to give their views. But what actually constitutes an acceptable majority has often not been thought through. Sometimes a mere majority may be no more than another form of tyranny if the interests of those in a minority are permanently ignored. In other cases, the decision may be handed to those who received under 50% of the votes cast, because no other group managed to get a higher percentage. Ultimately, the threshold set for any voting arrangement is only acceptable if there is no built-in bias against anyone. So if any process for the democratic selection of representatives or proposals is to command the confidence of those involved, it needs to be backed by mutually respectful relations. In this chapter, we will look at why mutual respect must be safeguarded to ensure democracy is workable, what clarifications are needed for concepts such as 'rights' and 'respect', and how mutual respect can be better secured in practice.

Why democracy must be underpinned by mutual respect

When the threshold set for what is to constitute a sufficient majority appears to change so as to help some people but hinder others, it raises the question of whether the voting rules are concocted to diminish the influence of certain groups in society.

For example, the Conservative government passed the Trade Union Act 2016 on the basis that strike actions must have proper democratic mandate as they could seriously disrupt people's lives.

As a result of the new legislation, if a union ballots for a strike in an important public service,[1] at least 40% of those eligible to vote (not just of those who actually voted) would have to back the proposed strike. Since strike actions in the UK have been at a historical low for decades,[2] and just fell from 788,000 days lost in 2014 to 170,000 days lost in 2015, the government's argument rested solely on the purported aim of securing greater democratic legitimacy for actions that could disrupt others' lives.

But the Conservatives who brought in the EU referendum had no such concern for securing a similar degree of democratic backing for the outcome of the referendum. Given the turnout was 72%, and 52% of those voted to leave the EU, it means that among all those eligible to vote, only 37% backed the 'Leave' option. If a similar threshold had been set at 40% – and no one would argue that pulling the UK out of the EU causes less disruption than a few days' strike – then the Leave vote would be deemed insufficient to trigger Brexit.

Furthermore, the Conservative government that passed the Trade Union Act and committed itself to implementing the EU referendum outcome, came to power itself in the 2015 elections with a turnout of 66%, winning 37% of the votes cast. In other words, out of all the eligible voters, only 25% gave their backing to the Conservatives to form a government.[3] Not only is this far short of the 40% requirement it imposes on trade unions to call for strike actions, it is indisputable that what it does as a national government can potentially disrupt people's lives on a far larger scale.

Superficially it may sound convincing to say that trade unions should have a 'proper' democratic basis for calling strike actions, or that it would be antidemocratic to question the legitimacy of the EU referendum. But once the relevant specifics are

---

[1] The category of 'important public service' includes the health, education, transport, border security, and fire sectors.

[2] The annual number of days lost to industrial action reached peaks of 30 million days in the late 1970s and 1980s, but since the mid-1990s they have rarely risen above 1.3 million.

[3] This does not even factor in the estimated 15% of the UK population who would have been eligible to vote but have not registered to vote, and thus are not included in the 'did not turn out to vote' figures.

exposed, it becomes clear that without consistent ground rules, majoritarian decision making can be easily manipulated to marginalise particular groups of people.

If we look back on how democracy evolved as a solution to the problem of choosing between strategies without permanently favouring some at the expense of others, we can see that the ground rules for its operation need to reflect its core concern with maintaining the mutual respect among those under its jurisdiction. With any other mode of governance, the interests of some people can be treated as less worthy of notice or disregarded altogether. With democracy, however, no one is supposed to be singled out for any rewards or penalties on terms that are withheld from others.

Mutual respect is in essence the expression of reciprocity. It is a precondition for democratic relationships, because only when people recognise each other as moral equals would they be prepared to accept the preponderance of views emerging from their fellow members as a reasonable guide to what should be done. This recognition may be captured in terms such as seeing others as 'of similar standing', 'not inferior', 'counting as much as oneself'.[4] This is not to say that everyone is regarded as having the same merits or faults. On the contrary, the assumption is that everyone is on a par by virtue of being a member of the group in question, and rewards and penalties will only be handed out in response to any relevant positive contributions or harmful violations displayed.

Attitudes towards those who fall outside the circle of mutual respect may help to illustrate the difference they can make. Ancient Athens initiated the democratic experiment, but infamously excluded women and slaves. For the male Athenian citizens, these other types of people were not comparable to them because they lacked something that would have rendered them deserving of the same respect given to male citizens. So while an Athenian male would have to show signs of madness before he was kept out of a public debate, or be convicted of a crime before he was denied a vote in a decision affecting the city,

---

[4] The notion of respect has been illuminatingly explored by Richard Sennett (2003).

women and slaves were simply deemed unfit to participate. If pressed to define that 'something' which is missing and which is essential for anyone to be counted an Athenian citizen, nothing coherent would be forthcoming. The difficulty for Athenian men is that they would either come up with some irrelevant characteristics or conjure up some untenable hypothesis about women and slaves being inherently incapable of being concerned about civic matters.

The dynamics of democratic self-governance depend on the mutual respect which commits the members in question to accept others as others will accept them in sharing the responsibility of steering their group for the good of all. But once some people are denied respect without adequate reasons, the overall system is vulnerable to creeping corrosion. If some individuals or subgroups are arbitrarily set higher bars for participation, what is to stop others from being discriminated against as well?[5] When that suspicion spreads, partial democracy disintegrates into tribal rivalry or gang rule. Anyone who does not fit the profile of what it takes to be accepted into the dominant set will not be treated with respect. Outnumbered, or outmuscled, 'outsiders' will be rewarded less well even if they contribute as much as anyone else to the group, and penalised more harshly when they commit any wrong (or, on occasions, when they have done no wrong at all).[6]

Historically, democracy has never been able to flourish until the barriers to mutual respect have been removed. Persistent tribal divisions or polarised religious sects have repeatedly hampered attempts to develop democratic governance in many countries across Africa and the Middle East. They ruined countless lives in the partitioning of Pakistan and India because no promise of a democratic electoral process could overcome the legitimate fear of a minority being viciously discriminated against.

But these are not problems unique to people living outside the West. When Britain embarked on its very gradual journey towards more democratic governance, it struggled with its

---

[5] One of the core features of the Counter-Enlightenment was its unrelenting opposition to the extension of respect beyond its narrow traditional confines (McMahon, 2001).

[6] Or required to meet a higher percentage threshold than others to qualify as winning a vote.

longstanding discrimination against Catholics and Non-Conformists. The founders of the US, well aware of the need to avoid similar chasms from undermining the unity of the country, decided to keep state and religion as completely separate realms. But their proto-democracy, like that of the Athenians, was dragged down by their exclusion of women and relegation of a large number of the population to the status of slaves. Yet if by the end of the 1960s discrimination on the grounds of gender, professed religion, or apparent skin tone appeared to be on the retreat, the dawn of the 21st century has witnessed a resurgence of the craving to stamp out mutual respect.

Even as the old hierarchical prejudices that accorded less respect to women, people with different ethnic origins, people who do not subscribe to what was previously the dominant religion, and anyone with some form of disability or with different sexuality from the conventional 'norm' were being rolled back, the resentment against such social (and legal) changes were channelled into what came to be known as the 'culture war' (Hunter, 1991). Starting with sarcastically dismissing concerns with tackling the manifestation of these prejudices as 'political correctness', the onslaught gathered momentum in the form of campaigns to 'take back control' of one's country, to 'make it great again', or, more bluntly, to once more put women, foreigners, and 'deviants' in their place.

One of the key components of the New Right fusion has been to appeal to people whose self-esteem was intertwined with the sense of superiority they held over those they deemed not to be their equals. As the economic component of their self-esteem came to be increasingly undermined by plutocratic redistribution of wealth from the majority to the rich elite[7] – aided by laws designed to weaken trade unions – many people with their self-image shaken were encouraged to turn their frustration into rage and direct it at both the targets of their long-held prejudices and anyone who dared to speak up for them. Negative identities are

[7] Largely as a result of the New Right's economic policies that have consistently widened the gap between rich and poor (Harvey, 2007; Reich, R., 2009).

projected onto target groups who are then viewed as deserving of contempt (Rapport, 2013).

But while New Right politicians tend to consider the stoking of prejudices as primarily a means to achieve plutocratic ends,[8] the more recent right-wing demagogues regard riding the wave of prejudice-led politics as an end in itself. In the UK, the Brexit campaign was driven in large part by the rhetoric against EU citizens, refugees, and immigrants for ruining the quality of life in Britain. In the US, the Trump presidential campaign took aim at Mexicans, Muslims, and other minority groups as threats to the American way of life.

In the run-up to the EU referendum, Nigel Farage, speaking for the Leave campaign, claimed that if they lost the vote by a small margin such as 48% to 52%, they would press for another referendum.[9] When they won the vote – by a margin of 52% to 48% – they said there could be no going back. An immediate impact of the Brexit vote was a 41% surge in hate crime in the following fortnight (Forster, 2016). After the final presidential debate before the 2016 election, Trump was asked if he would accept the results of what he had repeatedly referred to as 'rigged elections', and he said he would accept them if he was the winner. Meanwhile, his repeated warnings against the legitimacy of the electoral process, especially in areas where there were large numbers of African-American or Latino residents, led to many of his supporters talking openly about intimidating non-white voters and even rebellion if Trump did not become president (Hayden, 2016).[10]

The fuelling of prejudice and hatred, the use of democratic procedures when it suits them, and the denouncing of collective decisions if these should turn out to be unfavourable are familiar features of far right politics going back to the 1930s. Its resurgence in the US and across Europe poses a direct threat to

---

[8] Not all Conservative or Republican politicians subscribe to the New Right approach, but only a small minority vote against the party line.

[9] Farage's claim was made in an interview with *The Mirror* newspaper: www.mirror.co.uk/news/uk-news/nigel-farage-wants-second-referendum-7985017

[10] After Trump won the presidential race, there was also a surge in hate crime against minorities in the US (Milam, 2017).

democracy. For too long the liberal-minded have thought that tolerance should be extended even to the intolerant, and the media believed that those daily condemning 'political correctness' would make for amusing stories about anti-establishment mavericks; but the celebration of bigotry and disrespect would inexorably fuel the rejection of inclusive politics and undermine the culture of democracy (Kintz, 1997; Frank, 2006).

Rights, respect, and reciprocity

The mentality that can give rise to the politics of rampant discrimination is not some rare psychopathic condition, but all too common, if latent (Arendt, 1979; Burdekin, 1985). If we are not vigilant in keeping it at bay by nurturing the growth of mutual respect, it can be exploited by the unscrupulous and hand power to those who have no compunction about ruling with extreme prejudice.[11]

Memories of the atrocities committed by the Nazis led to the development of institutional tools such as the UN Declaration of Human Rights and the European Convention on Human Rights. But after only 50 years, the post-war consensus on not compromising on the respect to be accorded to all human beings was already crumbling. Under Republican President George W. Bush, people (with a Middle Eastern profile) were sent to and held indefinitely in a US detention facility without being charged with any crime, let alone put on trial. They could also be tortured. More recently, the Conservative government in the UK narrowed the remit of the Equality and Human Rights Commission, imposed a reduction of its staff by 60% from 455

---

[11] Apprehensive of the spread of fascism in Europe, Sinclair Lewis wrote his 1935 novel, *It Can't Happen Here*, about a charismatic US presidential candidate full of 'clownish swindlerism' and who counted members of the Ku Klux Klan among his supporters, winning power and turning the US into an oppressive regime. It was staged as a play in New York when the story's parallels with Trump's 2016 presidential campaign were widely noted.

to 180 (Ramesh, 2012), and cut its overall funding by 73%, from £62 million to £17 million (Pring, 2016).[12]

These symptomatic reversals suggest that rights-based protection of mutual respect can all too easily be eroded when the notion of reciprocity drops out of sight. Civic-communitarian thinkers have emphasised the human need for mutually respectful relations to underpin collectively binding rules. Individual rights matter, but only if they are structured to assure people that none will be shielded from the consequences of their behaviour towards others. If the defence of human dignity is to be reinvigorated, we need to dispel some of the problematic thinking around rights and respect.

People are often given the impression that rights are absolute. But having the right to life, liberty, and the pursuit of happiness cannot mean that individuals must be left alone to do as they please regardless of the consequences for others. A man about to murder an innocent child may well be rightfully shot dead by police marksmen arriving on the scene if there is no other way to save that child. A sadistic torturer whose pursuit of happiness leads him to inflict suffering on others should be deprived of the chance to live his life as he desires. The terms of reciprocity required for genuine mutual respect in relation to a wide range of issues can only be specified by the rules established in each type of case. But far from any individual being given unconditional respect and protection regardless of their behaviour, the respect must be conditional on it being mutual.

One-way rights demands have led some people to claim that their 'right' to speak their mind should always be respected, even if that involves them in directing abusive, demeaning, and threatening expressions towards others. They forget that the relevant right in such a case is one that is already accorded to them, namely that they and their loved ones will not be verbally intimidated and humiliated by people capable of doing so. Thus, on a reciprocal basis, they must respect others and hold their vitriolic tongues.

---

[12] These moves were made as the Conservatives announced their intention to abolish the Human Rights Act.

However, when reciprocity is taken out of the equation, the shielding of respect as an absolute right can lead to a breakdown of mutual esteem. The togetherness that underpins democratic co-dependence is unlikely to be maintained if some feel that rights only offer a one-way protection, leaving them more disrespected than ever. But if our governance procedures always make explicit the dimension of mutuality, fewer may fall into the trap of conceding to those who do not reciprocate others' respect.

Furthermore, by predicating the right to respect on mutuality, we can more readily expose misguided objections that view inclusive policies as discriminatory. For instance, there are frequent complaints made about suspects in criminal cases (especially if they allegedly involve terrorist activities) being 'overprotected' by rights, when for the sake of everyone's security they should be locked up indefinitely, or even beaten severely until they give up vital information about their plans. Attempts to defend suspects' rights in terms of what they are inherently entitled to as human beings tend to provoke rejections of rights-based arguments altogether. However, if it is pointed out that the protection is based on how all of us would want to be treated should we be accused of a crime, and there is no evidence to convict us, people may view things differently. Since they would not find it acceptable for them or their children, if they were the ones named as suspects, to be harmed even though nothing has been proven against them, they could see why it would be a mistake to call for such treatment to be allowed.

The institution of legal rights is an important means of securing mutual respect. But these must make sense in the context of people's everyday attitudes and relations. Otherwise there is a real risk that they will be seen as a hindrance rather than an aid to sustaining healthy social interactions (Kagan et al, 2002; Breslin, 2004). By contrast, explicating rights as the formal guarantee of reciprocal behaviour makes them more readily understandable and relevant to people's lives. Importantly, it can also help to correct false assumptions of favouritism that would otherwise fuel unwarranted resentment.

Even as campaigns for gender equality advance, reactions against them grow among those who fear they will miss out unfairly as well as those who just want to cling to the old male-dominated hierarchies (McClain, 2001; Fitzgerald, 2010; Allen, 2013). But how can we tell if any changes put forward are themselves discriminatory or not? At first glance, for example, paid maternity leave may be regarded as favouring women exclusively, or even just women who have children while they are in employment. Yet the issue is in fact about how we want our society to support its members who undertake the task of bringing the next generation into the world and caring for them in those critical early months. Even those of us without close relatives who will have children imminently can appreciate that we would be living in a worse society if infants did not get the fullest care and attention from day one. So if anyone chooses to have a child, we would expect support such as maternity leave to be forthcoming. Indeed, if the partner of the mother is to play a large role in helping to look after the baby, they should be provided with a degree of support too.

Public policies that focus on the rights of minority ethnic groups without reference to their wider concern with mutual respect have also led to misguided backlash. Programmes designed to redress the deprivations that were caused by a mixture of racial discrimination, plutocratic shift of resources to wealthier areas, and under-regulated business decisions had been taken forward as though they were exclusively to help people with certain ethnic backgrounds. People not belonging to those ethnic categories end up feeling (or at least susceptible to being misled into suspecting) that they have been discriminated against. But a large part of the misconception was due to the issue being dealt with as though it was solely connected with a person's ethnic identity, when it was in fact also about people's daily experiences of socioeconomic disadvantages and how anyone caught up in such circumstances needs to be supported. Only by positioning regeneration programmes more clearly as structured to help areas where people have been suffering from any form of persistent discriminatory or marginalising practices, and emphasising how the improvements will help neighbouring areas as well, can a better level of understanding and appreciation be achieved (Tam, 2007a).

Another group of people whose receipt of any kind of support is often presumed by some to be disrespectful to others is convicted offenders. Unlike gender and ethnic differences, the divide between criminals and the rest of society is widely seen as morally relevant in treating them in contrasting ways. Having broken the law can readily be cited as a justification for depriving offenders of a wide range of support that the rest of us would give and take on a mutual basis. But there is a question of proportionality that none of us would want to be ignored if we or anyone close to us were to be convicted of any criminal offence. Stealing bottled water worth a few pounds is hardly comparable to defrauding hundreds of people of millions of pound.[13]

Unfortunately, the intensification of plutocratic hierarchies has driven many people nearer the bottom to vent their frustration at those classified as criminals and thus seemingly suited to being the object of derision and deprivation. This is not helped by talk of the rights of criminals as though their violation against others can somehow be discarded as inconsequential. What is needed instead is a sense of proportionality that can be readily seen as mutually relevant. In other words, the responses to any type of criminal violation would be recognised as appropriate for that type if oneself or a member of one's family were found to have committed it.

Questions of how much should be taken away financially from offenders who caused financial losses to others, what penalties should be handed to offenders to acknowledge the social damage done, or how long they should be kept away from others to prevent them from repeating the offence in question will have to be answered through rule-setting processes that are transparently reciprocal. As we have seen, from the treatment of offenders to demands to outlaw certain offensive types of corporate action, all too often not everyone is given the same hearing when concerns are raised. Democracy cannot function if those handed the power to set policies use it to benefit themselves and/or their corporate friends, with patent disregard for the wider public.

---

[13] Yet the former offence may have more chance of landing one with a prison sentence than the latter as one 23-year-old student discovered after he was convicted of stealing £3.50 worth of bottled water: www.theguardian.com/commentisfree/poll/2011/aug/12/riots-water-theft-punishment

For example, the UK Conservative government relegated public objections to commercial schemes for fracking to the point of total irrelevance. It organised a formal public consultation on its proposal to change the law to allow fracking for shale gas under people's homes, and despite 99% of the 40,647 responses being opposed to the proposal, the government changed the law (Carrington, 2014). And when the democratically elected Lancashire County Council, having received over 18,000 objections, rejected an application for fracking to be carried out in the county, the government stepped in to overturn the decision and approved the application (Johnston, 2016).

The manipulation of democratic procedures to help corporate interests, and keep those with the least power in society marginalised, are even more blatant in the US. Republican-dominated state legislatures have been at the forefront of bringing in stringent ID requirements for voters in the name of preventing impersonation and voter fraud (Wilson, 2016). While research found that such laws might have prevented up to 31 cases of voter fraud out of a billion votes cast between 2000 and 2014, the Brennan Center at New York University estimated that 11% of eligible voters in the US lack the kind of photo ID that is generally required by these laws, and 'they are disproportionately black, Latino, low income, students and elderly voters' (O'Donoghue, 2016).

Such subversion of democracy has been aided by the confusion over the relation between rights and reciprocity. Resentment is stirred up against protection put in place for everyone, by insinuating that it is unjustly available to only some with no benefit for anyone else. On the other hand, discrimination against groups without enough power is disguised as rule adjustments to secure fair play for all. To expose such corrosive moves against democratic governance, we need to reconnect rights more visibly to their support for mutually respectful relations.

How to advance mutual respect

For those with governance authority or the power of scrutiny over people running public or private institutions, the advancement of mutual respect can be better supported with four types of intervention:

- tackling misunderstanding with reflective awareness-raising;
- exposing hidden discrimination with procedural consistency and transparency;
- providing rapid adjudication and correction; and
- making better use of reconciliatory exploration.

First and foremost, prevalent misunderstanding ought to be corrected with reflective awareness-raising. Members of any organisation or country should be in no doubt that rewards and penalties are to be allocated to everyone on the same basis, according to their actual behaviour and the established rules. No one is to be favoured or discriminated against just because some non-behavioural characteristics are highlighted out of prejudice. However, simply telling people they should not be prejudiced against others may have little impact.

Unimaginative diversity training can become a mere box-ticking exercise, and hearing what those discriminated against may feel is least likely to register with those who are most inclined to succumb to prejudices. Reflective awareness-raising, by contrast, holds up a mirror so people can see how they would feel themselves if they were at the receiving end of discriminatory behaviour. One of the most famous examples of this approach is of course Jane Elliott's pioneering lesson when, in 1968 after the assassination of Martin Luther King, she enabled a class of white children to understand what was wrong with discrimination with a simple experiment. Initially Elliott made children with blue eyes the 'superior' ones, which meant that unlike children with brown eyes, they could have treats such as second helpings at lunch, more free time at recess, and access to water fountains brown-eyed pupils were not allowed to go near. They sat at the front of the classroom, while the others were sent to the back rows. They were told not to speak with brown-eyed pupils, who would get told off for mistakes in class that were overlooked when made by blue-eyed children.

The experiment was then repeated with the two groups of children, reversing their roles. Elliott found that because the children were not just told how bad it was to discriminate against others, but experienced how they would feel themselves when discriminated against, all of them grasped far more readily why it was baseless, hurtful, and wrong. Elliott went on to develop more sophisticated awareness-raising sessions for employers in the US.

While some have expressed reservations about Elliott's method with children as young as eight, contemporary application of reflective awareness-raising techniques can be guided by pedagogical experts. For example, since its establishment by UNESCO in 1953, the Associated Schools Project (ASP) had by 2016 worked with over 10,000 educational institutions in 181 countries to foster understanding of human rights and intercultural dialogue. In Panama, one experiment took place over two years with nursery school children aged five and six being asked to welcome a new classmate with cerebral palsy, and engage with parents and staff in working out ways to be supportive to their latest member. As older children could be cruel to others who were different, involving five- and six-year-olds showed how early awareness might help to promote a deeper appreciation of why adjustments and extra support should be provided to those with particular needs (Meyer-Bisch, 1995, pp 38–39).

To ensure the people under their jurisdiction have the appropriate emotional understanding of why mutual respect has to be safeguarded, those in governance positions should provide appropriate opportunities for everyone to discover what it could be like to be ignored or mistreated as a result of prejudiced perception. When made more acutely aware of what being neglected or discriminated against would be like, people might tune in more readily to why no one should be put in that position, and why they would want an impartial body to step in to help anyone who was, as they would want to be helped themselves in a similar situation.

Secondly, there should be procedural consistency and transparency to keep out any hidden discrimination. Whether it is the Conservative government targeting union workers in the UK, or Republican legislators seeking to curtail voting by low income and minority ethnic citizens in the US, the superficial rationale for imposing more stringent controls on those discriminated against must be exposed and overturned. Politicians, especially those who still rely on securing power with just 20-30% (or less) support from all those eligible to vote, should face up to the challenge that they must either lower the threshold for victory in all voting contests to the same level they need to reach themselves, or accept they too should only be able to claim victory after reaching a genuinely majority threshold.

This may require a minimum participation rate among the members, and it certainly should demand that of those who do participate, an overall majority (that is, over 50%) must give their support to whichever candidate (or policy proposal) is to be declared the winner. It should rule out procedures which translate votes cast into a format that can hand victory to the candidates with the support of fewer voters.[14] Where there are more than two options, it will need to be supported by some form of proportional representation so either the majority is to be counted at a higher level (for example, allocating seats to a regional or national list by the same proportion as the votes cast), or second preferences would, if necessary, be transferred to the remaining candidates after the ones with the fewest first-round votes are eliminated.[15]

The exact procedures will vary between institutions, but the hurdles to get past to register for a vote, to turn out to vote, and to have one's vote counted as much as anyone else involved in the same local or national election must always be minimised unless there are genuine reasons for having such hurdles in place so that all comparable elections will also need to have them. Electoral discrimination by proxy is not difficult to detect, but it needs to be rectified more swiftly. We have seen how voter ID laws are sledgehammers that, in the name of cracking invisible nuts, are actually designed to break any bridge that can connect marginalised groups to the voting booth. It is by

---

[14] The US electoral college vote system has on six occasions given the presidency to a candidate with the support of a fewer number of voting citizens than their rival (Wasserman, 2016). Unless the US president is supposed to represent the states rather than the American people, the system needs to change.

[15] We will look further at electoral arrangements in Chapter Nine, 'Participatory decision making'.

no means the only method. In some states in the US, a felony conviction would prevent one from having a vote even after one has served one's sentence. For example, in 2010 23% of Florida's black voting-age population (that is over half a million African Americans) could not vote because of a past felony conviction (Rumbaugh, 2012).

The Republican strategy of capturing state legislatures in order to change electoral district boundaries to favour themselves led to the Democrats losing more seats to the Republicans in subsequent elections despite winning many more votes, because large numbers of non-white voters who were likely to be supporters of the Democrats were packed into fewer electoral districts. Although explicit racial gerrymandering is illegal in the US under the 14th Amendment and the Voting Rights Act, the Republican strategists used a proxy for race by identifying the wards where President Obama received the highest returns in 2008 (Dickinson, 2013).

The Conservative government in the UK deployed another tactic to reduce the number of people from certain groups voting in elections. When a new voter registration system was put forward, the government was asked to bring it in cautiously over a long period of time to avoid people missing out because of the transition. Instead of listening to the advice of independent bodies such as the Electoral Commission, the government accelerated the process, and almost 2 million people dropped off the electoral register – comprising mainly those who were among the most disempowered in society, such as students, the poor, and minority ethnic groups in inner cities (Lowles, 2015).

Thirdly, in addition to eliminating procedural anomalies in voting systems that unintentionally or deliberately discriminate, we should provide rapid adjudication and correction. Within the jurisdiction of any organisation, it is vital that appeals can be made to an impartial authority to assess and, if necessary, rectify any alleged behaviour that encroaches on the respect for any individual or group of individuals. The 'political correctness' smokescreen aims to trivialise behaviour that demeans people by dismissing it as 'innocuous banter' and reject attempts to challenge such behaviour as humourless and meddlesome. At the same time, uncertainty over what is objectionable encourages some to make false claims of discrimination, which undermines overall efforts to tackle prejudices.

To counter these related problems, an inclusive adjudication panel (comprising of, for example, managers and workers, politicians and selected citizens, public officials and local residents) should always be in place with the power to examine complaints about behaviour that intentionally or otherwise makes those at the receiving end feel unwelcome in the organisation/ neighbourhood in question. Such a panel should not be tied to discriminatory matters of an exclusively racial, gender, disability, or any other single issue.

The key to effective investigation and assessment is to subject the behaviour in question to an in-depth mutuality test. This means it is not enough to dismiss concerns superficially by claiming, for example, that one would not mind 'jokes' being made about one's name or appearance. The question would be what one would make of expressions that routinely signal that others do not accept one. Similarly, it will not be sufficient to shrug off overlooking someone for promotion on the grounds that one has also missed out on promotion opportunities oneself from time to time, when the critical point is the wrongness of not getting promoted despite being better qualified and more experienced than all other candidates, and excluded just because of some irrelevant or imagined characteristic fixated on by a prejudiced mind.

The adjudication panel must be given the authority to take action against both those who act in a discriminatory manner towards others and those who make false claims of discrimination. It should also have the responsibility to explain its decisions, which will include why in some cases it has to rule that a claim of discrimination is neither proven nor falsely put forward. The credibility of an antidiscrimination panel is strengthened by its readiness to recognise that there are occasions when the available evidence is simply not enough to judge the claim as valid or fabricated.

As to how much is to be left to generic panels and how much has to be handed to specialist panels set up with dedicated powers to deal with discrimination in, for example, law enforcement agencies or military organisations, that is for those with oversight responsibilities in government to determine.[16] But even where there is justification for specialist investigative capability to be brought into play, there should be an option for generic panels to ask for an explanation of how any specialist case is dealt with, and compare it with the level of thoroughness and impartiality attained in other sectors.

Public discontent and protests following police killings of unarmed black US citizens are symptomatic of a widespread sense that some Americans are treated with far less respect and due care by the political establishment. In 2015, five times more unarmed black people were killed by the police in the US than unarmed white people. Charges were brought against those responsible in under 10% of the cases, and only two cases resulted in criminal convictions for the police officers involved.[17] When citizens feel deeply disrespected by the system that governs their lives, it is understandably difficult for them to respect it as something in which they can play a meaningful part.

So we turn to our final suggestion, namely the better use of reconciliatory exploration. Unresolved disagreement can fuel distrust, which may in turn breed ever deepening prejudice and disdain on both sides. The disagreement may stem from opposing views on public policies, incompatible interpretations of police actions, conflicting behaviour in a neighbourhood, or a breach of legal expectations. Democracy is committed neither to treating all sides as simply entitled to their views, nor imposing a majority position on everyone. It seeks to build a consensus that can overcome the initial differences.

Of course there are differences that are created by people who display utter disregard for the dignity of others, and their attitudes and behaviour ought to be unreservedly curtailed. But in many other instances, beneath the surface dispute and anger, there is potential common ground that can help bring opposing sides together to cultivate a new understanding, which can lead to increased, rather than diminished, mutual respect.

---

[16] We will look at the relation between democracy and the need for public accountability in Chapter Eleven.

[17] Source: Mapping Police Violence (USA): http://mappingpoliceviolence.org/unarmed/

Reconciliatory exploration is an approach whereby experienced facilitators encourage and guide people with contrasting views and clashing perspectives to come together to find out more about each other so that they can deal with their differences more constructively. It can be used in diverse situations, and the key is to maintain the focus on steering away from longstanding suspicion and moving instead towards greater mutual respect.

The Advocacy Institute in the US, for example, developed the Common Ground initiative to bring together pro-life and pro-choice groups to explore the issues affecting women with unwanted pregnancies (Boyte et al, 1994, p 15). It was recognised at the outset that neither side was likely to change their position on whether abortion should be allowed. But instead of allowing any kind of routine confrontation to develop, the facilitators pointed them towards problems faced by the women they all wanted to help, and guided them in exploring what they could do to improve the arrangements for adoption, foster care, and the provision of adequate prenatal services, where these are sought. Consequently, groups previously divided by a lack of shared understanding learnt to collaborate with each other.

In the UK, the Thames Valley Police Force pioneered the Community Conferencing technique which helped to resolve rancorous neighbourhood disputes by bringing the residents concerned together in reconciliatory meetings facilitated by trained police officers (Strang & Braithwaite, 2001). Those attending are able to air their grievances, explain their actions or reactions, and, most importantly, find out how others are affected by events in the area. Having learnt at the outset that shouting and exaggerations would not impress the police officer, participants accept that a genuine sharing of concerns and exploring of feasible adjustments going forward are what they must focus on. Prejudices are filtered out, and practical issues about rubbish disposal, car parking, hedge trimming, noise level, and so on are directly addressed. According to the Chief Constable, instead of disputes recurring and escalating – leading to police officers having to be repeatedly deployed to the area – in most cases the residents came to a shared understanding and some form of mutual accommodation prevailed; and the costs of training facilitators for and running community conferences paled in comparison with diverting police resources to respond to recurring and heated neighbourhood disputes.[18]

Some may assume that such an approach would only work for relatively low-level antagonism. If people's sense of being discriminated against runs deep or they are consumed by longstanding disrespect of others they have to deal with, would reconciliatory exploration be doomed to fail? There is no evidence to support such a pessimistic view. On the contrary, with appropriately trained facilitators and long-term commitment, it is more likely to secure mutual respect and understanding than any other method.[19]

In the years leading up to 2007, for example, the youth justice system in Washington, DC was reaching breaking point, with half of the black population under the age of 35 overseen by correctional services (in prison, on parole, or on probation). The social innovator Edgar Cahn applied his ideas on how people could earn time credit from giving their time to specific activities valued by others to the development of the Time Dollar Youth Court. Henceforth, any young person arrested for the first time for a non-violent offence in Washington would most likely be sent in front of a jury of other teenagers, who would question the accused and decide what should be done. One of the sentencing options was to require the person found guilty to serve on a jury in the future. For young people caught up in criminal behaviour, especially those who felt strongly that their racial profile meant they would never get a fair hearing, the experience was transformative. Trust and respect in the justice system were enhanced. In 2007 the youth court dealt with 80% of all first-time offences in Washington DC, and its work halved the reoffending rate to 17% (Boyle & Harris, 2009, p 13). This model was successfully replicated in Jefferson County, Wisconsin.

At the national level, the approach of reconciliatory exploration has also been applied to help end 30 years of internecine conflict

---

[18] Based on discussions between the Chief Constable of Thames Valley at the time, Charles Pollard, and me in my capacity as Crime Reduction Director (East of England) at the Home Office in the early 2000s.

[19] Without well-facilitated engagement and discussions, however, surface involvement may have little real impact (Jones & Roberts, 2007).

in Northern Ireland. The Belfast 'Good Friday' Agreement of 1998 was the culmination of talks facilitated with the purpose not of laying blame on who caused what wrongs in the past, but of finding ways for future generations to live in peace alongside each other. For decades, the Protestant unionists and Catholic republicans had no respect for each other's position, while their paramilitary wings engaged in intimidation and terrorist acts. A majoritarian electoral system could not on its own have delivered democracy, merely a governance structure that would alienate the minority even further. Building up mutual respect through structured dialogues to enable both sides to comprehend the concerns of the other, on the other hand, effectively paved the way for genuine power sharing and cooperation.

Remedial checklist: mutual respect

With reference to any group the governance of which you are concerned about, you can use the checklist below to identify what requires the most improvement in relation to the need for mutual respect:

☐ Do some members feel that they are discriminated against due to some irrelevant characteristics they possess? Is enough being done to tackle the roots of prejudiced attitudes? Are there enough accessible and trusted adjudication mechanisms to deal with claims of discrimination impartially?

☐ Is there sufficient awareness of how selective invocation of traditions or religious beliefs can be used to lower the esteem for particular categories of people, and are labels like 'political correctness' deployed to deflect criticisms of disrespectful behaviour? Should there be more reflective awareness-raising carried out to help those who do not see the hurt caused to others, to enable them to attain better empathy?

☐ Are the procedures by which collective power is exercised checked for their actual impact on different members? When new barriers are introduced, or old criteria shielded from revisions, are they actually designed to marginalise those the rule makers do not care for? Is there notable discontent with the lack of consistency or transparency in the treatment of certain members?

☐ Are there too many divisive issues that turn some members against others? Where distrust and disrespect have reached a level where they threaten to undermine the prospect of the group moving in an agreed direction, are there plans to use reconciliatory exploration to overcome the psychological barrier to democratic cooperation?

FIVE

Coherent membership

Democratic governance needs those under its jurisdiction to have a strong enough sense of togetherness to support and accept collective decisions that will be binding on everyone. We have seen that this requires the cultivation of shared missions and the development of mutual respect among those involved. One further factor that must be taken into account is the need for coherent membership. Any group – a local association, a business, a country – must have a coherent approach to managing its membership if it is not to lose its core capacity to function as a governable entity. In this chapter, we will look at why certain membership issues must be properly dealt with if democracy is to work, what problems may follow if various misguided ideas on group membership are allowed to take hold, and how coherent membership can be more effectively sustained.

Why democracy needs coherent membership

For any group of people to get along – as neighbours, co-workers, or fellow citizens – they must understand what counts as being a member of that group, and what that entails in terms of membership benefits and responsibilities. Without that foundational understanding, it could be problematic for people to govern themselves when they are uncertain what 'they' are.

Group membership is inherently bound up with a sense of belonging. The laissez-faire view of group membership ignores the fact that membership choices are often limited, and the associated terms may not always be satisfactory. Although the question of membership of a country has received considerable attention in relation to the issue of immigration, the decline of stable identity among many people is connected with other changes ranging from insecurity as a worker in a business organisation, to uncertainty as a resident in areas that are either not fit to live in or too expensive for one's children to afford to set up home.[1]

Human identity and the corresponding level of self-worth are derived from people's relationships with others in groups they consider important to them (Bellah et al, 1996). How they are regarded, valued, and accepted in those groups shape their perception of who they are, particularly how they see their place in the world. The different groups matter to them to varying degrees, but each one adds to their overall conception of their role in life. Some individualists may think that the truly free person is one unencumbered by any inclination to take others' thoughts and feelings into account, but such an 'ideal' type turns out to be little more than a total sociopath. At the other extreme, there are nationalists who believe all that matters come from being a member of a nation, but that may only be true in exceptional circumstances, when one's nation is under imminent threat or one has hit rock bottom in one's relationship with all other groups to which one belongs (or wishes one belonged). Besides, what is projected as a nation is in turn a social construct that is often contested (Gellner, 2009; Smith, A. D., 2010).

For the vast majority of people, for most of their lives, the approval they seek and the support they are willing to offer are intertwined with the multiplicity of groups which count them as members. Where their membership provides them with regular opportunities to pursue shared goals with others, overcome particular differences, and nurture mutual respect, they can readily cooperate on working out rules and practices that will help them achieve together what they could not have done individually. However, if membership is precarious and the terms appear to be arbitrary, then instead of looking out for

---

[1] One of the key factors behind the public outcry over the fire at Grenfell Tower in 2017 was that for years many people had experienced being left behind in housing facilities that were grossly neglected, including in terms of their safety.

each other, people focus more and more on what is 'owed' to them, and they become highly sceptical about there being any common good for the group they ought to serve.

In the early post-war decades, the combination of steady economic growth generating decent jobs, and a burgeoning public sector providing a reliable safety net against ill health and financial difficulties meant that most people had stable families, reliable places of work, familiar local organisations, and a country that was entrusted to be governed by one or the other of two established political parties. Membership of overlapping groups was taken for granted. One belonged to a wide range of human associations, and few felt the need to question the basis or implications of that belonging.

But from the late 1970s on, with the New Right's ascendancy and the further concentration of power in the corporate elite, the relationships among the members of numerous groups at all levels came under increasing strain (Hertz, 2001). With fewer constraints on big business and more controls for trade unions, the mantra of labour flexibility became code for corporate irresponsibility. Businesses were free to make large numbers of their employees redundant, move operations abroad, slice jobs into part-time positions or zero-hour contracts, freeze pay despite rises in productivity, hire cheaper workers from abroad, and close plants irrespective of local impact. Workers were obliged to adjust accordingly.

Consequently, the decades leading up to the beginning of the 21st century were characterised by an increasing number of people who lost their workplace identity, with jobs for life diminishing; membership terms were shaken, with progression through accumulated experience becoming a thing of the past; family stability was undermined as people were expected to move around to chase after jobs; parents and grandparents had to work longer hours and supplement part-time work with more part-time work; and whole neighbourhoods slumped into economic deprivation when a major employer moved elsewhere (Gilpin, 2000; Reich, 2009). Local newspapers, radio stations, shops, football clubs, and other amenities that gave people a sense of belonging were bought by national and global corporations with their own agendas, leaving local people feeling like outsiders in their own towns and cities.

Just as people's sense of attachment to social entities that had previously anchored their relationships to others was in a state of flux, the reduced powers of trade unions to negotiate reasonable terms for their members meant not only that union membership itself declined, but also that employers could set pay at lower levels and bring in workers from abroad to fill vacancies. In 1995, seven EU countries moved ahead with the Schengen Agreement which abolished the internal border controls between them. Even though the external border was strengthened, right-wing politicians and their backers in the media began to attack the freedom for low-income people to move around European countries. The attacks continued to escalate when the EU pressed ahead with further enlargement in 2004 and 2007, inadvertently aiding the New Right in diverting attention from the role played by multinational tax-avoiding corporate powers, and focusing it instead on the negative portrayal of multi-ethnic tax-paying migrant workers.[2]

But while there will always be a minority who harbour fear and hatred for people who do not fit into their insular conception of normality, most people are not racist just because they have concerns about membership changes to their group. There needs to be some form of shared mission to give purpose to uniting different people into a common system. That mission can evolve over time, and mutually respecting members ought to be able to reflect on the terms and conditions for any future member of their country. Historically, this has seldom been a straightforward question. For example, France in the 19th century was so concerned about many people living there without taking the responsibility of being a citizen that eventually it pressed all residents to become full French citizens (Weil, 1996, p 77). By contrast, by the early 1980s many in West Germany felt that ethnic Germans who had come from the communist east were

---

[2] The 2004 EU enlargement was the biggest in terms of population added since the EU/EC was founded. The 2007 enlargement further brought in Romania and Bulgaria.

not culturally assimilated enough to be regarded as true nationals of their country (Fulbrook, 1996, pp 94-95).

Membership questions also relate to population control. Towards the end of the 1970s, China concluded that its population growth was too high to be sustained at its level of economic development, and adopted the one child policy.[3] The policy was reconsidered in the light of China's rapid economic growth in the 1990s and 2000s, and it was phased out from 2015. Many other Asian countries later also prioritised population control, with state-sponsored campaigns on sex education and the distribution of contraceptives.

If any country wants its members to govern themselves, then it is essential they have a clear and shared understanding of the process for determining their membership. To achieve the key objectives of their shared mission, they need to know what resources and skills are required, and if more or fewer members should be in the group in future years. Although xenophobic politics thrives on scaring people with claims of foreigners 'flooding in' from abroad and taking up precious jobs and resources, any reality check would pick up on problems associated with an ageing population, such as labour shortages, skills mismatch, and insufficient support from outside the country to generate new jobs and resources.[4] If inward investment can be vital for a country, and import of goods essential to meet basic needs, then the incoming of workers may be indispensable too under certain circumstances.

Furthermore, the clarity required for members to see their proper role in collective decision making goes beyond the expansion or shrinkage of the overall membership. It must reveal what members are under a duty to do; what they can expect as their due; what additional responsibilities/rewards may be earned; and what penalties may be incurred in relation to what failures to act. The answers to these questions affect nearly all

[3] The policy only applied to the Han majority ethnic group. Ethnic minorities were allowed to have more than one child per family.

[4] Fred Pearce (2011) has argued that instead of an irreversible population explosion, the world should be preparing for the eventual decline of global population. In time, more people may come to realise that they should be concerned with increasing, rather than reducing, immigration.

other forms of membership in society. Their overall impact can either further fragment social bonds and render civic cooperation even less likely, or strengthen the building blocks for large-scale collaboration on a national and international level. There are at least four sets of issues that can shift citizens' dispositions in one or the opposite direction.

First of all, what are the basic rules for 'joining and excluding'? A democratic country would not allow any group under its jurisdiction to exclude members on grounds that are not connected to relevant behaviour or abilities. Anyone should be allowed to apply to join an educational institution, work for a company, or stand for political office. Their selection should be based solely on the relevant aptitudes, as should any subsequent exclusion if those selected are found to breach the criteria for their retention. So if, for example, one is told that one's children cannot go to a state-funded school just because one does not subscribe to the 'correct' religion, that casts doubt over one's democratic membership.

Secondly, since membership covers a wide range of roles with different responsibilities, powers, privileges, and compensation, the question arises as to what the criteria are for attaining the more prestigious positions. As the wealth gap has widened, the rise to higher ranks is increasingly dependent on how rich one's parents are or how skilled one is at the task of buying and selling goods, services, or financial deals to maximise one's gains. But for most groups, many of the attributes and contributions they depend on to flourish are rarely adequately remunerated.[5] Despite the common rhetoric about the value of 'hard-working families', the mobility for obtaining higher rewards/responsibilities is extremely limited, and for many people hard work barely guarantees even subsistence-level pay.

Thirdly, membership of a state is supposed to bring with it a range of direct support for all citizens, and a further set of indirect protection via the regulations placed on groups under that state's jurisdiction. For example, the direct support may

---

[5] For example, caring for relatives, giving encouragement to those losing hope, sharing difficult but unpaid burdens, or organising for those necessary but thankless tasks beyond financial transactions.

include free education for children, a health service, a safety net from extreme poverty, basic environmental cleanliness, policing and judicial functions; while the indirect protection may help to curtail incidents such as sexual harassment at the workplace, refusal by local amenities to make allowances for people with disabilities, or a residential organisation intruding into the privacy of its tenants. But since the 1980s people have been increasingly told that the tax revenues and regulations needed to deliver such membership terms are too much of a burden on people and corporations, and that the benefits they offer ought to be cut back so people can learn to manage their own lives. When enough people buy into this rhetoric and thus vote for those who then bring in policies that repeatedly cut down on the benefits of membership, insecurity in almost every sphere of life rises, and the downward spiral heads towards the Mandeville mantra of 'look after yourself, forget about everything else'.

Finally, there is the question of partial suspension or total disqualification of membership. Being a citizen entitles one to be protected directly and indirectly from a wide range of negative situations, but the protection is not unconditional. Unfortunately, what factors may lead to what withdrawal of protection is seldom clearly explained. This can lead people to think that there is not in fact any coherent rationale behind the single most serious issue for any of them – the possible loss of their identity, their security, their future prospects as a member of their country, and the related implications for their relationships with other groups to which they belong. Since any group, from a business to a nation, depends on its members fulfilling their roles without doubting that their membership entitlements may be arbitrarily reduced, uncertainty over the loss of those entitlements can lead to a group losing the dedicated support of its members. The only way to counter this is to have a set of reasonable criteria that members accept as applicable to all without exception. For instance, people may lose the protection from being detained if they pose a threat to public health because they have contracted a dangerous and highly contagious disease. The evidential threshold for assessing if these conditions apply in any situation, and the proportionality of any authorised response, must be carefully calibrated if the group and its members are not to end up with worse problems than those the responses are meant to solve.

Contested notions of group membership

To improve the democratic governance of any group, it is essential for the members of that group to understand and broadly agree with the terms of their membership. Otherwise they may doubt if they truly belong, or for that matter want to belong, to that group, let alone help it make the right decisions. But how those membership terms are to be formulated depends on a deeper conception of what kind of group it is.

One common assumption is that any group is important to the extent it constitutes the identity of its members. The more a group determines how its members see themselves, especially the attitudinal and behavioural boundaries they feel they must accept, the more significant and commanding it is. What leads people to comply with the extensive, and even rigid, demands placed on them by such groups can take many forms, but they share one crucial characteristic – they offer a unifying force that in the minds of the members is so strong that their allegiance to it is unalterable (Anderson, 2006). This force could be a shared belief in a deity; a revered monarch/emperor (past or present); a skin tone perceived as a proxy for blood ties; a language/dialect; a set of customs; a flag and related monuments; a religion or a sect/denomination of it; territorial boundaries from one designated historical period; a collection of cultural dispositions; or some combination of them.

For some, a group bound together with such 'unbreakable' bonds is the only group worth belonging to. Everything else must be subservient to it, and anything it enjoins can only be rejected at the risk of one being marginalised or punished, if not altogether expelled. This is true of how certain religious congregations, tribes, and countries have at times behaved. But many other groups at all levels of society do not. Just because some people are desperate for a single all-absorbing identity and demand, on occasions successfully, that others in the group follow their lead, it does not mean that everyone else feels the same. People can have a multiplicity of social identities, a plurality of commitments, and an evolving network of reciprocal relationships that enrich their lives emotionally, and connect them to robust mutual support with others. They can love their country even though most of their fellow citizens do not share their religious devotions. They can dedicate themselves to outperforming a business competitor, but passionately join with some of the members of that rival business in supporting the same environmental cause. They can routinely seek to raise funds for a political party, and treasure their involvement in a Haydn appreciation society where members belong to different political parties.

And not only is it wrong to insist that to have a meaningful sense of belonging one must be completely pinned to a fixed position in a monolithic group; to succumb to such a worldview has wider negative consequences. People may end up becoming convinced that their sense of belonging can only be sustained by excluding others who do not meet some criteria for imagined purity. Racism, misogyny, or homophobia can become badges of the 'hard core' true members. Ironically, the underlying aspiration to be an all-encompassing group that can deal with every key issue in life is thereby thwarted by its narrowing vision. Instead of embracing diverse contributions for different concerns, such groups want to slot people into hermetically sealed categories irrespective of what the issue is. As a result, they refuse to engage with others whose help would otherwise prove invaluable (as nurses, teachers, technicians, and so on, or just as friends and neighbours), just because of some irrelevant factors that have ossified into absolute barriers in their minds. When others want to change membership terms – for example, to get rid of old restrictions on what women can do, or open the door to new members to help save the group from its limitations – those obsessed with 'preserving' the group end up aggravating its weaknesses and hastening its decline.

Such fundamentalist group mentality can turn a religion of love into a cult of intolerance; displace an honest assessment of the need for immigration by routine harassment of immigrants to placate those who resent 'aliens' (Shanahan, 1999); and, where it sweeps through society in the form of tribal nationalism, it can impose a rigid hierarchy wherein some are given the group's 'blessing' to look down on, intimidate, and ill-treat anyone in the category of 'others' (Tam, 2015a, pp 116-137).

Against this ethos of total group absorption, a diametrically opposite outlook has developed from the time of the Daoists, through Mandeville's unapologetic individualism to modern-day rational choice theory. One of the early Daoists, Yang Chu, famously claimed that if he had to pull one hair off his own body and that would help the rest of the world without any benefit accruing to him, he would not do it (Chan, 1963, pp 309-313). According to rational choice theorists, human beings are best thought of as logical calculators of their own interests, on the basis of which they will make decisions as to what they will do. The membership of any group, far from carrying any unquantifiable value that stems from a unique sense of belonging, is considered a purely instrumental matter. One joins if the benefits outweigh the costs of joining, and leaves if that is reversed. Similarly, others are welcome to join if that is assessed to be overall advantageous to securing what one wants, but new membership should not be given out if that diminishes the narrowly defined returns one has hitherto been counting on.

The psychological assumptions behind this outlook, and its limited predictive powers when access to information is often highly restricted, have been widely criticised (Foley, 2008; Green & Shapiro, 2012). Few people in any case actually behave in the manner of a 'rational choice' maker, except for the economics lecturers and graduates who try to practise what they preach.[6] But where these experts of economics attain influential policy positions, they shape proposals that in effect treat membership issues as though everyone would come together or move apart on a basis of purely self-centred functional calculations.

Redevelopment of neighbourhoods, for example, is premised on what the quantifiable gains and losses (often restricted to what can be expressed in monetised terms) are for individuals, and presented as justifiable even if people actually feel that

---

[6] Economics students often perform worse than others in Prisoners' Dilemma games because of their mistaken assumption about human behaviour. In one case conducted by two university economists, the students did worse than actual prisoners (Nisen, 2013).

radical changes to the area will strip it of the familiarity and mutual helpfulness they associate with the old place, or if the most vulnerable end up being displaced (Lees, 2013). When wider social relationships are ignored, and obligations to fellow group members are not given due consideration, then any group is reduced to nothing but the individuals who only think about what they can personally get out of the group. It is no coincidence that such a conception of 'society' breeds the 'cut my taxes, but spend more on the public services I use' attitudes. If community cohesion ebbs away, it is because the internal bonds are relentlessly corroded by the spread of 'what's in it for me' individualism.

Beyond national borders, there are transnational institutions and partnerships set up around the world to facilitate business deals and security operations (Held & McGrew, 2002). People were told to appreciate the City of London or Wall Street boosting the economy with their global investment; cheaper goods produced by factories abroad with low-paid workers; and improvements to the balance of payment through greater profits made from arms sales to the Middle East and elsewhere. But when the economy was wrecked by another international banking crisis; jobs were lost when more production plants were moved abroad; and escalating conflicts in the Middle East, fuelled by weapons bought from the West, led to more refugees seeking sanctuary, there was no group mechanism to come up with satisfactory solutions. Many concluded that whatever transnational group or arrangement they had gone along with so far, it was time to pull out (James, 2016).

In order to steer through monolithic group absorption as well as superficial grouping of laissez-faire individuals, we need a pluralistic form of membership that combines the pursuit of a shared mission with mutual respect among diverse members. Democratic group formation enables people to hold on to what they personally regard as important to them (and that may be different for different individuals), but requires them to abide by certain rules and procedures so they can cooperate in defining and pursuing common objectives. The mere fact that people have divergent beliefs, values, and customs is not in itself a cause for concern. Indeed, such diversity may help to test old assumptions and generate new ideas, and thus strengthen the group's ability to innovate and adapt. However, when differences lead to direct conflicts between members, or disputes over what the group should do, these must be resolved through processes supported by prior democratic decisions.

Over time, procedures are established for electing representatives, selecting judges, appointing officials, passing laws, investigating infringement, conducting trials, implementing sentences, and assessing appeals. But what if some members refuse to abide by them on the grounds that they are incompatible with their conscience or their allegiance to some higher authority? Most challengingly of all, what if someone uses the procedures to obtain sufficient power to dismantle them?

Since the rise of the New Right in the 1980s, strands of tribal nationalism have been increasingly invoked to attack the inclusive intentions of democratic governance. Patriotism was co-opted for a political strategy that deflects discontent with rising income inequalities and socioeconomic insecurity caused by corporate irresponsibility, towards foreign elements that need to be put in their place at home and abroad. From the show of military prowess in defeating enemies over at the Falkland Islands or Grenada, to repeated innuendos that immigrants were damaging the WASP[7] culture that characterised true Brits and Americans, the flame of imagined purity was fanned until it started to burn down democratic safeguards, and membership cleansing entered mainstream politics by the late 2010s.[8]

How to improve democratic membership

Democracy's promise of collective self-governance can only be delivered by members who are prepared to safeguard its core commitments, and support the development and implementation of common policies. This is unlikely to happen if the group in

---

[7] White Anglo-Saxon Protestant.

[8] This can take many forms, from Prime Minister Theresa May's stance post-Brexit vote that drove many EU nationals living in UK to leave (O'Connor & Warrell, 2017), to President Donald Trump's crackdown against millions of law-abiding residents in the US who originally arrived in the country without due authorisation (Roberts, 2017a).

question is misguidedly boxed into a rigid, isolated hierarchy; diluted into a loose collection of detached individuals; or left without enough safeguards against exploitation by an unscrupulous few. The kind of group that can sustain democratic governance needs membership arrangements that are pluralistic, fair, and nimble enough to adapt to changing circumstances without losing sight of its shared mission.

Any group concerned with having members capable of using the meta-strategy of democracy to guide its policy development should give consideration to at least four areas where improvements can be made to the relationship between the group and its members. These involve:

- providing comprehensive induction for all members;
- subjecting disputes to a civic compatibility test;
- committing to member-led revisions of terms and conditions; and
- improving processes for the suspension and restoration of membership.

Let us first look at what is involved in providing comprehensive induction for all members. Despite widespread talk of the rights and responsibilities of citizenship, the tendency is still to leave it to individuals to find out what being a member of any given society means. And even when someone is keen to discover more, it is often not easy to find the relevant information.

For example, the US Citizenship and Immigration Service sets out the rights of a US citizen as including 'the freedom to express yourself; freedom to worship as you wish; the right to a prompt, fair trial by jury; ... and the freedom to pursue "life, liberty, and the pursuit of happiness"'.[9] The responsibilities are listed in terms of the duty to 'support and defend the Constitution; stay informed of the issues affecting your community; ... pay income and other taxes honestly, and on time, to federal, state, and local authorities; serve on a jury when called upon; and defend the country if the need should arise'. The various rights

---

[9] See www.uscis.gov/citizenship/learners/citizenship-rights-and-responsibilities

and responsibilities are open to contrasting interpretations, and there is no indication of what one can expect if one's rights are violated or if one fails to live up to one's responsibilities.

Many other governments adopt a similar basic listing approach.[10] The UK supplements it with an A–Z guide. But none of these lists provides citizens with an in-depth understanding of what it is to be a member of one's country. For immigrants applying for citizenship, there is a formal process comprising a simplistic knowledge test and a one-off public ceremony. The test is usually made up of questions for immigrants, though many existing citizens will not know the answers to them. The ceremonies vary in size but are all aimed at giving public recognition to the conferment of the new civic status. Very few new citizens will learn from these experiences what their rights and responsibilities really mean in practice, and there is nothing equivalent for those who are already citizens of the country since birth.

Singapore is one of the few countries where there is a more extensive programme of induction for new citizens. It brings together 'an online self-study component, a tour of historical landmarks and national institutions, and a community engagement session, culminating in a citizenship ceremony' (Mathews & Soon, 2016). If such an approach is linked to a more interactive A–Z type guide to what citizens can expect to receive and are in turn expected to offer, and made available to all, not just new citizens, then we may begin to have the building blocks for comprehensive induction.

The Citizenship Foundation in the UK has shown how a wide range of learning resources, teacher training guides, and interactive exercises such as mock trials and political debates can help schools play a key role in ensuring every member of a country, from an early age, can develop a practical understanding of what it means to be a citizen. Citizenship education even formally entered the curriculum in England and Wales from 2001, potentially enabling young people to learn over time at growing levels of complexity until they are ready to make the

---

[10] Canada, for example, adds 'taking responsibility for oneself and one's family' to the list of responsibilities, while it makes it clear that serving in the military is noble but nonetheless optional.

fullest use of government information online relating to their democratic membership.[11] Unfortunately, citizenship education was subsequently downgraded after Labour lost the 2010 election, and any hope of developing it post-formal education was lost through cuts to public funding for lifelong learning. But despite the withdrawal of political support, it has been shown that educators can generate the core components of an ongoing induction programme. With longer-term support, more learning activities in schools can be integrated with public information services to provide a gradual induction programme to ensure people are engaged in learning about what they should or should not do as citizens, what are contested areas, how they may be involved in resolving them, and why they need to keep up to date with relevant information on their rights and duties.

Secondly, support for group diversity and resolution of disputes should be aided by a civic compatibility test. Only a totalitarian state would attempt to subsume all its members into a single group in society. By contrast, democratic openness welcomes a multiplicity of groups which people can form or join to cultivate common interests and pursue a variety of shared goals. However, this openness has often been exploited by groups that seek to achieve objectives which are incompatible with the core mission of protecting all citizens from harm, and the requirement of mutual respect which rules out the subordination of some members of society to gratify others.

A civic compatibility test would permit groups to set their own terms for their members provided they do not act unilaterally regardless of the threat they pose or the harm they may inflict on others, who may or may not belong to those groups. Any group which is likely to fail such a test cannot hide behind a demand for autonomy to persist with its activities. For example, a private club may claim that members share photographs of naked children for their own enjoyment and it is no business of anyone else to infringe on their liberty. Members of a sect may claim that they must stay true to a doctrine which forbids them or their families to have anything to do with modern medicine,

---

[11] Citizenship education in England and Wales was advanced by Bernard Crick (Crick & Lockyer, 2010).

even if a refusal to receive treatment can cause the death of an infant or spread an infectious disease to the wider population. Members of a militia group may claim that they will refuse to comply with any law passed to regulate the purchase and use of deadly weapons because they consider it an unacceptable affront to their rights.[12] In all such cases, a group cannot be allowed to continue its practices. For people to share a democratic way of life, they must abide by the commitment to mutual respect we considered in the previous chapter. Just because some people believe that what they do is right or has been hallowed by time, if they threaten or harm other citizens, they cannot shield themselves in the name of group autonomy.

To govern democratically, a government has to be ready to intervene where necessary. If a group seeks to engage in activities that are totally incompatible with the protection due to democratic citizens, it should not be allowed to have any members. Where there is no such incompatibility, membership ought to be open. Between these two ends of the spectrum, there will be others that require varying degrees of monitoring and regulation. So-called 'culture wars' are often initiated by groups that maintain an all-or-nothing position about their freedom to operate. Invoking disputed rights or contested customs, they insist on rejecting regulatory oversight, because allegedly they would otherwise be extinguished altogether. But in these cases, the governing body must dismiss the false dichotomy.

For example, a commune is free to draw up its own rules and practices, but there are still limits the government can reasonably set as to how it treats its members. A firm can determine its own terms for those who work for it, but if these include any that would effectively place workers under duress to comply with degrading conditions, those particular terms would have to be removed. A country may want to standardise its internal communications with one single language, but in some cases,

---

[12] The Second Amendment to the US Constitution has been invoked in arguing that citizens' right to bear arms cannot be infringed by any kind of government regulation, when the need for regulation has in fact always been accepted, otherwise anyone could purchase, carry and use any type of arms, from a sniper rifle to a missile launcher, without any legal control (Waldman, 2014).

such as Canada (with about 22% of its population speaking French as their first language), it needs to accommodate the use and provision of another language in everyday life and official business (Maris, 1995).

Thirdly, it is important to establish member-led revisions of terms and conditions. Many destabilising factors for democratic governance come from members feeling helpless about some unsatisfactory membership terms that are in place, or members alienated by changes to those terms without their involvement. The situation should be reversed so that members' informed views are sought about current terms, and opportunities are provided to them to influence any changes that will be brought in.

In the UK, for example, polarisation between the old and the young is brewing because those approaching what were the previously set pension ages for men and women were told they would have to wait longer before they could retire, while the young are told that a wide range of support that their parents' generation took for granted, such as free university education and housing benefit, has been withdrawn from them. The two sides of the age divide are encouraged by some commentators to blame the other – the old are having to work longer because the young are less dedicated to finding work; the young are losing financial support because the elderly are getting 'all the benefits'. In reality, changes to their membership terms were made to deal with the longer lifespan of people (resulting in higher costs to cover pension payments) and the cutting of public expenditure to accommodate the accumulation of the country's resources in the private wealth of the richest in society.[13] If people were given a chance to consider the different options for distributing the country's resources to fund existing membership entitlements, they might arrive at alternative offers, and they would most likely take greater ownership of the outcomes.

[13] Tax changes that came into effect in the UK in 2017 resulted in 80% of the gains from tax cuts going to the richest in the country while the poorest became worse off. For example, a high-income couple with two children, earning £100,000 a year, will be £480 better off; but a low-income single parent with a baby, earning £17,300 a year, will be £530 worse off (Helm, 2017).

The detachment of membership changes from current members poses an even more critical problem in relation to people coming to a country from abroad. Immigration has become a highly exploitable issue that can be used to channel citizens' discontent towards newcomers without addressing the real causes of socioeconomic insecurity. People with precarious jobs and low pay are susceptible to propaganda about the level and impact of immigration. But unless they have a sense of ownership of the criteria and process for deciding who should or should not be brought into the country, they are less likely to believe that decisions relating to immigration are the correct ones.

Given the complexities of the issue – which covers shortage of skills and willing contributors in a number of key sectors; the implications of an ageing population; the appropriate timespan for cultural integration; marriage and family ties across borders; the importance of maintaining international cross-fertilisation of ideas and outlooks – it would be counterproductive to reduce discussions to a simplistic dichotomous referendum. Instead, member involvement should be developed through the comprehensive induction outlined above, so that people can learn about why members have certain rights and responsibilities, how changing circumstances mean that more or fewer members are needed, and what criteria make sense for administering the assessment process.[14]

Instead of compartmentalising the issue of immigration, the continuous learning and sharing of informed opinions should be integrated with discussions about other closely related matters. For example, if the pros and cons of new members joining a country are to be considered, so should the pros and cons of existing members leaving the country, especially if they have taken advantage of what the country has given them (training, opportunities to accumulate wealth from others in the country, and so on), and take the assets they have built up away with them. Questions can be raised about if one's country should support or even lead the bombing in another region of the world, what

---

[14]   For a useful guide on how to facilitate a sensitive and deliberative discussion about immigration, see Katwala et al (2014).

responsibilities should follow when refugees try to escape from that region and seek sanctuary in one's country.

Membership changes can also be brought about on a large scale when merger/demerger options surface. We have seen how the ad hoc handling of the UK's relationship with Scotland and the EU has led to greater discontent, uncertainty, and instability. The polarising assumption that one can become a member of a group and withdraw unilaterally without taking into account the impact on the rest of the group can only lead to interminable tension. Many British citizens outside Scotland felt that the future of the UK should not be put at risk by a decision that was to be made exclusively by people in Scotland, but a large number of them were content for the future of the EU to be jeopardised by a referendum held exclusively in the UK.

Finally, we should improve our arrangements for the suspension and restoration of membership terms. There is no better indicator of arbitrary rule than the random imposition of penalties and the deployment of wholly disproportionate punishment. Members of a democracy should rightly expect to be treated with the same respect that is accorded to everyone else, and the rules stipulating the consequences of any particular type of violation would be applied to all without exception.

Although trial by jury has an important role in ensuring that justice is administered by one's peers without bias, it actually has a small part in the overall system for law and order. Most arrangements for determining what are violations, how they are to be detected, and what should be done with those accused are shrouded in bureaucratic mystery that few can penetrate. Against this backdrop, it is not surprising that some may regard any form of enforcement as top-down social control (Dreyfus & Rabinow, 1982; Foucault, 1991).

To counter the ignorance and misunderstanding of what membership terms may be suspended under what conditions and explore how to restore them, members must be given a wider role in reviewing these issues. Extensive research carried out for the Esmée Fairbairn Foundation found that the involvement of lay members (that is, not professionals of criminal justice organisations) in deliberating options helps to generate more constructive proposals for what to do with those accused of having violated the trust of their fellow citizens (Rethinking Crime & Punishment, 2004). One notable discovery was that although tabloid propaganda may lead some people into thinking criminals in general should be punished more severely, informed explorations with expert testimony can shift opinions away from prejudiced positions towards approaches that are far more likely to lead to a safer society and a reduction in reoffending.

These approaches in turn share a focus on connecting community experiences of violations with the perpetrators' experience of the consequences of their actions. Community-based judges have sought the views of local people in a deliberative environment to understand better the impact of offences before passing sentences. In youth justice, volunteers from local communities across England and Wales have served on panels to discuss with youth offenders what would be the most effective actions to reduce the likelihood of their reoffending (Davies & McMahon, 2007). Communities have also been invited to put forward suggestions and indicate their preferences for community reparation work to be carried out by prisoners under supervision. These have included restoring neglected open spaces, growing food, and other landscaping projects, where the work and consequent benefits to the wider community could be seen by all.[15]

Facilitating engagement of offenders with their victims has also been an important pathway back to civic normalisation. One of the biggest stumbling blocks for offenders to reintegrate fully into community life is the stigma of not being forgiven, and an underlying cause of that is the belief that they have not truly experienced any remorse. Locking offenders away or keeping them under supervision by probation officers does little to address this problem.

By contrast, restorative mediation that brings offenders and victims together provides an opportunity for offenders to face up to what they have done, learn from their victims, and respond accordingly. It is easy to dismiss this approach in the abstract as something that will lead to either heartless offenders upsetting

[15] See, for example: www.uclan.ac.uk/research/explore/projects/assets/ GOOP-Impact-Report.pdf

their victims even more, or devious culprits pretending to show remorse to get better treatment. In practice, the evidence shows that while some offenders are not prepared to engage with their victims, many do go through the process with transformative results for themselves, their victims, and (as a result of their greater readiness to avoid further violations) society generally (Crosland & Liebmann, 2003).[16]

Although there are serious offenders who will need to be detained for long periods or kept under tight supervision even after they are released, there are degrees of rehabilitation that should nonetheless be considered. The neglect of this issue has allowed, for example, the virus of racial hatred to spread in prisons, and infect wider interactions in the community. Instead of aiding the transition from criminality to respectful citizenship, prisons thus become host bodies where more virulent strains of racist animosity are bred (Phillips, C., 2007). But any democratic society that is too ready to push large numbers of its members beyond a point of no rehabilitation, with no offer of intervention, counselling, or reconciliation, will find itself producing ever more people who feel cut off and act accordingly. The UK's insistence on denying prisoners convicted of non-serious offences their right to vote, and the US states that will not restore the right to vote to those who have served their time for a serious crime, are further symptoms of this harmful neglect.

---

[16] For more on the applications of restorative justice, see the information provided by the Restorative Justice Council: www.restorativejustice.org.uk/what-restorative-justice

Remedial checklist: coherent membership

With reference to any group the governance of which you are concerned about, you can use the checklist below to identify what requires the most improvement in relation to the need for coherent membership:

☐ Is there a coherent membership system in place that is generally understood by the members in terms of how it will recruit, induct, reject, and expel members? Is it functioning effectively enough to secure a membership that is suitable to meet the group's needs? Can existing and new members count on going through a comprehensive induction programme to understand what membership entails?

☐ Do members welcome or have reservations about who is joining or leaving the group? Are they involved in considering why changing circumstances may require appropriate changes in the overall membership? Are informed views being developed and sought in order to guide decisions over issues such as merging with or separating from other groups? Are revisions to the terms and conditions of being a member made with the input of the members themselves?

☐ Is it clear to all members that they can participate in any group the aims and activities of which are not incompatible with the overall civic mission that is underpinned by mutual respect? Or in cases where a group is being set up or supported with the intention to undermine social harmony or inflict harm on others, are there sufficient barriers to prevent such a group from operating or recruiting members?

☐ Are members sufficiently supported in carrying out their roles so they merit what they are entitled to as members and steer clear of the designated range of violations? Are there dependable mechanisms to prevent those who have broken the rules from reoffending, enable them to learn from their mistakes, and help restore them as far as possible to full membership status?

PART THREE

How to underpin democratic objectivity

SIX

Collaborative learning

In the last three chapters we have looked at how democracy can only function well if it manages to engender sufficient togetherness through establishing a shared mission, robust defence of mutual respect, and coherent membership arrangements among those who seek to govern themselves. In addition to these elements, for any group to steer itself democratically, its members must be able to discuss options and resolve differences with a high degree of objectivity. Without a common basis on which conflicting ideas can be explored and assessed, people will have no means of deciding what claims should be taken into account, or what demands are groundless. Between the autocracy imposed by some imperious know-it-all and the anarchy of perpetual disputes, democracy can offer a viable alternative, provided it operates with the objectivity that comes from collaborative learning, critical re-examination, and responsible communication. In this chapter, we will consider why collaborative learning is indispensable, what lessons should be learnt from past attempts to acquire reliable knowledge, and how the development of collaborative learning can be better supported.

Democratic objectivity and collaborative learning

When the arguments over whether or not there should be universal suffrage intensified in the middle of the 19th century, John Stuart Mill cautioned both sides about the need to build democracy on proper foundations. If rule by a few should not be risked because it could open the door to being controlled

119

by fools and knaves, he observed, majoritarian rule could also be dangerous if public decisions were driven not by informed debates, but by rash or ignorant assessments. In his *Considerations on Representative Government* he maintained that while the vote should be extended to all adult men and women, there should be basic requirements to ensure that people had some rudimentary skills in digesting information presented to them before they were eligible to vote (Mill, 2008).

Mill's suggestion of testing people on the ability to read, write, and do simple arithmetic to determine if they should be admitted onto the electoral register drew criticisms from all quarters. The conservative-minded insisted that people needed much more than the basic skills Mill mentioned to be able to judge what they should vote for, and hence the franchise should be restricted to the minority who had the luxury to cultivate the necessary understanding. Radical reformists, on the other hand, rejected any educational hurdle as an elitist and unacceptable barrier to granting the right to vote for all.

Leaving aside the adequacy of any single test of democratic competence, Mill was right to be concerned with expanding the right to vote along with advancing the ability to learn about what one is voting on. If people had no idea of what the options before them really entailed, they could not weigh the pros and cons presented to them. If they were unable to see through the lies and red herrings served up to deflect them from the pertinent issues, their votes could lead to decisions that were harmful to them and many others besides.[1]

Since the mid-19th century, the right to vote has gradually been extended to all adults, while the ability to learn about what one is voting for or against is left to take care of itself on a wing and a prayer. In 2016, the chasm between voting behaviour and voters' grasp of issues became so shockingly wide in both the Brexit and Trump victories that Oxford Dictionaries announced 'post-truth' as its word of the year. Referring to any state of

---

[1]　The legitimate concern with voters' understanding of political issues should not be overlooked just because there are blatantly illegitimate attempts to use contrived tests to curtail voting by targeted groups. For an example of a discriminatory test, see the one concocted in Louisiana in the 1960s (Onion, 2013).

affairs wherein 'objective facts are less influential in shaping public opinion than appeals to emotion and personal belief', the term points to the emerging disjunction between reality and what people imagine it to be (Stewart, 2016). The campaigning for Brexit and Trump was characterised by the twin traits of an outpouring of falsehoods (anything from overblown claims about what the UK paid as a member of the EU, or climate change being a hoax invented by China, to the blaming of immigrants for every conceivable problem in the UK and US) and the dismissal of any unhelpful finding by experts as worthless exaggeration (Gore, 2016).

But post-truth is not a new phenomenon. Steve Tesich used that very term in a 1992 article to describe Ronald Reagan's handling of the Iran-Contra scandal (Economist Briefing, 2016). A leading figure of the New Right, Reagan as US president authorised members of his administration to break the law in selling arms to Iran, and further defied explicit Congressional rules by using the proceeds to fund Contra rebels fighting against the Nicaraguan government. When more information came out about Reagan's role in the affair, he managed to convince the public he was not culpable despite all the evidence to the contrary.

The ideological formula that incorporates fundamentalist rhetoric, military adventurism, and plutocratic policies has always echoed elements of far right politics in Europe during the 1920s/1930s, which stirred millions into embracing demagogues who lied to them and ultimately led them to ruin. Although New Right proponents in the 1980s and 1990s thought they could keep it from becoming too extreme,[2] by the 2010s the UKIP and Tea Party influences on the Conservative and Republican parties respectively had pushed them further towards positions welcomed by contemporary far right advocates. Thus terrorist threats were attributed exclusively to one religious group, Muslims; economic woes were blamed on Eastern European/

---

[2]   In 2002, Theresa May, then chair of the Conservative Party, warned delegates at the party conference that they had come to be reviled by many as the 'Nasty Party'.

Latin American migrants; and social instability was routinely blamed on the arrival of refugees.

It is often pointed out that not all those who voted for Brexit or Trump indulged in the disparagement of minorities or delight in xenophobic vitriol. Many were just motivated by their belief that leaving the EU/having Trump as president would give them better jobs. Some suspected their vote could cause problems but somehow the shock to a complacent 'establishment' would be worth the cost. Quite a few, who were actually well-off members of the establishment, thought their own financial interests would be better served by their chosen option. But for all their differences, the majority of them shared notable post-truth tendencies in being relaxed about the incomparably high number of false claims and distortions coming from the side they supported, and unmoved by the contrary findings put forward by experts, who were just dismissed as out of touch or unreliable. As Jacob Rees-Mogg, Conservative MP and staunch Brexit supporter, said, 'Suspicion of experts goes back into antiquity. Experts, soothsayers, astrologers are all in much the same category' (Elgot, 2016).

The assumption that any person's claim is as good (or bad) as anyone else's, regardless of the objective basis for that claim, is incompatible with the goal of cooperating to achieve common ends. And its resurgence strikes at the heart of democratic governance. But the very ascendancy of the notion of post-truth may suggest that individual preferences cannot ultimately be tamed by the systematic quest for justifiable assertions. To show why such a view is misguided, we should take a look back at the societal mindset that may be termed 'pre-truth'.

Since imperial regimes were first set up across the world with the backing of military might and the legitimising interpretations of venerated texts,[3] ordinary people had for centuries believed in broad terms whatever they were told by the ruling elite in society. Official doctrines sanctioned by those in power would set out what the world was like, who was rightly in charge of the empire, what would be deemed admirable and what should be

---

[3] For example, the Bible in Europe, the Quran in the Middle East, and the Confucian Classics in China.

condemned, and what would secure the wellbeing of all. These would not be questioned however much they appeared to be self-contradictory, run counter to people's experiences, or have no evidence whatsoever to back them. People went along with them out of a mixture of fear that disbelief would be punished, and hope that compliance would give them the certainty they needed in life. Beyond the formal doctrines issued from on high, people also grew accustomed to their own folklore, rituals, and superstitions.

Pre-truth societies transmitted prevailing beliefs but took little interest in learning about how to differentiate what should be believed and what ought to be discarded. It is no coincidence that they were ruled by governance strategies that were selected by those at the top of the power pyramid, based on their personal dispositions, without any critical debate of whether or not the adopted strategy was indeed the most appropriate for the circumstances. But from around the 16th century on, the late Renaissance revival of interest in the enquiring ethos of democratic Athens and republican Rome gave rise to an intellectual revolution that established objective scientific learning as the basis for assessing truth claims (Easlea, 1980; Tam, 2014). During the 17th century, the collaborative approach to experimental enquiry championed by Francis Bacon and others started to shift a growing number of people away from pre-truth attitudes towards a more critical mindset that would subject beliefs to the test of shared analysis and evidential scrutiny (Urbach, 1987; Faulkner, 1993).

The shift in outlook was further accelerated during the Enlightenment of the 18th century, leading to the modern development of democracy as a meta-strategy for assessing and selecting the most appropriate options for people's collective self-governance (Bronner, 2004; Pagden, 2013). Democracy as we know it today descended from the displacement of unthinking embrace of groundless claims by conditional acceptance of assertions validated through systematic research. The pre-truth mentality, which once appeared to be an impregnable citadel, was not only overturned, but its demise paved the way for the acquisition of testable and hence far more reliable knowledge claims in every sphere of life (Gay, 1973). Not surprisingly, when the Enlightenment inspired intellectuals in China to call in 1919 for an end to that country's feudalistic pre-truth outlook,[4] they rallied their supporters around two 'teachers' – Science and Democracy (Schwarcz, 1986).

The most extensive exposition of the connection between the scientific ethos and democratic governance is to be found in the works of John Dewey, whose educational ideas were highly influential in both the West and the East in the early 20th century (Dewey, 1921, 1973). Dewey's ideas explain why people must learn to differentiate justifiable truth claims collaboratively if they are to select appropriate proposals for effective governance for everyone. When people need a reliable guide in life, blind faith in the words of soothsayers and rash dismissals of expert analyses as being no better than astrology are as useless as each other. The reason why collaborative learning is the only dependable way to advance knowledge beyond mere dogmas and outmoded assumptions is that it enables a multiplicity of minds to add to, cross-check, and potentially remove elements from what at any given time constitute the objective consensus of warranted beliefs (Campbell, 1995). One person may be delusional, two may be compounding each other's errors, but an open forum of learning means that over time, oversights and mistakes get to be corrected, and a better tested and more reliable set of working hypotheses emerges. It follows that education at all levels should inculcate collaborative learning so that citizens are capable of sustaining democracy rather than becoming mere pawns in others' attempts to win power to serve their own ends (Dewey, 1944).

The overcoming of pre-truth proves that there is no ineradicable barrier in the human mind to thinking with critical objectivity. But emotions are an essential part of being human, and while they can make us passionate and resolute about discovering the truth, they can also lock us into prejudices or overwhelm us with groundless suspicions. And while democracy is predicated on the pursuit of our individual aspirations being guided by our shared knowledge and common understanding, those who prefer to destroy or subvert democracy have always

---

[4] During the May Fourth Movement.

sought to use irrationality as a tool to prevent people attaining a proper grasp of how they should be governed.[5]

The fomenting of post-truth tendencies began in earnest when the impact of the Enlightenment provoked reactionaries of every shade into denouncing it as a threat to religious faith, time-honoured traditions, and patriotic sentiments (McMahon, 2001). They decried its audacity in supposing that human reasoning could usurp the deeply held feelings people had for their God, their customs and their own country. In short, they preferred not to have collaborative learning among citizens getting in the way of mass manipulation of people's beliefs. The anti-Enlightenment developed in subsequent centuries into a refuelling station for any clique in fear of losing their dominance[6] in the face of concerted actions by informed citizens. By attacking systematic efforts to sift truths from falsehoods as no different from any arbitrary claims, they keep the door open for the unscrupulous to deceive enough people to secure majority control of political offices.

To counter the derationalisation of politics and reconnect democracy to collaborative endeavours to learn about real problems and genuine solutions, we should highlight the areas where the nature of learning can be misconstrued, and ensure any plan to promote objective learning is not taken down the wrong path.

Learning about learning

One of the most significant factors in displacing the pre-truth mindset is the scientific emphasis on treating the pursuit of warranted beliefs as an ongoing collaborative exercise. There is no definitive collection of truths accessible to just a few individuals, and there is correspondingly no expectation that everyone else should accept the views of the few. At any time,

---

[5] Both George Orwell and Ray Bradbury, in *Nineteen Eighty-Four* and *Fahrenheit 451* respectively, showed how absolute control could be maintained with ease once people were prevented from learning objectively and conditioned into not thinking critically about their society.

[6] The dominance may be in terms of wealth, religious authority, self-proclaimed racial superiority, or their place on the prevailing social hierarchy.

there will be a framework for information sharing and mutual examination, and those seeking to discover what may warrant their conditional acceptance can join together to see where it leads them. The framework, procedures, participants, input, and findings may change over time in the light of new experiences, but those changes should be guided by critical deliberations with reference to coherent arguments and testable evidence.

Unfortunately, if the approach of collaborative learning is not continuously reinforced, it is liable to become too opaque and lose its credibility, or worse, regress to pre-truth levels of arbitrariness. Although Mill was correct to draw attention to the need for participants in any democracy to acquire the basic tools of learning such as reading, writing, and arithmetic, he did not go far enough when he overlooked the fact that effective participation required people to learn about how to learn. People do not have time to join with others to learn about everything, but that makes it even more important for them to understand how the learning they access is derived from the appropriate collaboration carried out by other learners. Without this understanding, the distinction between what one has reliably learnt and what one happens to believe starts to collapse, and democratic discourse will soon give way to subjective disputes incapable of being resolved.

The accelerated growth of technological complexities following the Second World War raised the profile of scientific research, but also ironically sowed the seeds of 'white coat distrust' syndrome. In a single generation, democratic governments in the West had overseen the harnessing of nuclear power, the mass production of penicillin, the development of electronic computers, and the mastery of supersonic flight. The temptation was there to entrust experts with the solving of all key problems. The process of collaborative learning faded into the background, and what remained visible resembled a knowledge machine that kept churning out new discoveries and inventions. In the decades that followed, the public learnt less and less about what made the scientific approach of collaborative learning preferable to other modes of knowledge acquisition, and more and more about the impressive achievements of indefatigable researchers.

With so much coming off the conveyor belt of new facts and findings, it became fashionable to call for a return to rote learning (Orlin, 2013). The exploratory and discursive approach favoured by teachers who recognised its centrality in critical learning came under fire as being unfocused and time-wasting. But the more people were steered from an early age towards viewing knowledge as a pre-packaged product from a not to be questioned supplier, the less they understood how belief evaluation was dependent on participants engaging cooperatively in a trial and error enterprise. And having been told to place their complete faith in modern wizards, they did not know what to think when those idols started slipping off their pedestals.

The thalidomide disaster revealing how hubristic the pharmaceutical industry could be; the use of Agent Orange in the Vietnam War, leading to decades of deadly contamination and birth defects; the partial nuclear meltdown at the US plant at Three Mile Island; the panic caused by the unexpected spread of AIDS – these and other incidents began to cast a shadow over the reliability of experts. The Enlightenment ethos of advancing democratic problem solving through collaborative learning came to be sidelined by a mix of deliberate or unwitting distortions.[7]

After decades of expert knowledge being presented as the work of a few outstanding individuals – and not as the provisional outcomes of an ongoing process involving many – it was not difficult, once negative stories hit the front pages, to discredit those individuals as arrogant and flawed. From then on, sound research no less than arbitrary claims can be brushed aside with the same cavalier attitude. One individual can persuade countless parents to reject the MMR vaccination for their children despite the substantial collaborative findings of others; a few groups funded by fossil fuel businesses can cast doubt over the consensus regarding the dangers of human-induced climate change, even though that consensus is being sustained by vigorous critical

[7]   The emphasis on the need for cooperative cross-checking in belief evaluation was either overlooked or simply rejected (see, for example, Goldstein, 2015).

exchanges among scientists;[8] and a vocal minority with no expertise in biology can demand that creationism be taught as a scientific theory in schools irrespective of the overwhelming support for evolution as the core explanation for the emergence of humans and other species on Earth.[9]

In parallel with the rise of the New Right, and buoyed by the support actively lent by many sympathetic to one or more elements of the New Right agenda, two trends in reorientating learning gathered momentum as the new millennium approached. The first trend echoed the classic disciplinarian strategy for governance. Since the 1980s, its champions have ridden successive waves of indignation that found expression through some self-styled 'moral majority', 'back to basics' rallying calls, campaigns against the permissive society, revival of 'traditional' values, love of 'God and country', and, more recently, disdain for multiculturalism and contempt for 'political correctness'. In schools, the model teachers are the ones who will teach key facts (that is, facts welcomed by the people who matter), ensure pupils accept what they are told, steer clear of topics beyond those mandated, and drill their class into passing the standard tests prescribed for them. Former soldiers with no teaching experience were even singled out by the UK Conservative government during the 2010s as ideal candidates for taking charge of lessons in schools (Camden, 2016). Reinforcement of respect for a single religious faith is encouraged, while subjects such as sex education would be frowned upon.

The role of universities in promoting intellectual exploration of diverse ideas, or questioning conventional modes of thinking, has also come under attack. Higher education is reframed as the training ground for future workers with skills and knowledge in demand by employers. The sciences are valued in so far as they produce graduates and postgraduates who can carry

---

[8]   Judging by the findings on global climate published by scientists, there is almost a 97% consensus on harmful climate change being caused by human activities: www.skepticalscience.com/global-warming-scientific-consensus.htm

[9]   If creationism is to be treated as being on a par with the theory of evolution to be taught in science classes, then the same could go for the teaching of babies delivered by storks or any other idea with no empirical support.

out commercially important research work. Business and management courses are shaped by corporate expectations. Degrees linked to professional qualifications such as law and medicine are backed to the extent their holders will be in demand in the corresponding field. But the humanities bear the brunt of funding cuts (Hutner & Mohamed, 2013; Preston, A., 2015). The cultivation of the mindset to learn through collaborative exploration with others, to test out contrasting perspectives, and to appreciate truths as provisional tools for problem solving is relegated to the lowest rung of academic priorities. After decades of widening access to higher education, the inexorable escalation of tuition fees for attending university led many to believe that unless young people were likely to get a well-paid job to help them pay off the debt, it might make more sense for them not to go to university at all.

More widely across society, thoughtful probing of hypotheses and constructive exchanges of provisional ideas have come to be regarded as too boring, tentative, and uninstructive. Reviews of the strengths and weaknesses in the findings of people who have actually engaged in the relevant field, investigative journalism, and in-depth documentaries are deemed ponderous and only suited to a tiny minority that most media would not cater for.[10] The focus shifted instead to giving a platform to televisual personalities whose charisma, flamboyance, chutzpah, or entertaining pomposity, combined with their ever-ready ability to spout provocative claims and polarise people, render them gold for ratings and headlines. Farage and Trump were just two of the more notable examples of how the media platforms given to them because of their bombastic outbursts and immunity

---

[10] Or in the case of the BBC, most programmes with a learning dimension are steadily moved from BBC One to BBC Four; the former has a weekly reach of 75% of the viewing population, the latter has just 14%. 2013-2014 figures: http://downloads.bbc.co.uk/bbctrust/assets/files/pdf/regulatory_framework/service_licences/service_reviews/television_services/performance_analysis.pdf

to having their lies regularly exposed by fact checking enabled them to convince millions that they deserved to be believed.[11]

By contrast, the second trend in reshaping learning draws from ideas to be found in any minimalist strategy. In essence, since the scientific approach of collaborative learning was presented as no more reliable than any other approach, people should be left alone to figure out what they want to believe. Superficially it may even sound like an endorsement of Kant's conception of the Enlightenment ethos as the intellectual readiness of daring to know. But the self-liberation promoted by Kant and other Enlightenment thinkers is not about individuals cutting themselves off from everyone else and just adopting whatever beliefs they personally fancy. It is predicated on people learning to think by opening their minds to the arguments and evidence submitted by others, exchanging critical assessments to see what stands up best to ongoing scrutiny, and developing their own understanding on the basis of what is emerging from a community of thoughtful enquirers to which they belong (Schmidt, 1996).

The last thing minimalist libertarians want is to recognise the authority derived from collaborative learning. For them, there should be no more trust placed in the cooperative efforts of people who have over time cross-checked and reviewed provisional claims than any other output from anyone inclined to assert their beliefs. They go from the sound premise that no one is infallible and leap to the absurd conclusion that no one's assessment can ever be better than anyone else's. Their refusal to acknowledge that the errors arising from individual fallibility are most reliably identified and corrected through the dedicated scrutiny and critical cross-fertilisation of a group of learners open to further input from others leaves them sliding down a spiral of epistemological anarchy. When there is supposed to be no authority to question the legitimacy of any belief, then anything goes.

---

[11] Boris Johnson is another example of how jovial fabrications helped to sustain a political career that encompassed becoming mayor of London and the UK's foreign secretary.

Supporters of this trend rally behind the cry for freedom from indoctrination. In practice, it means that some of them feel free to indoctrinate their own children or group. Others are of the view that people can adopt any belief without having to justify it to anyone. In the past, this development has often been blamed on 'progressive' educational ideas associated with the teachings of John Dewey (Evers, 1998). But there is a crucial difference between the distorted applications of Dewey's philosophy of learning and what Dewey himself consistently emphasised. While some zealous advocates of pupil-centred learning took it to mean that the learners, whatever their age or background, should individually choose what and how they learn without any external guidance, Dewey was unwavering in explaining how successful learning came from instructive interactions between those who have studied a subject extensively and those who are beginning to engage with it (Dewey, 1944). Neither side should dominate the process. Those with more experience would have more to share, but they must be receptive to queries and criticisms, and respond to them by drawing on existing evidence and/or new findings. Those with less experience should take note of what has been discovered so far, but should be ready to question what they are told if these do not cohere with anything else they have been learning.

For Dewey, the starting point of learning is where the collaborative efforts at evaluating beliefs have taken us to so far. It establishes a provisional basis for differentiating truth from falsehood. It can be revised, but until there are sound reasons for its revision, it would be unjustifiable to cast it aside. Diametrically opposite to this Deweyan approach, libertarian learning insists that any view can be rejected or embraced without reference to any kind of objective justification. Far from being a pillar of freedom in support of democracy, it is an outlook that promotes free-for-all irresponsibility that destabilises democratic decision making.

Under the cloak of freedom, children can be led to believe any absurd claim put forward: medical science is a scam, while miracle cures are real; the blood of diverse ethnic groups is fundamentally different, and pigment density is a morally relevant indicator; historical records depicting atrocities by one's own country are fabricated, but heroic accounts of its triumphs are beyond doubt; hypotheses explored by physicists are flimsy, while the interpretations of one's favourite sacred texts by fervent preachers are eternally correct. There is no end to arbitrary and deceptive teaching unless collaborative learning is safeguarded by institutions and procedures designed to prevent its marginalisation.

Democratic governance has often implicitly relied on schools, the teaching profession, and the statutory bodies overseeing educational policies and practices, to ensure the minimum standards of genuine learning are met. However, without an explicit commitment to support them in carrying out this vital civic role, they can be undermined themselves. For example, in the US, fundamentalist Christian groups not satisfied with scientific ideas that challenge their objectively untestable beliefs, or open discussions that may question their assumptions about a wide range of issues, have for decades organised themselves to capture local school boards. They have not won in every contest, but where they have succeeded in taking over a school, they have replaced teachers and altered curriculum content (Deckman, 2004; Claassen, 2015). Christian fundamentalism is itself just one strand of the New Right alliance behind the Republican Party dating back to the rise of Reagan. And where local groups could only go so far in winning over more school boards, when Republican politicians manage to take control of a state, they step in directly themselves. While state takeovers of schools were once a rarity, they have become increasingly common as the number of states controlled by Republicans doubled between 2010 and 2014 (Layton, 2016).

In the UK, the New Right has through successive Conservative governments treated the teaching profession and local education authorities as barriers to the advancement of its agenda. Teachers would be repeatedly branded as ineffective. Local education authorities, which provided democratic oversight to ensure all schools deal with their pupils fairly and keep their minds open to critical learning, were deemed obstructive. So they were abolished (like the Inner London Education Authority), diminished by having powers removed from them, or systematically undermined with schools in their jurisdiction pressurised into converting themselves into independent academies.[12] Furthermore, 'free schools' could be set up by any group, and these would be run as deregulated businesses using public money, with no teaching qualification requirements for their heads or the teaching staff.[13]

As groups and individuals are given ever more leeway to teach their members in their own schools or their children at home, what they teach may not only depart from the most robust findings currently sustained by collaborative learning across society, but may entrench an anti-rationality mindset that rejects the need to cross-check claims with diverse sources or assess their veracity in terms of the extent to which they have withstood open scrutiny. It is revealing that the standard response to concerns about children not being taught what is backed by the latest research consensus is that research consensus in any field changes over time and no special value should be attached to it at any given moment. This shows an uninformed, or worse, deliberate, misconstruction of how learning attains its objective reliability. Our beliefs should not be locked up permanently, but nor should they be chopped and changed arbitrarily. Provisional consensus cannot be dismissed without cogent arguments, critical shifts in evidence, or replicable experimental findings backing the move to a new assumption.

If politicians constantly taking aim at the danger of radicalisation of young Muslims by fundamentalist groups take off their blinkers, they will see that it is not a problem connected exclusively to one religion. Once you facilitate the disengagement of learning from collaborative scrutiny and development across society, insular indoctrination will be free to spread its toxic influence, and misguided doubts and facile ideas will take root in impressionable minds over issues ranging from race hate and sexist disparagement to contempt for gays or asylum seekers.

---

[12] New Labour unwittingly helped to undermine local education authorities with its drive to develop academies.

[13] According to the Department of Education's figures, the number of teachers without teaching qualifications in academies and free schools in England went up between 2012 and 2013 by 207% to 8,000 (Adams, 2014).

How to develop collaborative learning

Despite the flagrant bypassing of facts featured in both the Brexit and Trump campaigns, collaborative learning is still embedded in many areas of contemporary life. Some businesses may give financial backing to New Right politicians who regard the disengagement of individuals from truth assessment as a major campaign asset. But commercial realities remind them daily that unless they have workers and suppliers capable of learning to solve problems and improve their products and services, they could lose out to competitors who are better at promoting a learning culture.

To prevent the post-truth mindset from becoming the norm, we should avoid seeing it as an irreversible tide, but tap into the considerable interests the majority of people have in differentiating the reliable from the groundless, and reinforce the practice of collaborative learning at every level of society. There are five approaches that should be pursued:

- establishing a collaborative network for giving practical guidance;
- providing training for teaching collaborative learning approaches;
- removing institutional barriers to collaboration;
- placing sufficient investment in collaborative research; and
- promoting better understanding of scientific enquiry.

First, there should be a collaborative network for practical guidance. For too long the public have been informed about scientific announcements and expert findings without a sense of how these were arrived at. And when some of them were found to be flawed or superseded by better hypotheses, the impression is given that such changes would from time to time come about even if it is not clear why they should be accepted. Among those directly involved in research, however, the understanding of the key methodological components has been steadily improved and refined. From explorations of scientific procedures to academic studies of cooperative problem solving (Urbach, 1987;

Tam, 2013), there is a self-correcting consensus on the broad parameters for truth acquisition.

Established research institutions and peer-respected theorists should pool their generic knowledge and provide a network that others can plug into for practical guidance. Unlike trying to land a lunar module on the moon, differentiating a process that brings people together to work out testable scientific proposals from arbitrary pronouncements is not rocket science. It is the common wisdom of people who have collaborated with others, and opened themselves to evidential challenges and reasoned critiques.

As universities provide academic supervisors for potential doctoral students, the network can provide advice to guide wider group efforts at the pursuit of learning. Just as PhD supervisors can advise on what is feasible or promising, and what is misconceived or incoherent, but cannot deliver the actual content of the research, the collaborative learning network can help sift sound from misguided learning processes, without taking on the task of determining what is to be learnt. It will not get involved with assessing the truth or falsity of any contested claim, but its guidance will enable others to evaluate the reliability of the learning process underpinning the claim.

The practical advice from the network will address what ought to be involved in ensuring participants can operate without coming under undue pressure from others with power advantage over them; facilitating input from anyone with useful contributions to make; putting in place a trusted facilitator or referee to keep at bay any unwarranted disruption; sourcing relevant witnesses and experts; keeping a watch over vested interests or emotional turmoil deflecting from clinical scrutiny of the evidence; welcoming diverse hypotheses and interpretations, and subjecting them to rigorous testing; rating, in the light of how well the ideas have stood up, the findings in terms of their reliability from the unfounded to the probable; and declaring openly what the current consensus position is, while reserving the possibility of future revision.

Secondly, we need more training for the teaching of collaborative learning approaches. The employers' body, CBI, has criticised the UK government for its narrow focus on testing pupils and warned against a return to rote learning (Downs, 2012). Their concerns reflect a wider recognition that the readiness to accept claims because of one's personal inclinations is not at all helpful in a complex society with fast changing technological development. People need above all the aptitude to work with others to discover what ideas most warrant their belief. It is vital that schools should resist the demand for generating a compliant workforce, and not programme their pupils to submit to selected facts and doctrines.

Michael Fielding, for example, has observed that both academic achievements and the ethos of democracy were enhanced in schools where collaborative learning was mainstreamed (Fielding, 2011). Through practices such as peer mentoring and teaching, pupils learnt more effectively by supporting each other, and improved academically and behaviourally. Student–teacher learning partnerships encouraged young people to think and act like co-researchers in working out what they would take on board as provisional findings. Schools as learning communities enabled students to explore curriculum topics and also wider school issues, and helped them understand what could be done differently and why certain arrangements had to be in place.

However, such improvements could not be replicated without those leading the learning developing the necessary skills to facilitate collaboration. Those with teaching responsibilities need to encourage curiosity without letting the demand for novelty dictate enquiries. They must be able to manage tensions and frustration without allowing disappointment or anger to deflect from where the most reasonable analyses are heading. They should be firm in holding back forceful individuals from hijacking discussions, but also thoughtful in reining in an impulsive majority from pushing their views on others when these are not well formulated or backed by sound arguments. The research into these skills and how to promote them ought to be much more extensively shared (McGregor, 2005).

One aspect that requires particular attention is the supposed difference between objective sciences and subjective interpretations. Many in the past have wondered if it is true that while subjects such as physics or biology deal with concrete facts that can be established with complete certainty, other studies relating to cultural constructs such as literature or the law are ultimately dependent on the weight of opinion (Bleicher, 1980; Brown, S. C., 1984). In recent decades, the absence of a single methodology for guaranteeing scientific claims as well as the practical similarities in all systematic enquiries in search of acceptable assertions have pointed to a convergence of ideas on how collaborative learning underpins the quest for sound beliefs in all fields (Miller, 1987; Brandom, 2000). The key is enabling the uncoerced interplay of ideas and counter-suggestions to shape provisional hypotheses at any given time.

The training will have to go beyond teachers in schools and universities. Parents who want to home-school their children will need to grasp that there is no text or doctrine that they can take as absolutely unquestionable in transmitting it to members of their family. They and their children need to engage with others in order to approach learning as a collaborative enterprise. Without that experience, dogmas and prejudices could simply be perpetuated, and the art of learning with others would be overlooked. The same applies to lifelong learning, where it is not just the acquisition of new knowledge that is valuable, but the active involvement in a shared pursuit of justifiable beliefs, and adjustments made in response to collegiate criticisms that help to strengthen people's ability to think as citizens about the many issues that crop up in democratic deliberations (Mayo & Annette, 2010).

Thirdly, more should be done to remove institutional barriers to collaboration. Leaders sometimes make the mistake of assuming they cannot bring people from across organisational divides to discover new ideas and approaches because the divisions are too entrenched. But this can be overturned by active intra- and inter-organisational initiatives designed to produce joint findings. With cooperative leadership and process redesigns, different departments can be brought together to engage in joint problem solving (Goss, 2007; Tam, 2007b). Public officials should be left in no doubt that, regardless of their own functional roles – across all relevant teams and departments – they will be judged on how they work with others to find answers to cross-cutting problems, and their action planning and performance reviews will be reorganised to ensure that exchange of ideas across old silos become the new norm (Quirk, 2011).

Lack of trust and fear of losing credit are often behind systemic reluctance to join forces to achieve more. So investing time in building mutual understanding and praising individuals for their contributions to collective results are important. In the UK's Together We Can programme for community empowerment, 12 government departments collaborated over a seven-year period (2003–2010) to develop better opportunities for citizens to influence public policies to improve the quality of life in their communities (Tam, 2015b). The commitment was given by the prime minister in conjunction with the relevant secretaries of state, and communicated to all the policy teams involved. Citizens in diverse areas were able to learn about different options and their implications, assess their likely impact and the relative costs and benefits to where they live or work, and reach a consensus on what would appear as the best solution under the circumstances. Changes to policing priorities, support for community health projects, youth-orientated initiatives, review of environmental improvement schemes, and so on, led to better outcomes and higher public satisfaction.

Dovetailing with internal government corrective action to promote collaborative learning, a focus on cooperative problem solving in adult education can also play a key part in helping to develop citizens capable of becoming informed and constructively critical in working with public officials. Policy makers should take lessons from the WEA (Workers' Educational Association) which has run many projects such as bringing ex-miners and asylum seekers in South Yorkshire together to learn what kind of policies are needed to address their respective predicaments; enabling people to learn through art projects about the implications of contrasting housing provisions for those living close to each other; and facilitating shared experiences for young people and elected councillors as they learnt about the problem of travelling to and carrying out unpaid work placements without an income or reliable transport (Walker, 2013).

Fourthly, the government must take the lead in ensuring there is sufficient investment in collaborative research. Public funding should be channelled into independent institutions accountable to their community of researchers and critical reviewers, but protected from state intervention should any findings prove inconvenient for government policies. Even more importantly, the independently supervised funding stream should protect research from private commercial or fundamentalist interests if any of these attempt to undermine public understanding of what warrants belief.

For decades, the New Right's mantra that private is better than public has been echoing down the corridors of research institutions (Brown, W., 1993). Instead of relying on the state to fund research from tax revenues, learning institutions are told to turn their attention to private funders, or become fully privatised. This is meant to direct their attention to what is 'really' needed, as opposed to following the broad steer from 'ignorant' politicians or indulging in their own favourite topics. But once the direction of research is set primarily by people motivated by making more money than their rivals, the research that will get their support will be what in their opinion would help them most in securing financial advantages against those rivals. And since misleading information can, for example, deflect concerns about a company's damaging products and activities, or cast doubt over what the regulators or one's competitors are doing, epistemological resources could very quickly be depleted.

The danger of commercialisation of research may also take a subtler form. Without crudely steering research towards narrowly conceived business goals, the mere prospect of corporate interest and thus promises of funds can distort collaborative learning. There is evidence emerging of what has been dubbed the 'natural selection of bad science' (Devlin, 2016). In order to compete for media interest, which in turn helps to attract/sustain funding, many researchers are tempted to concoct novel, odd, high-profile hypotheses that have little support from others, and are rarely replicable. Claims about the health impact of little-known food, homeopathic cures, or psychological manipulations are put forward without clear test conditions or corroborative observations. But with ever more fanciful theories getting the headlines and interest in their potential for commercial exploitation, proper collaborative scientific research is pushed further back down the queue. The only safeguard is to pool public resources that will go into backing sound approaches to expanding our learning.

Finally, those in governance positions should promote better understanding of scientific enquiry. In a complex world guided by layers of hypotheses, Mill's concerns with people's ability to understand political options can only be addressed by raising public awareness not of the multitude of claims that exist, but the basics of how claims come to be validated. People need to understand better what questions they should ask to differentiate claims with varying degrees of reliability. This should distinguish the collaborative approach that underpins scientific enquiry from dogmatic claims made in the name of 'science'. It is in part the exaggerated halo effect attached to scientists that provoked the reaction against 'so-called experts'. The essence of scientific research is in the exploration of diverse perspectives amid the available evidence by people collaborating to test out what most warrants belief at any time. It does not have an indubitable answer for every conceivable question. It is a tool for assessing the case put forward for any given theory, but it does not follow that every aspect of life should be reduced to a scientific examination. Poetic expressions or contemplative introspection connect people to different kinds of experience, and except where they make assertions about alleged facts, there is no reason for them to be constrained by science.

Understanding the limits of scientific enquiry is also essential to comprehending what may lie beyond those limits. Where scientific enquiry reaches provisional conclusions, future revisions depend on further collaborative learning. Where the reliability of a belief is set in terms of probability, nothing should alter that probability except through more joint efforts in considering new evidence or overlooked arguments. Where no conclusion can be reached, then suspended judgement is all that is warranted. A common post-truth line goes from science not being able to give a definitive answer to 'therefore' something else with no scientific basis whatsoever can step in to fill the void. Another favourite is that since the current scientific consensus is 'only' 90%, a view that has less than 1% support from those working in the field in question should command equal assent from the public. Once these tricks of the trade are routinely exposed, the derailment of learning in ascertaining what deserves to be believed should become less frequent.

Aldous Huxley's *Brave New World* is often cited as a warning against trusting scientists to run the world. But the real danger comes from not understanding what scientific enquiry can and cannot do for us. We would do well to remember Huxley's even more alarming, if lesser known work, *Ape and Essence*, in which a post-apocalyptic society is limping along without the basic necessities and, worse still, lacking the research know-how to advance human knowledge from the primitive state it has regressed to. Unsurprisingly, with widespread ignorance, authoritarian rule became the norm.

Remedial checklist: collaborative learning

With reference to any group the governance of which you are concerned about, you can use the checklist below to identify what requires the most improvement in relation to the need for collaborative learning:

☐ Can members distinguish between claims made with little or no basis in any form of sustained collaborative enquiry and those that are backed to a significant extent by an open, cooperative approach to learning? Do they have a basic understanding of what constitutes sound, scientific enquiry?

☐ Is collaborative learning the norm for discovering and assessing justifiable beliefs, and do most members in practice adopt it? Is there a culture of lifelong learning that enables members to continuously improve their comprehension of how knowledge is expanded and revised? Do all those with a teaching role have the necessary training to explain and support collaborative learning?

☐ Are there arrangements in place to bring together those with proven experience and respected expertise in advancing research to provide practical guidance to all members, and challenge those who seek to deceive or mislead the public in what warrants their beliefs? Where those who have impartially studied a topic are genuinely and evenly divided about what merits assent, is it recognised that belief should be suspended unless further collaborative learning can lead to a new consensus?

☐ Are sufficient resources made available to sustain independent research so that those with vested interests cannot buy the production of findings to suit their private agenda? Can research to resolve contested claims or establish dependable solutions be advanced without institutional barriers intentionally or unwittingly getting in their way?

SEVEN

Critical re-examination

Anti-politics and post-truth tendencies are symptoms of alienation from objective discourse. Democracy is premised on people governing themselves through shared learning and collective assessment. On the assumption that people are willing to review ideas in the light of the evidence and arguments in front of them, what the majority of them choose as the most convincing option on any given occasion is taken as a reasonable choice to follow. However, when a substantial part of the population steps back from reasoned deliberations with others, and insists that their own views are unquestionable, then democracy cannot function. In this chapter, we will look at why all claims and assumptions affecting any group must be subject to critical re-examination, what that should not be taken to mean lest it leaves us with no basis for collective discussion, and how a system of critical re-examination can be embedded in the way we govern ourselves.

Why democracy depends on critical re-examination

Unlike other approaches to governance, democracy as a meta-strategy is distinctive in its focus on reviewing options and selecting what the cooperative intelligence of the people deems most likely to lead to improvements. It rejects the notion that any set of commands or policies can be appropriate for all time, and actively seeks to come up with better solutions. Consequently, while non-democratic regimes may hold on to ideas and practices regardless of how well they might have stood up to scrutiny, democratically governed groups are disposed to check for opportunities to revise and improve.

In the post-war years leading up to the 1970s, most developed countries shared a sense of modernity, democratic openness, scientific progress, and a technologically sustained rise in prosperity. But with the emergence of the New Right as a political force, plutocratic policies began to reverse the decline in income inequalities, accelerate the concentration of society's wealth among the rich elite, and leave the rest to become increasingly less secure (Freeland, 2012). By the beginning of the 21st century, for the first time in decades, many people were beginning to wonder if their children would end up worse off than them (Taibbi, 2014).

Intensive globalisation and rapid technological advancement had left all too many feeling that everything was changing too fast, and these people were shaken by losing all the certainties they could once take for granted. Increasingly, many yearned for unquestionable truths to anchor their lives. And they were prepared to grasp at any straw thrown in their direction. Fundamentalist preachers, con merchants selling get-rich-quick schemes, reactionary ideologues, shameless trickle-down advocates, all spoke with utter conviction and drew ever larger crowds.

When the dogma of banking deregulation led to the financial crisis of 2008, and public money went into bailing out the banks while public services were cut and job prospects worsened for those earning the least, that dogma was not dismantled. Instead, people's disorientation by the threat of permanent economic crisis was greeted by a resurgence of dogmatic disdain for scapegoats – immigrants, feminists, trade unions, benefit claimants, and liberal-minded people who reject such disdain.[1]

Once the disdain becomes widely promoted, it is shut off from every conceivable form of critical re-examination. It did not matter what contributions immigrants brought to the countries they worked in, how many women's lives were endangered by

---

[1] There have been sustained narratives to shift the blame for the economic woes caused by bankers' irresponsibility to those who were the victims (Gross, 2008; Milne, 2014).

violent spouses, how pay deals and working conditions worsened without union negotiation, or why many people and their children were suffering because of inadequate social security to compensate for low pay or lack of jobs. For many people, it was enough to have a version of events they could believe in without any doubt whatsoever, and which could guide them in their behaviour no matter what contrary evidence might surface.

For example, some may contrast Trump's promise to end the dominance of the political establishment by Washington insiders and their wealthy backers with the fact that he was appointing to his cabinet Washington insiders, millionaires and billionaires who had exerted substantial policy influence for years and decades, and conclude that his was the same old plutocratic agenda. But many of Trump's followers would hear nothing of it. For them, it was better to have an unshakeable faith in Trump than to feel lost and hopeless.

The Trump phenomenon is of course not unique. 'Miracle cures' are sold all the time to people who despair of the limits of medical research. Similarly, with cults that prey on irrationality, the offer of an unquestionable way forward fills the void of insecurity for desperate souls. Although not everyone is susceptible to such deception, the psychological need for total assurance is far from rare (Reich, W., 1970; Arendt, 1979), and when societal changes put pressure on people to deal with widespread instability, many will reach out to whoever is ready to tell them that everything will be alright.

When the twin onslaught of fascist and communist regimes threatened to destroy democracy in the first half of the 20th century, Karl Popper set out in *The Open Society and its Enemies* (1966), how the institutionalising of dogmatic arguments would jeopardise society's ability to think through what should be done. He warned that once we allowed a system of governance to close off critical re-examination because absolute certainty was conferred on selected claims by someone with 'unquestionable' authority, there would be no escape from pervasive falsehoods and deception.

Popper connected intellectual trends that privileged an arbitrary set of ideas as indubitable to the spread of dispositions that passively go along with the most incoherent and groundless assertions. From ideological dogmas about the supremacy of the party to routine dismissals of evidence that the applications of those dogmas were causing problems and large-scale suffering, so long as the tipping point had been reached, the masses would stay compliant as individuals would be too exuberant, numb, or scared to contradict the dominant views.

If we were to avoid sliding towards more nightmares like the Third Reich or Stalinist Russia, Popper proposed we immunise ourselves with the help of systematic falsification tests. This means that we should check the veracity of a claim not simply in relation to what may appear to support it, but by actively searching for counter-evidence. If a claim or doctrine can withstand robust attempts at demonstrating its vulnerabilities, then it can be retained. But even then, it does not acquire a permanent status of unquestionability. It is deemed provisionally acceptable, on the understanding that it could be revised or rejected subject to further scrutiny in the future.

Unfortunately, Popper's advice was turned on its head by the New Right and presented as antithetical to any doctrine concerning how social problems could be tackled. Instead of subjecting large-scale policy proposals to the test of falsification, defenders of the plutocratic status quo invoked Popper to dismiss all such proposals as reckless. But not only was such a stance, as it sought to close off enquiries a priori, at odds with Popper's philosophy for an open society (Burke, 1983); by promoting the rejection of rational exploration of social change options it fuelled the revival of fanaticism and dogmas.

By the 2010s, many processes for critically reviewing claims for their objective justifiability were no longer widely valued. For example, because biological theories included components that were revised over time, it was claimed that it had no greater right to be taught in schools than any other account of human origins some people might happen to favour. Appeals in criminal cases, especially where the death penalty was involved, as in the US, were seen as being soft on murderers regardless of evidence showing that many innocent people had already been wrongfully executed.[2] Fact checking of the lies that dominated the EU referendum and the 2016 US presidential campaigns was dismissed as a feeble attempt to besmirch the names of those rare politicians who dared to speak the 'truth'. Any suggestion that potentially false claims made by one or more individual military personnel should be investigated was decried as unpatriotic.

Trust is once more pulled in the direction of shameless showmen and raving fundamentalists. Religious and nationalist extremism offer total certainty. Doubt is condemned. The warnings of Popper, Orwell, and Arendt are pushed to one side. For decades, those who have democratic power on their side could have fought back. They could have more thoroughly exposed the lies put forward by the unscrupulous. They could have introduced tougher checks and made violations more financially prohibitive. But they just conceded ground by acting as though it was only fair that anyone could make any claim about anything – irrespective of evidence, arguments, and proper scrutiny. Instead of ensuring there is an open system that will without bias subject contestable claims to critical re-examination, 'impartiality' is turned into an open invitation to give airtime, a seat on any media panel, and every public platform, to people who spout false and misleading views to get wider attention and build their political base.

In order to defend democracy, some think that the way to counter absolute certainty that deceives is to bring forward absolute certainty that is rightly beyond question. So they look to religious leaders or some foundational document like a constitution to lay down what must be accepted. But this would be to forget that democracy takes root only because there can be no absolute certainty. What one religious leader says, another may contradict. And the more inviolable a constitutional document is set out to be, the more problematic it becomes as a guide to what should or should not be allowed. The supporters and opponents of every major cause in the US have turned to their Constitution for definitive backing one way or another.

[2] One study found that at least 4.1% of death row inmates would have been exonerated if there were enough time and resources to review their convictions thoroughly (Grossa et al, 2014).

In practice, this means that on a major range of issues it is how the thoughts and intentions of a group of 18th century men are interpreted, rather than the options and consequences that may impact on contemporary lives, that determines what is acceptable. Like theological disputes, disagreements over the Constitution are often settled because those who had the power managed to get more of their supporters into the relevant arena. Indeed, since the late 1980s, in virtually all the cases where the most politically contentious issues were decided by the Supreme Court on a tight 5-4 majority, members of the court backed the position favoured by the party of the president who nominated them[3] (Kuhn, D. P., 2012; Rodriguez, 2016).

If a religious leader is prepared to offer advice without invoking divine infallibility, or a constitutional document is to be produced as a deliberative aid rather than a quasi-sacred text that commands total submission, we can at least dispense with any dubious claim to certainty. This is crucial because revisability, far from being a weakness, is the strength of democratic governance. It is only by recognising that we can never be so sure as to close the door completely on all future enquiries that we can be as certain as circumstances allow in any given situation (Dewey, 1930). Effective governance requires the assessment of numerous claims and assumptions, on the basis of which policy choices then have to be made. Every time a revision is held back for no good reason, another opportunity to form a more accurate view or improve on the available option is cast aside.

The minimalist rhetoric of the New Right may suggest that if the routine and sensible checking of claims is generally beneficial to society, then it should be left to proceed spontaneously without any collective arrangements to sustain it. But in practice a laissez-faire approach means that it is far more likely that any critical re-examination needed to expose complex corporate deception or unsound policies driven by vested interests would lack sufficient funding or organisational capacity to proceed. It is no coincidence that thinkers as diverse as Jurgen Habermas and Paulo Freire emphasise the oppressive dangers posed by any

---

[3]   Between 1986 and 2012, the US Supreme Court decided by a 5-4 majority in over 20% of the cases.

epistemic authority that seeks to leave individuals oblivious of the need to openly and collectively review that authority (McCarthy, 1981; Freire, 1996). The task of questioning any authority is too much to be shouldered by any single person. If it is not to end up as nobody's business, it has to be systematically arranged so that everyone has a stake in it.

Before we turn to how this systematic arrangement is best embedded in our approach to governance, we need to take a closer look at how misapplications of critical re-examination can severely damage prospects for democratic cooperation.

What is wrong with hyper-critiques

What we refer to here as 'hyper-critiques' began as cautious warnings against technocratic tendencies, but ended up dismissing all ideas for improving society. In the course of the 19th century, thinkers such as Auguste Comte suggested that a distinct class of scientific experts could take charge as rulers because they would be able to work out methodically what should or should not be done in any situation.[4] The notion that there was one correct, rational, scientific blueprint for examining what warranted belief, and that one group of people should be entrusted to make key decisions for society as they alone could grasp this blueprint, impressed on some people that a technocratic utopia was almost upon us.

What this Comtean philosophy promoted was the rigid codification of scientific exploration, which would in effect transform it into a new form of religion. An elite with the grasp of the 'essence' of science would then be relied on to oversee what should or should not happen in society, and make arrangements to secure the appropriate outcomes. Such a philosophy substituted the unquestionable dogmas of theocratic priests by the indubitable dogmas of technocratic experts. Its inherent hubris was mocked in works such as Kurt Vonnegut's *Cat's Cradle* and Margaret Atwood's *Oryx and Crake*. The idea that anyone with the ability to come up with some scientific

---

[4] Comte was criticised by J. S. Mill for distorting the nature of scientific enquiries and for promoting antidemocratic technocracy (Mill, 1993).

discovery or technical invention must thereby know and care about what would work best with other people was exposed as not just laughably naïve, but potentially catastrophic if it was ever taken seriously. It was dismantled by those who studied how systematic enquiries were actually carried out. Major shifts in scientific theories, for example, were found not to be determined by immutable procedures, but shaped by changes in paradigms which are influenced by a multiplicity of factors that can themselves alter over time (Kuhn, T., 1970). Assessment of claims made in diverse fields such as market research, criminal investigation, medical diagnosis, and quality control displayed a variety of techniques that need to be refined contextually and adjusted through ongoing trial and error (Cohen, 1977; Levi, 1984).

As Larry Laudan observed:

> It is time we abandoned that lingering 'scientistic' prejudice which holds that 'the sciences' and sound knowledge are co-extensive; they are not. Given that, our central concern should be with distinguishing theories of broad and demonstrable problem-solving scope from theories which do not have this property – regardless of whether the theories in question fall in areas of physics, literary theory, philosophy, or common sense. (Laudan, 1981, pp 153-154)

In other words, where a theoretical claim or set of ideas is related to the solving of a problem – for example, reducing suffering, bringing coherence to two related equations, producing more insightful interpretations of a text, or building a bridge that can withstand tremors – its reliability cannot be judged by some preconceived methodology, but only by how well it manages to solve the problem in question.

During the 1970s/1980s, scientistic assumptions about a supreme epistemological methodology were so thoroughly criticised that they could not provide any further intellectual succour to Comtean or any form of technocracy. Unfortunately, in some quarters, the rejection of scientism was not enough. The battle had to be moved to a new level against science, collaborative problem solving, and any form of rational enquiry associated with the ethos of the Enlightenment. At a time when the erosion of democracy was gathering pace, and society needed more than ever to challenge flawed assumptions put forward in the public realm, the emergence of hyper-critiques undermined the credibility of critical re-examination.

Hyper-critiques tend to take one of three forms: anarchic permissiveness, grand incoherence, or relentless despair. A leading exponent of anarchic permissiveness, Paul Feyerabend, would not accept that any form of enquiry should be given greater support than any others since none could possibly be more reliable. He went from the perfectly reasonable assertion that there is no single methodological blueprint for advancing knowledge, to the groundless insistence that all methods were essentially on a par (Feyerabend, 1975, 2010). For him, practices such as astrology and traditional rituals should not be dismissed as unreliable sources of information. Although he might have encountered some professional scientists who were disdainful about any attempt to seek truth outside formal research institutions, he assumed they must therefore be mistaken in their negative appraisals. But where particular practices have been critically examined, and their pronouncements routinely found to be no more reliable than random guesses, then it is only sensible to treat them with due scepticism.

Feyerabend also popularised the idea that since people could get interesting ideas in innumerable ways (from dreams to rereading mythological stories), there should be no presumption as to the validity or otherwise of anyone's ideas. He overlooked the fact that allowing people to come up with ideas in diverse ways did not mean that those ideas should not be tested for their veracity. And the systematic testing and re-examination of claims and theories do over time reveal the greater reliability and coherence of some compared with others. It is his refusal to acknowledge the emergence of such differences that led him to argue that the state should not favour any kind of approach to enquiry over others. The supposition that society can be governed without greater reliance being placed on some approaches to enquiry is not only naïve, but could be highly damaging if it is translated into the total suspension of public investment in scientifically promising research, or the replacement of, for example, forensic and judicial investigations by whatever crystal ball gazing method some individuals may prefer.

Feyerabend never seemed to have appreciated the importance of differentiating between claims that have stood up to systematic scrutiny and those that routinely fail whatever problem-solving test they were meant to satisfy. When the conceptual richness of theories of genetic mutation is treated as no different from the simplistic claims of creationism, or when a diagnostic procedure that is reliable for over 90% of cases is dismissed as no more accurate than the ramblings of a self-styled clairvoyant, Feyerabend's type of blinkered permissiveness does not support the development of an open society, just the proliferation of arbitrary assertions that undermine democratic governance (Lakatos & Musgrave, 1970; Peterson, 1996).

The next form of hyper-critique exhibits itself in grand incoherence, and has become increasingly popular among many who are dissatisfied with the way they are governed, and yet are reluctant to commit themselves to any definable alternative. It chimes with the mood of anti-politics where perpetual protests take the place of constructing a preferable future. A representative figure steeped in this milieu is Slavoj Žižek. Everything is fundamentally flawed, and nothing is worthy of being designated, even provisionally, as the alternative to be pursued. Indeed, there can be no coherent substitute, because any proposal can be taken apart rhetorically. Typically, Žižek celebrates the contradictory messages he sends out. He cites the fact that he has been attacked for being anti-Semitic and spreading Zionist lies; for being a nationalist and unpatriotic; for being a defender of Stalinist terror and a bourgeois enemy of communism; and concludes that 'so maybe, just maybe I am on right path, the path of fidelity to freedom' (Žižek, 2011, p xiv).

Like others who treat intellectual commentary as a performance art, Žižek has no interest in clarifying what he is actually advocating. He throws out remarks like glittering confetti – from dismissing Marx as insufficiently radical to endorsing Trump for the US presidency – with the aim of entertaining his audience without ever specifying what policy and institutional changes should be pursued to bring about improvements for any group or groups of people. It may be objected that philosophical critics should have the freedom to turn everything upside down and foster new perspectives for reviewing current beliefs. But that freedom does not imply that they can say anything and not be shown up as misleading and vacuous. By comparison, Richard Rorty, whose writings were also filled with clever metaphors and provocative debunking, showed that far from degenerating into grand incoherence, a commitment to critical re-examination could aid the process of improving social outlook and political organisation. Instead of attacking every theory and practice he came across as inescapably not good enough, Rorty highlighted misguided standards set for 'truth', illustrated how we managed to check out the reliability of claims in different contexts, and reminded us that the reduction of human suffering served as a guide to social actions (Rorty, 1998, 1999).[5]

Although 'capitalism' serves as a catch-all target for Žižek's vitriol, he has nothing tangible to offer to tackle this problem. This did not escape the notice of a reviewer who was no friend of capitalism either, when he concluded that 'achieving a deceptive substance by endlessly reiterating an essentially empty vision, Žižek's work ... amounts in the end to less than nothing' (Gray, 2012). Ironically, John Gray's indictment of Žižek's vacuity flowed not from a concern with the lack of effective transformation proposals, but from a broader project to demonstrate that no transformation proposal can ever be effective.

Whereas civic-communitarian thinkers want to subject prevailing assumptions to critical scrutiny in order to identify options for improving governance arrangements in society, Gray believes that any attempt to reason out a way to a better future is ultimately a lost cause. He is not the first to blame the Enlightenment for its alleged arrogance in supposing that human beings can work out with the aid of reason how to make the world a better place. But he has established himself as the leading exponent of relentless despair.

---

[5] See also Walzer (1993) for an insightful approach to social criticism, albeit without the flamboyant prose style.

In his book *Straw Dogs: thoughts on humans and other animals*, Gray blames all the ills of life on Earth on that 'exceptionally rapacious primate' known as human (Gray, 2002, p 7). He is convinced that every time human beings have come up with another theory or practice to secure some kind of improvement, it has somehow ended badly yet again. This sweeping dismissal of intelligence-based progress runs counter to any evidential review, but of course Gray would cast any such review aside as another symptom of our delusional attachment to 'reason'. While he lambasted Žižek for having nothing to offer behind his rhetorical façade, Gray's own position was that no one could reasonably have anything to offer because human reason was irrevocably flawed.

Astute commentators were quick to point out that Gray did not bother to subject the products of human reason – policies, inventions, reforms – to any meaningful evaluation of their impact, but simply projected his anti-rationalist and misanthropic assumptions in precisely the universal manner he condemned as a sign of intellectual folly (Eagleton, 2002; Postel, 2003). For him, there could be no hope of reasoned deliberations guiding us to more opportunities for a fulfilling life or any tangible reduction of suffering. This proclamation of relentless despair suggests that it is futile to try to assess and select policy options since no such effort can possibly lead to better outcomes. Gray's ideas reinforce the proclivity for pessimism just when plutocrats buoyed by bigotry are on the ascendant, and encourages people to abandon the Enlightenment ethos of cooperative deliberations, without which democracy will wither.

Raymond Tallis has traced the ideological pessimism in Gray, and others such as Dudley Young and Jacques Derrida, to their refusal to recognise the span of human capacity for conscious deliberations (Tallis, 1999, 2011). Towards one end of the spectrum, there are undeniably occasions when particular individuals can barely articulate their meaning, or make coherent judgements. But moving closer to the other end, there is ample evidence that many people in all ages have used their individual and collective mental resources to solve problems and create better forms of life. Progress may not always be permanent, yet it is patently possible and frequently obtained.

The problem with the spread of hyper-critiques is that it diverts attention and energy from what Dewey called the development of cooperative intelligence to deal with the challenges we face. Instead of subjecting key claims and assumptions systematically to critical re-examination to differentiate which should be retained or revised, people are urged to believe that nothing can escape from being exposed by some form of radical criticism or another to be no better than anything else. And if nothing can stand up to such criticism in any case, there is no point in trying to be reasonable in differentiating proposals one should back from those one ought to shun.

Academics and intellectuals who weave hyper-critiques may enjoy the limelight without worrying about the cul-de-sacs they lead others into. But their success reinforces the 'anything goes, nothing matters' outlook that undermines democratic endeavours. As Tallis has noted in frustration,

> That's fine to be pessimistic about the future of humanity if you're a nice, comfortable professor in a tenured chair … If you're a bloody child grubbing in the dirt, and you knew those buggers over there were saying, 'There's nothing we can do about the world,' while they're drinking their claret, it wouldn't give you much hope in the dirt, would it? (Quoted in Parry, 2011)

How to embed critical re-examination in the way we govern

Proponents of hyper-critiques not only turn the questioning of claims affecting society into empty gestures, they also encourage the perception that all criticisms display rhetorical style rather than corrective substance. For many who are shaken by the divisive changes driven by plutocratic policies, it becomes all the more important to have some absolute 'truths' they can hang on to. Under such circumstances, it may be tempting for some to think that it would be wise to concede to fundamentalist cravings and allow particular beliefs to go unchallenged.

But once the favoured dogmas of one section or another of society are granted immunity from critical re-examination, they can spread and be exploited further to undermine open evaluation of what should be done. Dogmas such as those relating to one religion deserving to be privileged above all others; immigrants being assumed to weaken rather than strengthen community life; that businesses will always behave more responsibly the less they are regulated; that the bargaining powers of the rich justify their taking however large a share of the revenue generated by their poorly paid workers – once they take hold, any attempt to question these dogmas would be repudiated as outrageously antibusiness, unpatriotic, or sacrilegious.

To counter such inimical development, effective critical re-examination must be systematically reinforced in the way we govern ourselves at every level. Only then can we hope to be in a position to differentiate what claims should be provisionally adopted pending further investigation, what must be jettisoned, and what ought to be left as an open case unproven in either direction.

Learning from the deficiencies and loopholes that have hampered democratic governance in different contexts, attention should be paid to four aspects of critical re-examination to ensure they are robust enough to root out policy mistakes, false claims, and outmoded beliefs. These cover the following:

- embedding a responsive trigger mechanism;
- developing sufficient capability for re-examination;
- nurturing the cultural readiness to challenge assumptions; and
- organising the strategic re-examination of re-examination processes.

Let us first take a look at what is involved in putting in place a responsive trigger mechanism. Such a mechanism has to meet two objectives: to enable legitimate concerns regarding any prevailing assumption with significant implications to be addressed with a proportionate re-examination of that assumption; and to keep at bay groundless, vexatious, or simply devious attempts to raise doubts about well-founded claims and theories.

It would be a mistake to suppose that democratic 'neutrality' somehow requires those in governing positions to stand aside and leave people to manipulate critical re-examination to suit their private agendas. Real neutrality is only secured if there are rules and referees to regulate the contesting of beliefs that may guide individual and collective behaviour. Contrary to the picture of science painted by thinkers such as Feyerabend, since the 17th century scientific pioneers and research institutions have developed through progressive revision approaches that provide a systematic basis for assessing the reliability of claims made in diverse fields. While these range from claims regarding engineering precision or verifiable predictions in astronomy to the health impact of different substances or the causes of psychological trauma, the underlying assessments share important features such as being susceptible to accuracy comparison and correction. So although some assessments may not be as accurate as others, the fact that the relative deficiency can be identified, and that it is open to revision if a better approach is forthcoming, show that they offer a dependable means to check particular claims.

By adopting the peer review approach scientific researchers use to keep check on each other's new claims, a trigger mechanism can be developed to target attention to where an established claim should be critically re-examined because of the relevant reasons and evidence cited, and where a request for a comprehensive review can be put aside as it is not accompanied by any cogent argument for reopening an investigation.

This approach is of course already used in corporate and judicial governance in, for example, responding to calls for product recalls due to safety concerns, or for appeal hearings to overturn an allegedly wrongful conviction. But it is not systematically embedded in all governance arrangements. Blatant lies by self-styled 'maverick' politicians, instead of being officially exposed as false, are actually promoted as entertainingly provocative claims by ratings-chasing media. Other dubious assertions, such as those about the efficacy of certain types of treatment, are defended as though it would be antidemocratic to warn the public about their total lack of credibility. In the film *Dallas Buyers Club*, for example, the US Food and Drugs Administration was presented as unreasonable and meddlesome in ruling against certain untested 'cures' for people infected with the HIV virus, when in fact those 'cures' included expensive 'supplements' that had no tangible beneficial effects, and substances that were found to be extremely harmful (Matthews, 2013). The FDA was not itself infallible, but crucially it was prepared to subject its recommendations to critical re-examination so it could improve its advice as time went on. The film's tenet, however, echoed the minimalist stance of wanting to leave individuals to 'judge' for themselves when the experience of the FDA was testament to how people on their own could be deliberately fooled, or simply misled by someone with the best intentions, without the broader investigative and research resources of a public agency.[6]

A trigger mechanism is particularly needed where claims are positioned as exempt from falsifiability. For centuries after the Enlightenment, many who resent being reined in by empirical research and logical reasoning have tried to argue that their beliefs are inspired by unquestionable, divine sources which are beyond any mortal method of verification. In short, they alone know what is true, and no one can possibly cite anything to cast doubt on their claims. Democratic advocates have at times been hesitant in tackling this defiance of objectivity for fear of being regarded as disrespectful to religious people. Yet the issue is not about religion versus secularity, but about whether any claim (made by anyone with whatever personal beliefs) is to be subject to objective scrutiny. And if a belief affects the lives of others, then it is unacceptable that one person can claim that God is on their side and no one can query the reliability of that belief. To concede immunity from criticism to claims such as God is ordering the faithful to drink deadly poison or slay divinely chosen victims, it is God's will that a child should die rather than receive a blood transfusion, or young females should have their bodies mutilated in accordance with some ordained

---

[6] Prince Charles' documented attempts to press the NHS to channel more public funds into homeopathy remind us how arbitrary claims can shape our lives if not for the systematic checks offered by institutions rooted in objective research.

tradition[7] is to grant an open licence to behaviours regardless of how harmful and groundless they are. Some may think that we do not have to question the veracity of such claims, but just intervene on the grounds that they threaten serious harm. But the problem is that the people who make such claims are quite prepared to assert that what everyone else can see is harmful is in fact 'good' as far as their God is concerned.[8] The only way to intercept irresponsible claims and stop them having what any objective examination will consider as harmful effects is to trigger an official assessment which, in many of the cases with a touch of 'I know because my God told me so' in them, can lead to swift and unequivocal dismissals.[9]

Secondly, to ensure the scrutiny triggered can be carried out effectively, we must have sufficient capability for re-examination. This requires systematic support to be provided to the participants in diverse fields of enquiry, to develop the relevant experience and expertise. It is not feasible to bring together a group of people without the understanding and skills needed to dissect a particular type of problem, and expect them to carry out a thorough assessment of some claim made relating to that problem.

Experts are neither remote minds cut off from the world nor people who merely dress up their arbitrary opinions in esoteric language. From plumbers and electricians to brain surgeons and supercomputer programmers, it is those who have been immersed in a given field, learnt from their engagement with the issues that arise, and convinced their established peers of their competence that have the status of experts conferred on them. Ensuring their development and availability is vital in having a supply line for conducting critical re-examination.

---

[7] Although female genital mutilation, for example, is associated by some with Islam, it is in fact a practice adopted by some people who subscribe to the Christian, Muslim, or Jewish faith, but abhorred by others who see no connection with it to their religion.

[8] Another type of response would be that what (they claim) 'God' wants is beyond human understanding and everyone should faithfully accept it.

[9] And criminal prosecution if the injunction to refrain from acting on the rejected claims is not complied with.

It may be argued that people who do not engage in certain practices such as those tied to particular transcendental beliefs or insular cultures would be unqualified to judge those practices. But that would be confusing the experience of those practices with the experience of examining those practices. People can study and become skilled in problem solving in relation to the behaviour of reptiles, subatomic particles, sociopathic killers, or planets in distant galaxies without having behaved as any of those entities. Expertise is not derived from acting like whatever one is learning about, but from observing patterns, testing out interpretations, and connecting explanatory hypotheses to the available evidence and arguments.

What would disqualify people from serving as experts to carry out critical re-examination is the lack of skills and understanding to differentiate unsubstantiated and incoherent claims in the given field from those which merit the appropriate degrees of assent. So those who profess that their devotion to some beloved tradition means that they cannot ever entertain the notion that people with different ethnicity or gender can be equally competent in anything, or their exclusive communication line to God rules out any point in listening to others who hold different views from their 'divinely sanctioned' ideas are the ones who thereby confirm that they are in no position to overcome their prejudging disposition to be part of any serious process of re-examination.

On the other hand, while there may be a case that those who might obtain financial or other tangible gains from backing or rejecting a claim under review,[10] or who have been known to hold an incorrigible assumption regarding the issue,[11] should be kept away from the review, people who have expressed a provisional view about a subject they have studied should not be excluded. It is a commonly made mistake to consider anyone who has in the past been favourably disposed towards a certain

[10] Many members of the House of Lords, tasked with scrutinising the Health & Social Care Bill, were able to vote in support of it though they would gain financially from the enactment of that bill from the shares they owned in private healthcare companies (Dorling, 2013, p 92).

[11] For example, people whose faith tells them homosexuality is unforgivably wrong.

claim to be automatically unfit to be involved in any critical re-examination of that claim. But the key factor is why the person is so disposed. If it is because most expert assessments up to that point make a sound case for backing it, rather than the presence of any inherent bias or vested interest, then participation in the re-examination will offer an opportunity for an informed review of the case, taking into account any new evidence or arguments presented.

The setting up of a critical re-examination process should, in addition to selecting members with the relevant know-how, be supported with the resources (for example, time allocation, remuneration, administrative backup) that are deemed commensurate with the requirements of the case when it is cleared by the trigger mechanism. For example, a judicial re-examination of a government policy under challenge or a criminal conviction subject to appeal cannot succeed without the analytical assistance and evidence-checking authority necessary to carry out its task. Unrealistic timetables, media attacks on judges, or inadequate management support are just a few of the vulnerabilities that can undermine a review. Similar concerns have to be addressed in other forms of critical re-examination, from arbitrations to resolve disputes over a policy that has been introduced, to formal inquiries set up to take a fresh look at current practices and mistakes that might have been overlooked up to now.

In all such cases, once the team that will carry out the re-examinations has been constituted with members who have a track record of the relevant expertise, the team members should be left to apply their experience to devise the appropriate methodological procedures, without any presumption that there is a single correct procedure to be followed. What those in governance positions should do throughout the process is to ensure that the review team members can stay focused on the objective of their re-examination, without being bribed, duped, or intimidated in any way.

However, probity may not be secured just by curtailing individual attempts to exert undue influence over those involved in the re-examination process. There are potentially broader difficulties that can only be tackled through our third proposal, namely, long-term cultivation of the cultural readiness to challenge assumptions. As Thomas Kuhn's analysis has shown, even with the most rigorously tested scientific theories, isolated counterevidence may be interpreted as anomalies or absorbed through adding qualifications to a hypothesis, rather than lead to the rejection of the theory in question (Kuhn, T., 1970). It could take cumulative findings and a steadily growing interest in alternative explanations before the weight of expectations tilt towards a paradigm shift.[12]

Rather than withholding a requested re-examination for fear of offending the easily offended, we should ensure the public appreciate why and how critical re-examinations should be carried out to protect us from overlooking errors or outmoded thinking that can damage our wellbeing. The teaching of history provides an opportunity to showcase how mistakes in the past were corrected – slavery, torture on grounds of religious disagreement, use of children as factory workers, abuse of women by male 'heads of households', and so on. But the advancement achieved is too often presented as a fact simply to be celebrated as a notable feature of the past, and not as a process which in transforming uncritical assumptions is instructive for the future.

Citizens need to be brought up with the understanding that while it is helpful to have a range of doctrines and beliefs to guide us in life, no individual can be infallible in declaring any of them to be absolutely unquestionable. History is full of examples of how the subjecting of many claims to systematic scrutiny by those with the relevant learning and experience has led to their revision or complete abandonment. This does not mean nothing can be relied on, only that what may be provisionally assumed to be correct may nonetheless require a thorough investigation at a later date.

Without paving the way for wider cultural acceptance of the value of critical re-examination, those tasked with overseeing their respective group's governance may be hampered by deep-

---

[12] For example, limitations in Newton's theory of gravity were brought out in Einstein's general theory of relativity in the early 20th century, but it was not until the 1960s that Einstein's theory was widely recognised as having superseded Newton's.

seated resistance to long-held beliefs being questioned. For example, the ending of the conflicts in Northern Ireland did not come about solely from diplomats and security strategists rethinking how to work with the IRA, but also from politicians and victim representatives setting out over time why the old assumption of no negotiation must be reconsidered. Similarly, the cultural readiness for new thinking over same-sex marriage was promoted through political leaders and celebrity figures linking challenges to prejudices in the past to contemporary obstacles to loving relationships. By their very nature, entrenched beliefs form strong emotional ties to those who have embraced them. Instead of threatening to dismiss any one of these beliefs as symptoms of flaws in their believers, we should ensure that people appreciate how critical re-examinations can help to improve assumptions that affect society, and everyone benefits from the new perspectives engendered by revisions over time.

Finally, we need to organise strategic re-examination of re-examination processes. And the greater potential impact any given re-examination body has, the more thorough a re-examination of how able it is in carrying out its function should be planned and implemented. Such reviews should consider if its terms of reference are still relevant and feasible; if it is equipped through effective recruitment and resource allocation to carry out its duties; and if its personnel possess the expertise and credibility to back their findings.

Democratic governance depends on there being arrangements that will ensure public policies are not shaped by misguided assumptions or erroneous judgements. But if these arrangements are not functioning well, it would discredit collective policy making even more. For example, the Advisory Council on the Misuse of Drugs, set up by the UK government in 1971, was tasked with guiding ministers in reviewing current policies to tackle the physical and social harms, and dependency problems associated with drug misuse. But it was criticised by the Science and Technology Select Committee in 2006 for not drawing ministers' attention sufficiently to evidence that the prevailing drug classification system was flawed. Yet in 2009 its recommendations to change the classification of cannabis and ecstasy was rejected by Home Secretary Jacqui Smith, and its chair was later sacked by Smith's successor, Alan Johnson, for expressing views contrary to government policies on drugs. Later in 2011, the new UK government removed the legal requirement for the Advisory Council to have people with the relevant scientific expertise as its members.[13] Without a critical review of its role and assessment of its capability, this body cannot be relied on to carry out any re-examination of drug policies.

Institutional inertia is common in holding back proposals to re-examine a body set up with critical re-examination responsibilities. This means that those in governance positions must be vigilant in convening a review as soon as the need arises, regardless of when the body in question was first set up. For example, the UK's Independent Inquiry into Child Sexual Abuse was set up in 2014, but by 2016 three successive chairs had already resigned and one leading staff member had left amid rumours of inappropriate sexual behaviour. Under such circumstances, it should be urgently re-examined to determine what must be changed if it is to deliver on at least some of its objectives. On the other hand, the US Supreme Court has been around for over two centuries, but the total politicisation of its appointment process in recent decades means that if it is to function as a non-partisan body steered by legal expertise alone, then its composition, appointment procedures, and remit ought to be critically re-examined.[14] In either of these types of cases, instituting a thorough review of the body in question is essential for dispelling any doubt about its ability to deliver the impartial and reliable findings it is tasked with producing.

---

[13] Jacqui Smith and Alan Johnson were Labour secretaries of state; while the post-2011 UK government was a Conservative-led coalition with the Liberal Democrats.

[14] To secure bipartisan appointments, one option would be to require candidates to be jointly backed by the two largest parties in Congress (as opposed to being dependent on the support of just one party).

Remedial checklist: critical re-examination

With reference to any group the governance of which you are concerned about, you can use the checklist below to identify what requires the most improvement in relation to the need for critical re-examination:

☐ Are members aware of how they can seek to trigger a formal re-examination of key decisions, adopted policies, authorised claims, or established practices? Will most of them understand why it may not be triggered if there are insufficient grounds to open a particular case again?

☐ Are the arrangements for carrying out specific tasks of critical re-examination adequate in terms of the expertise available, management support, and the allocation of time and financial resources? Are there preventative measures to stop those involved in the re-examination from being bribed, deceived, or intimidated? Do members of the group generally have confidence in the competence and integrity of those carrying out the re-examination in question?

☐ Are there sustained efforts to promote recognition and appreciation of how erroneous assumptions, flawed claims, and misleading beliefs can persist unless they are subject to critical re-examination that will not allow any claim to be shielded from reviews by merely invoking some unquestionable tradition, custom, or divine source inaccessible to anyone else?

☐ Is there an adequate process for capturing the lessons from the success and failure of bodies set up to carry out critical re-examination, and applying them to improve their future performance? While vexatious objections to their operations should be dealt with accordingly, where there are reasons for checking over a particular arrangement for critical re-examination, is it likely that it will be subject to a thorough re-examination itself?

EIGHT

Responsible communication

One of the key pillars of democratic governance is the openness with which people can access and discuss information relevant to considering matters that concern them all. But it is often misrepresented as the freedom to say or show anything, in any manner whatsoever. Consequently, this freedom has been invoked as a licence for irresponsible communication, undermining objective deliberations and casting a shadow over the prospect of citizens attaining a shared understanding of what they should do as a group. In this chapter, we will look at why democracy needs to be able to count on responsible communication, what role should or should not be entrusted to those with media outlets, and how to foster responsible communication more systematically.

Why we need responsible communication

'No one is to infringe our freedom of expression' or 'The freedom of the press must be protected' – such sentiments are meant to reflect a firm commitment to democracy. But as with many shorthand slogans, they short change the truth. If there is no enforceable restriction on what and how people can communicate, those who use words, symbols, or images to promote, arrange, or facilitate any activities that damage others' lives will be able to do so without ever having to justify themselves, or face any possible penalty.

The notion that democracy is premised on the absence of limits on communication is simply at odds with reality, not only because democratic objectivity has to be protected from lies and distortion, but no form of governance can survive when trust in every sphere of society is shaken by everyone being given a licence to deceive. The pivotal question is what the appropriate requirements are to be in light of the informed concerns of society's members.

Even US lawmakers, constrained by a constitution that explicitly declares under its First Amendment that 'Congress shall make no law ... abridging the freedom of speech, or of the press', have no doubt that legal action is necessary against irresponsible communication when certain conditions are met. There are at least five distinct categories where there is long-established consensus that government intervention is required. There is certainly disagreement within the US and between different countries as to what the precise conditions for intervention are, and what sanctions may be appropriate, but a look at each category will show us why democracy can be jeopardised by libertarian overreach in shielding all acts of communication from judicial restraint.

The first category concerns the lawless effect that is likely to be caused by the communication in question. Since *Brandenburg v Ohio* (1969), the US has relied on 'inciting or producing imminent lawless action' as the criterion for intervention (Lynd, 1975, p 151). So if someone urges others to beat up someone walking by, or provokes an individual or group of individuals to react violently, that may warrant intervention. However, the impact has to be 'imminent', which means that if an extremist is setting out why people should look for opportunities in the future to inflict harm on certain groups, that is permissible. Furthermore, since racist abuse is considered protected under the First Amendment in the US, anyone spreading such abuse is safe from the law so long as the victim does not react immediately with violence (or some other 'lawless action'). Ironically, it means that those who are hurt by racist abuse but bear it stoically will thereby render the act beyond legal action, and the only way to bring it into the scope of state intervention is if someone is ready to engage immediately in some lawless action in retaliation. By contrast, in England and Wales any hate speech targeting a person's colour, race, disability, ethnic or national origin, religion, or sexual orientation is forbidden. Correspondingly, any communication which is threatening or abusive, and is intended to harass, alarm, or cause distress, is against the law.

This problem for US lawmakers does not stop with the expression of bigotry, but extends to the advocacy of antidemocratic ideas and practices in general. In the 1950s, the concern was with communist communication regarding the violent dismantling of the American political system. In the 2010s, white supremacists and Islamic extremists advocate changes that are incompatible with basic democratic inclusiveness and equal respect for all to participate in civic decision making. Yet the reliance on 'imminent lawless action' as the central criterion has meant that no intervention is allowed unless the advocacy can be convincingly linked to the *imminent* dismantling of democratic processes.[1] But the advocacy that can turn people towards blind hatred, misguided rage, and a determination to hurt others may not deliver its damage against the declared 'enemies' for many months, or even until years later. If only the US were prepared to rule against hate speech, it might more readily find a coherent path to halt communication that attacks mutual respect and radicalises impressionable minds into despising democracy and peaceful coexistence.

The second category covers communication that is unacceptable in itself – because it is deemed by contemporary standards to be obscene or offensive. Leaving aside cases that overlap with and can thus be covered by restrictions on communication that may provoke or produce violence, fear, or distress, this category points to a separate type of verbal or visual communication that people would generally find obnoxious, indecent, or disgusting. Those at the receiving end need not be hurt or intimidated by what is communicated, so long as their negative assessment of what they see, read, or hear is shared by others in the wider community.

At first glance, it may strike many that this is one category of communication that should have no restriction whatsoever.

---

[1] The US did previously, under Dennis v US (1951), draw the line at communication by any group that is closely associated with the promotion of antidemocratic practices, but Brandenburg v Ohio (1969) interpreted it as only applicable where it would bring about the damage in question imminently.

There is certainly a need for democracy itself to be protected from people who may halt any communication by decrying it as obnoxious every time they come across anything that does not fit in with their personal sensibilities. As Justice John Marshall Harlan once wrote (*Cohen v California*, 1971), 'One man's vulgarity is another's lyric'. Social attitudes also change over time. What many people might previously have objected to in relation to the use of swear words or the expression of affection between people of the same sex or different ethnicities can come to be considered quite differently just one generation later. And what one religion declares as blasphemous or profane may be perfectly acceptable to another, let alone to those who subscribe to no religion at all. Muslims may be told by the Quran that Jesus is just another human prophet, but to some Christians that could be interpreted as insulting to the Son of God. The US has from its inception kept religious disagreement out of the government's jurisdiction. Belatedly, the UK abolished in 2008 the criminal offence of blasphemy in England and Wales.[2]

However, it would be fallacious to leap from the lack of common judgement in some areas, and the changes of standards in other areas, to the conclusion that there are no general standards at all for acceptable communication. Our discussion of mutual respect in Chapter Four would point to the need to guard against behaviour that demeans others, and that includes verbal or visual communication that conveys derision or reinforcement of negative stereotypes. It may not incite hatred or violence but it can leave those targeted understandably feeling disparaged or disgusted. This provides one clear basis for tackling obnoxious communication, especially if it occurs at the workplace, in schools, or in a public space or building.[3] Additionally, one of the elements that will form any shared mission of contemporary societies is without doubt the concern for children in tackling the promotion of paedophilic ideas and images. Hence the

---

[2] Though it has remained so in Northern Ireland after the amendment to make it applicable there was withdrawn.

[3] It would cover hurtful remarks disguised as 'banter', and the many vicious psychological attacks deployed in cyber-bullying.

communication in any form that may facilitate or sustain such activities should fall into the category of legally unacceptable.

The third category deals with attempts to communicate what belongs to others. Just as the law does not permit people to take without justification the money or physical property of others and make use of them, it gives protection to the words, figures, imagery, ideas, and data that belong to individuals or groups of individuals, and under certain circumstances forbids them being communicated more widely without due authorisation. Patented ideas, written materials with copyright protection, confidential commercial documents, and a wide range of intellectual property cannot be passed without restriction in the name of free expression or communication. But even where commercial infringement may not be an issue, people are expected to have their privacy respected, so that their private conversations, their personal documents, their own records, and so on, are not something others can pass on without satisfying particular legal conditions. In the UK, for example, apart from defined groups such as accountants, solicitors, or journalists who are discharging relevant professional duties, anyone seeking to obtain and pass on information about others without their permission must first apply for a Security Industry Authority licence, or else their activities would be illegal.

The fourth category draws the line against the communication of false information. With the spread of groundless scepticism, a resurgence of fundamentalist rejection of objective evidence, compounded by the mainstreaming of post-truth advocacy by pseudo 'anti-establishment' critics, it may be easy to forget that the distinction between truth and falsehood remains key to the rule of law. And the law of any democratic system must unreservedly forbid the use of false information, regardless of attempts to claim that truth is just a matter of subjective opinion. As we have seen in the previous two chapters, collaborative learning and critical re-examination are essential for sustaining objective discourse, and our capability to tackle false communication is strengthened by their continuous improvement.

Some allowances ought of course to be made for the unintentional sharing of false information. If despite one's best intentions the information one puts forward turns out to be false or misleading, the infringement may be excusable. For example, the US Supreme Court ruled in *New York Times Co v Sullivan* (1964) that action should not be taken against the press on reporting false information unless those responsible knew it was false, or treated the issue of truth with 'reckless disregard'. However, the burden of checking for accuracy generally falls on the communicator, and depending on the potential harm, the due diligence expected can rise correspondingly. So anyone who wrongly declares someone an embezzler without any serious investigation having been carried out, or produces a leaflet about a drug that misprints the level for a safe dosage, may rightly be made liable for damages. And despite the libertarian commercial culture, it is widely accepted that advertising, the sole purpose of which is to influence people's behaviour by deploying persuasive forms of communication, must not contain what is false or misleading, or leave out important information relevant to what is being advertised.

The final category targets any communication that is damaging to national security. It is not necessary for the information to be taken from the government without permission. Someone might have witnessed an event that took place in an abandoned warehouse, and if it could be argued that any reporting of the event would bring about a situation that could seriously damage the security of the country, then there is a prima facie case against its disclosure. Two factors would have to be weighed in practice. One is whether there is a genuinely serious threat that needs to be avoided, or disclosure might cause nothing other than embarrassment to someone in government. The other is, granted there is a risk that aspects of the country's security might to some extent be compromised, whether suppression of the information could give rise to a high risk of some other core aspect of the country's wellbeing being badly damaged. For example, revealing the identity of security personnel involved in covert operations may put them and their mission in danger, but if they are responsible for torturing and killing people who are innocent bystanders, keeping it a secret may enable those activities to continue and put the safety of many more people in jeopardy.

Having established these five categories where irresponsible communication is expected to be placed under legal restrictions and subject to prosecution, it follows that anyone in a governance position ought to be similarly constrained. Hence a democratic government at any level must be required to communicate responsibly without expressing hatred or urging anyone to resort to violence; being offensive in breaching mutual respect or being obscene by widespread societal standards; using information that belongs to others except where a greater justification can be produced; lying, misleading, or intentionally omitting important information that is relevant; or endangering national security. If these requirements lead to conflicts, then they are to be resolved not by the invocation of some non-existent hierarchy of 'free expression', but by a practical assessment of the risk and impact of the specific factors in the given case. For example, a government has entered into a contract with a private company to deliver a major public health programme. If one member of that company is found guilty of vandalising the car of a neighbour, the government may rightly turn down a request from a journalist to disclose the public health contract just in case it has some relevance. But if the member of the company is arrested for bribing a corporate client to win a contract and then cut corners in its delivery to push up profits, there may well be a case for the public health contract to be openly scrutinised.

The question we must ask is why, if citizens, organisations, and government at all levels must comply with detailed requirements for responsible communication, those requirements never seem to be taken seriously in relation to those promoting political agendas and campaigning for public office. It should be clear by now that they cannot hide behind the rhetoric of 'freedom of speech'. What has protected them is a mixture of timidity and intellectual confusion. Those who have won power democratically for most of the 20th century have thought that if they used their power to hinder anyone else in making claims in support of a rival political offer they might be accused of acting undemocratically. In fact, because of the serious consequences that can flow from inveterate liars and charlatans taking control of government institutions, democracy should be safeguarded by robust legal measures against irresponsible communication in political debates and electoral campaigns.

Unfortunately, many took the view that a few inaccuracies on either side would just cancel each other out, and when it came to the lies told by some fringe, or extremist, advocates, the assumption was they would never win power anyway, so let them spout away. And thus when anti-establishment sentiments reached boiling point in the 2010s, the freedom to incite hatred against scapegoats, promote offensive denigration of minorities, use illegitimately obtained information, and spread false and misleading stories helped to tip contests in favour of those who had been waiting to hollow democracy of its inclusive substance, and leave it as a plebiscite device for demagogues to manipulate so as to advance their personal objectives.

Yet many are still reluctant to find ways to curb irresponsible communication in politics. A parallel myth to that of the absolute freedom of expression has been the irreproachable freedom of the press. And politicians who had wanted to keep regulation away from political communication might argue that so long as the media were free to report on what those promoting various political policies were up to, that would suffice. But is the so-called fourth estate really up to the task, especially when its neutrality in judgement has been increasingly eroded by plutocratic takeovers?

Media power's real impact on democracy

The media have an undeniable role in tracking and uncovering government activities, including what and how information is being communicated by those in public office. But just as it would be naïve in the extreme to assume that all citizens and government institutions will always be fully responsible in their communicative behaviour, it is untenable to suppose that all those with media power will never use that power irresponsibly.

When governments, corporations, or influential individuals issue statements or express their views on matters many others will be concerned about, the media's ability to expose any lies, criticise any distortion, and highlight any misleading omission is vital for public confidence that deception does not get a free ride in their society. The media have a critical role in helping to expose governments' attempts to disguise the serious underfunding of the health service,[4] paint a disingenuously one-sided picture of their foreign policy (Curtis, 1998), or deflect the public from the damaging consequences to young families caused by drastic cuts to children's centres (Jayanetti, 2016).

However, not all those with media power intend to use it impartially to serve the public interest. Media networks for news, entertainment, publishing, and data transmission have been increasingly bought up by a small number of large conglomerates.[5] Of those that have not been taken over, many are owned by businesspeople who have close financial ties with a range of commercial interests. And it is not unheard of for some of them to use their power selectively to damage a government under the control of a political group they view with hostility, or to minimise the criticisms that would otherwise be directed at a government in the hands of those they consider worthy of their support.[6]

Since the 1970s, the New Right has provided a political platform to bring together plutocrats, military expansionists, and advocates for social divisiveness. Those who sign up to increase corporate powers know that one way to help advance their alliance is to fan prejudices so those consumed by them will be more ready to vote for New Right candidates, who will in turn cut taxes for the rich and empower big business to push back regulatory constraints. Many have since used their media

---

[4] The false claims made in 2016 by the Conservative government were pointed out by the Conservative chair of the Commons Health Committee, and reported by some in the media: www.itv.com/news/2016-10-31/nhs-funding-to-be-cut-despite-government-claims-says-tory-head-of-health-committee/

[5] In 2017, six corporations controlled 90% of the media output in the US (Sanders, 2017).

[6] For example, viewers of Fox News would assume Democrats are responsible for pushing up the federal deficit, when it was Reagan who increased the deficit by 142%; Clinton reduced it by 1%; and while both George W. Bush and Obama increased it by 53%, the former inherited the surplus from Clinton, while Obama had Bush's legacy to deal with (Amadeo, 2017). As for the counterclaim that the wider US media were biased in favour of liberals/Democrats, the evidence is against it (Halbrooks, 2016).

empire to promote an agenda that is the antithesis of mutual respect (Dearden, 2016).

The way had been paved for both the Brexit and Trump's presidential campaigns years before with media attacks on 'foreigners' and cross-border institutions (such as the EU). For example, the Migration Observatory had tracked a sharp increase in negative coverage of immigration to the UK since the Conservatives won power in 2010.[7] Notably, instead of focusing on the problem of banking irresponsibility which had just caused a global financial crisis, the pro-New Right media intensified its daily presentation of immigrants as a major cause of the decline of Britain's quality of life.

Lord Justice Leveson, who chaired the public inquiry into the culture, practices, and ethics of the British press, stated that 'when assessed as a whole, the evidence of discriminatory, sensational or unbalanced reporting in relation to ethnic minorities, immigrants and/or asylum seekers, is concerning'. He added that there were enough examples of careless or reckless reporting to conclude that such reporting in the UK was a feature of journalistic practice in parts of the press, rather than an aberration.[8]

And while some in the media may act responsibly by, for example, keeping a watchful eye over what the UK government is doing through extended surveillance of its own citizens, especially after it secured the passage of the Investigatory Powers Act (2016),[9] others may indulge in their own intrusion into people's private lives. Phone hacking may have caused the Murdoch press some temporary embarrassment, but there remain many ways to dig up secrets that serve no public interest. Individuals who are targeted may not have the means to take media moguls to court. Worse still, when individuals are singled

---

[7] See the 2016 report, 'A Decade of Immigration in the British Press': www.migrationobservatory.ox.ac.uk/resources/reports/decade-immigration-british-press/

[8] Electronic Immigration Network (2012): www.ein.org.uk/news/leveson-report-finds-sensational-or-unbalanced-reporting-relation-immigrants-and-asylum-seekers

[9] The Act, labelled by many as the 'Snoopers' Charter', gave the government the right to monitor its citizens' private communication to a far wider extent than is permitted in any other Western country (Carlo, 2016).

out for their political stance, they have to retreat or face an uphill battle to clear their names from misleading stories that put them in an extremely bad light. Tom Watson, the Labour MP who was a staunch critic of the Murdoch press, was himself subject to threats of having damaging media stories published about him (Watson & Hickman, 2012).

Since it is empirically plain that no one becomes a saint solely by virtue of having control over media outlets, the reasons considered in the previous section for formulating and enforcing legal limits on what and how individuals, governments, and political advocates may communicate must also be applied to the media. Indeed, if the media are exempt from regulation themselves, then individuals, governments, and political advocates can circumnavigate attempts to curtail their irresponsible communication by getting supportive media to deceive others on their behalf.

Plutocrats use the media under their control to promote their favoured agenda by distorting the truth, misleading the public, and helping the politicians who back them get much more favourable coverage at the expense of their opponents. Rupert Murdoch, for example, never made any secret of his dislike of the EU because of its powers over his business dealings. It was reported that 'when asked by the journalist Anthony Hilton why he was so opposed to the EU, Murdoch is said to have replied: "When I go into Downing Street, they do what I say; when I go to Brussels, they take no notice"' (Martinson & Mason, 2016). So Murdoch's tabloids relentlessly attacked immigrants and blamed their 'flooding' into the UK on the EU, which was also portrayed variously as authoritarian, wasteful, and anti-British. In the US, the Koch brothers, with their substantial stake in the fossil fuel business, fund numerous bodies to publish and promote climate change denial stories every year (Sheppard, 2011).

One of the biggest hurdles to media regulation is that even those that on the whole practise responsible communication, such as *The Guardian* newspaper, oppose it as an encroachment on the freedom of the press. The argument is usually framed against a specific proposal, such as the one that was put forward as a result of the Leveson Inquiry. In this particular case, objectors have seized on the fact that they must either agree to join a government-approved low-cost arbitration service, or opt under Section 40 of the legislation to stay clear of that service and use the courts system, but will then have to pay all the costs of the hearing even if they win.

It is understandable why journalists would be unhappy about the Section 40 option since it would encourage corporations and unscrupulous individuals to take a news publication to court, knowing that even if the disputed report was deemed fair and accurate, they would have their costs covered. This in effect provides a free vehicle to drag the media into costly defences of their own reporting, regardless of its reliability. Far from enabling irresponsible organisations to hamper investigative journalism, the media should be shielded from unwarranted attacks. For example, in *Grant v Torstar Corp* (2009), the Supreme Court of Canada ruled that the law of defamation should give way to the rights of a party to speak on matters of public interest, provided the party has exercised a certain level of responsibility in verifying the potentially defamatory facts. A defence of responsible communication on matters of public interest was thus recognised.

Instead of using a clumsy and flawed tool such as Section 40 to 'incentivise' the media into signing up to an independent arbitration service, a wiser course for the UK government would have been to (a) require all media to accept the jurisdiction of a designated independent arbitration service and (b) ensure that there is such an arbitration service in place that is sufficiently affordable, independent, and effective. So long as the arbitration service on offer has vulnerabilities such as being financially supported by large contributions from individuals who had been embroiled with conflicts with the media, it can be presented as not fit for purpose.[10] However, the alternative is not to ignore the need for such a service, but to develop one which can facilitate

---

[10] For a critical perspective on Section 40, see: www.theguardian.com/commentisfree/2017/jan/11/section-40-british-press-regulation-investigative-journalism

trusted arbitration for all sides and help constrain irresponsible communication.[11]

Trump's alliance with media organisations such as Fox News in his repeated attempts to attack other news providers that report events responsibly shows that if an independent arbitration service is not properly established when power is in the hands of the democratically minded, then it becomes even likelier that irresponsible communication will spread when those who care little for democratic oversight extend their reach over public offices and private media outlets. Part of Trump's strategy is to undermine trust in those media that refuse to sign up to his political agenda, and the more people who are uncertain which side to believe, the easier it would be to get away with false and misleading statements.

Although it is by no means easy to develop an arbitration service for responsible communication, the same can be said about establishing an impartial judiciary. And just as Trump's attempt to undermine the judicial system with his attack on a federal judge because of his Mexican heritage is a reminder of why the system must be protected from arbitrary assault on its integrity (Trudo, 2016), his antagonistic attitude towards the media is not a reason for leaving the media unfettered, but confirmation that independent arbitration over the communication of powerful persons and organisations is vital.

Some may say that with the proliferation of social media, citizens themselves can through their blogs, tweets, Facebook posts, and other online communication fully take on the task of making sure lies are exposed and reliable information is properly shared in society. Unfortunately, this utopian view falls down on three counts. First of all, it assumes that on any issue many of those misled by established conventional media can be guided back towards more reliable facts and interpretations by the combined forces of social media. But in practice, the reach of social media as a news provider has clear limits. For example, according to a 2010 Pew Center Research report conducted

---

[11] For a rebuttal of attempts to dismiss the case for an independent arbitration
    service, see: www.theguardian.com/commentisfree/2017/jan/11/section-
    40-media-abuses-press-regulation-justice

in the US,[12] even among those aged 18-29, 25% did not have even one social media account. The figures for the rest of the population rose by age: for those aged 30-45 it was 50%; 40-64, 60%; and when it came to those aged 65+, 94% did not have any social media connections. And time pressures and, to some extent, fear of being hacked, are leading many young people to deactivate their social media accounts. Furthermore, just because one taps into social media, it does not follow that one will seek out information that helps one critically review what one has picked up from conventional media. In fact, many people log in just to keep in touch with friends, catch up on sports and entertainment, or read headlines and reports that reinforce the views they generally prefer to adopt.

Secondly, given the propensity for false stories to be generated and spread on social media, one cannot rely on them as the ultimate mechanism to correct the misinformation sent out by corporations, governments, or political advocates. If anything, social media have become a major source of unsubstantiated allegations and totally fabricated 'news'. To test how easily this could happen, Anders Colding-Jorgensen set up a Facebook group in 2009 to rally support in protesting at the (fictitious) demolition of a well-known fountain in Denmark. Within two weeks, the group's membership went up from 125 to 27,500.[13] As Colding-Jorgensen observed, the same phenomenon could easily happen with protests stirred up against the fabricated misdeeds committed by immigrants. Indeed, in the 2016 US presidential elections, Trump demonstrated through his Twitter feeds how false or misleading claims[14] about his political rivals, immigrants, foreign countries could be generated to convince millions that they were right to denounce and detest anyone deemed a treacherous enemy or a worthless scapegoat.

---

[12] 'Millennials: a portrait of Generation Next': www.pewsocialtrends.org/files/2010/10/millennials-confident-connected-open-to-change.pdf

[13] See 'Stork Fountain Experiment #1: Why Facebook groups are not democratic tools': http://virkeligheden.dk/2009/stork-fountain-experiment-1-facebook-groups-are-not-democratic-tools/

[14] Fact checking found 70% of Trump's claims during the 2016 presidential campaign were false (Konnikova, 2017).

Thirdly, social media and the wider internet in which they are embedded are highly susceptible to controls and manipulation by organisations whose agenda may conflict with the promotion of responsible communication (Morozov, 2011). The dominant tech companies have a business model that is dependent on capturing data that will reveal individuals' preferences, and working with others to generate more revenue from satisfying those preferences. Fuelling prejudices is one option, and any request to restrain communication that may undermine mutual respect because of its abusive or deceptive nature is rejected on grounds of freedom of speech. The same freedom is exploited through the funding of the production of reports and bulletins in support of everything from climate change denial to whitewashing the financial sector's role in causing the global economic crisis. Both public and private sector agencies may use online networks to mislead people about what they should believe. And even the disclosure of secret documents can become a potent tool in helping a favoured political candidate over another, as WikiLeaks' actions against the Democrats in the 2016 US elections demonstrated.

Ultimately, neither conventional print/broadcast media nor social media can be exclusively relied on to keep governments, corporations, and influential individuals from harming others and undermining democratic governance with irresponsible communication when they are liable to communicate irresponsibly themselves. In fact, the frontier mentality of social media businesses has lent itself to a lie-and-let-lie modus operandi that renders it far from being the ideal candidate to secure objective discussions and inform collective choice making.

How to foster responsible communication

Minimalist strategists often push their vision of a lawless order until their dream of spontaneous harmony is shattered by reality. Even in the Old Wild West, where rugged gunslingers would supposedly settle matters between themselves, it turns out that the law did not hesitate to step in. While contemporary libertarians are still trying to invoke the freedom that sprang up once upon a time in America to rebut gun controls at every turn, a photograph of a sign in Dodge City, 1879, captured a common practice of the time. It read: 'The Carrying of Firearms Strictly Prohibited' (Winkler, 2011). Whatever difficulties people might cite about attempts to bring in such regulation, they were introduced and effectively enforced by local sheriffs. And just as guns can be used to maim and kill, irresponsible communication can be deployed to destroy lives.[15]

As with all governance challenges, the key is to find the appropriate balance between harmful inaction and overbearing interference. To do this, a culture of collaborative learning and the availability of critical re-examination are essential to secure continuous revision and improvement. In order to tackle irresponsible communication more effectively, there are at least five types of action to be considered:

- rationalising the law on responsible communication;
- developing media arbitration services;
- setting legally recognised professional standards in journalism;
- recalibrating the conditions for anonymity; and
- advancing global oversight of communications.

First and foremost, the myth that there can be no legal restriction on what and how we communicate should be laid to rest, and attention directed to rationalising the law on responsible communication. Of the key categories we looked at earlier, no country has yet managed to apply their laws consistently to prevent their violation, especially by the most powerful individuals and organisations. A commission should be set up to carry out a critical re-examination of the laws on dealing with irresponsible communication, and identify what changes should be brought in. The penalties, from fines to imprisonment, must be proportionately sufficient to deter potential perpetrators, and reduce the likelihood of repeat offending.

Inciting or provoking people into lawless behaviour must be curtailed, not just if the effect is imminent, but whenever it is intended and the connection a foreseeable one. If a comedian is

---

[15] From suicides caused by cyber-bullying, to wars launched on the basis of distorted intelligence reports.

making a joke about how people unhappy about a government policy should blow up a bridge, and someone leaves the venue to make a bomb and plant it on the nearest bridge, the comedian is hardly culpable. But if a member of a paramilitary group suggests they should mark an event a year hence by blowing up a public building, the law should not wait to see how well they plan their action, but step in straightaway. It is notable that the shock sometimes expressed about such an 'infringement of the freedom of expression' often vanishes, to be replaced by impatience with intervention, when the communication in question is attributed to an Islamic extremist.

Similarly, offensive communication that breaches the level of mutual respect required for a democratic society should be subject to legal controls. While matters of pure aesthetics or inner spirituality can be left to individuals to pursue, as we have seen in the chapter on mutual respect, it is not beyond our everyday intelligence to see whether or not how one person communicates with or about another is reciprocally acceptable. Few would argue with the principle that private information should not be freely shared, and yet government surveillance and internet loopholes have increasingly encroached on what we thought we could have legitimate control over. As for the communication of false or misleading information, Trump's administration's proclamation of lies as 'alternative facts' is a stark reminder that judicial intervention is long overdue.

The law must be tightened in relation to all these categories and applied consistently regardless of the attempts by some to decry the loss of their 'freedom of speech'. In one further category, that relating to national security, the law must be made clearer as to what types of damage are relevant, how they are to be weighed against public benefits,[16] and what penalties can be expected. For whistle-blowing activities that exposed atrocities committed or supported by US operatives, Chelsea Manning ended up serving seven years of a 35-year prison sentence (before

---

[16] Following the publication of the information provided by Manning, US military personnel became stricter in reining in torture and other inhumane treatment of Iraqi civilians, which had previously further inflamed hatred against the US.

receiving a pardon from President Obama). For his involvement in leaking the identity of a CIA agent, Lewis 'Scooter' Libby, chief of staff to Vice President Dick Cheney, was sentenced to 30 months in prison but did not serve a single day as the sentence was immediately commuted by President Bush, who admitted that the leak came from his own team in the White House.[17] Since this latter case was tied up with who the White House did or did not want to be sent to check out claims about Iraq developing weapons of mass destruction, with the wrong finding leading to the war against Iraq, the national security risks could not be higher.

To avoid problems being ignored or persisting until they are taken to court, with all the cost implications, we should look to the second area where action ought to be taken, namely the development of media arbitration services. A simple comparison between the output of Fox News (with its unregulated and dedicated bias against anything its owners would like the public to reject) and Sky News (subject to impartiality rules enforced by Ofcom) would show the difference that having a recognised referee can make to contested claims about responsible communication.

But having a body that can rule on disputes is just a starting point.[18] Ofcom might have provided a check on blatant excesses in broadcast media (such as the vitriol and distortion one would read in the press without a comparable regulator), but it has generally taken a minimalist approach in relation to what constitutes a balanced discussion. So if a broadcaster wants to cover a claim supported by a few people with no relevant expertise or recognised track record in the field, it can invite one of them to the studio to discuss it with someone whose in-depth understanding is acknowledged by the vast majority of those who have genuinely studied the matter critically. But that does not constitute a balanced discussion. It provides a misleading platform to suggest that each side of this discussion carries equal weight.

---

[17] See the NBC report on the Valerie Plame case: www.nbcnews.com/id/19728346/ns/politics/t/bush-admits-administration-leaked-cia-name/

[18] Beyond fact checking by groups such as Snopes, media arbitration will need to involve assessment of intent and harm.

This is often compounded by the short and soundbite-driven approach that helps to hide the ignorance of the misguided and showcase favourably the art of entertaining charlatans. Another form of media bias is to give disproportionately more airtime to those who are likely to stir up resentment against people who cannot defend themselves (such as refugees and immigrants), but less to those who may challenge powerful organisations that prefer to be kept out of the media spotlight (such as corporations that heavily pollute the environment). For example, between 2009 and 2013, the BBC invited onto its flagship political discussion programme, *Question Time*, representatives of the established political parties on a fairly equal basis; but of the two emerging parties, it invited Nigel Farage of UKIP (a party with no MP) 14 times and, by contrast, Caroline Lucas of the Greens (and an elected MP) was invited just 8 times (Eaton, 2013).[19]

Any effective arbitration service must address any concerns about its own recruitment and staffing policies so its independence can be relied on (Preston, P., 2017). It must be able to rely on guaranteed public funding, rather than donations that can come from individuals or groups others may perceive as trying to influence the decisions of the arbitrators. And its binding judgement must be backed by legal sanctions if those involved seek to reject their conclusion. This will be challenging when those taken to task could be media platforms favoured by powerful people. But once again the evidence of how those who have managed to secure high public office manage to abuse their power through lies and groundless accusations should remind us how necessary it is to put effective scrutiny arrangements in place.

The third area for action concerns the need to develop legally recognised professional standards in journalism. While the proliferation of opportunities via the internet for ordinary citizens to report on events, comment on current affairs, and share their observations is to be welcomed in broad terms, it

---

[19] The BBC received the highest complaints (in relation to its party political coverage) accusing it of biased coverage in favour of UKIP during the 2014 European Parliamentary elections: www.theguardian.com/media/2014/may/30/bbc-complaints-ukip-election-coverage-bias It remains to be seen if Ofcom would do any better should it take over the regulatory role overseeing the BBC fully after the demise of the BBC Trust.

should be remembered that the passing on of false or misleading stories has also risen exponentially as a result. A key safeguard against patients being badly treated by people unfit to practise medicine is based on legally sanctioned professional rules to exclude those without proper training and qualifications, and to suspend those who have failed to act with due care despite their training and qualifications. Organisations such as the National Union of Journalists and the National Council for the Training of Journalists in the UK, and the Society of Professional Journalists in the US, should similarly establish professional standards that are robust enough to define a formally recognised journalist.

The standards would reflect a commitment to abide by responsible communication as outlined above, and any approved journalist could be suspended by a peer panel or even permanently lose their licence to practise if they were to intentionally or recklessly breach the commitment in relation to one or more of the categories. On this basis, recognised journalists should be given easier access to government and corporate information that may serve the public interest; and the signing off of a story by them should be an indication of its reliability. Any story that surfaces which cannot be traced back to a recognised journalist may still circulate, but until one confirms it, it will rightly be considered 'speculative'. Citizen journalism could benefit from this through aspiring reporters in the community taking the necessary training, and inviting recognised journalists to support them as volunteers to develop their output.

The fourth area for action is the recalibration of the conditions for anonymity. Communication can be problematic if the identity of some of the people involved is concealed. The general assumption is that if the negative consequences likely to befall the individuals in question cannot be outweighed by the wider benefits from disclosure, then people should be able to remain anonymous. But in practice, the weighing of the two sides is often far from consistent in different cases. Should anyone giving testimony as a victim against the accused in any type of crime be kept anonymous from the accused, or does it depend on the likelihood of the accused using the information to intimidate or directly harm the accuser? Why should the everyday financial transactions of most people be open to government scrutiny, but vast deposits and transfers by the wealthiest be shielded by internationally guaranteed anonymity? Does it make sense for anonymity to be given to individuals on the internet who would use it to abuse and ruin the lives of others, while corporations and governments can use their powers fully to uncover the identity of whistle-blowers even where the latter have performed a substantial public service by exposing serious violations that were hitherto hidden?

A systematic recalibration that removes unwarranted guarantee of anonymity in cases where it would be exploited to threaten or harm innocent victims, and safeguards it for those who should be protected from retaliation by exposed wrongdoers, would not only increase the level of responsible communication, but also counter public perceptions that anonymity is granted or withheld arbitrarily.

Finally, we must advance global oversight of communications. The rapid and extensive development of internet communications has led many to believe that it is not something anyone can regulate. But the large tech corporations and those that want to make more money from selling through their networks, advertising channels, and profiling algorithms are well aware of how controls can be put in place. Moreover, they are constantly tempted to segregate the internet into fast lanes for high-return commercial traffic and slow routes for everything else. Broadband access is already a dividing issue for communities split between those with ever increasing top speed and areas that are left behind. Global agreement is needed to ensure that a pseudo laissez-faire smokescreen is not put up to hide manipulation that will make it more difficult to get out information valuable in terms of public interest, while giving privileged speed and scope to the transmission of information promoted by the corporate elite for their private gains.

Since the 1970s, many campaign groups have tried to develop standards to ensure important issues get a public hearing, and to prevent powerful corporations and governments from deploying their propaganda to discredit critical reports from other sources. UNESCO sponsored the International Commission for the Study of Communication Problems, produced the

McBride Report, and adopted the Mass Media Declaration in 1978, setting out the responsibilities of mass media in global communication (Alleyne, 1997, Chapter 4). In the 1980s, the US and UK, both under New Right administrations, withdrew from UNESCO on the grounds that its work pressing for more responsible communication was infringing the freedom of the media. The resistance to setting global standards remains a major obstacle to be overcome.

The development of resource networks such as Wikipedia suggests that informal scrutiny can play an important role in identifying false and misleading information (Wales, 2017). But wider collaboration is needed to combat the outpouring of deceptive and unreliable reports. Ultimately, the task of securing effective international oversight would need the support of powerful countries, which means that when truly democratic-minded leaders win office, they should make it a priority to develop transnational cooperation to set up the appropriate controls, and not leave the challenge as one of low priority. After all, if it is not tackled, cross-border communicative manipulation will continue to distort what citizens ought to know, and feed them with fabrications. It has already reached the point where elections are influenced by the fake reports and messages sent out by hostile nations, making it increasingly difficult for pro-democracy politicians to succeed against unscrupulous opponents (Simmons, 2017).

Remedial checklist: responsible communication

With reference to any group the governance of which you are concerned about, you can use the checklist below to identify what requires the most improvement in relation to the need for responsible communication:

☐ Do most members want to see misinformation minimised and corrected? Are they convinced that serious violations of responsible communication will be rigorously pursued? Is there sufficient shared understanding of what differentiates objective information that should be accessible from false and deceptive materials that need to be restricted? Can people turn to a trusted and affordable media arbitration service to resolve disputes?

☐ How consistent and effective are the rules and regulations set down for preventing irresponsible communication, and protecting open communication in other cases? Do they transparently apply to government and corporations as they do to individuals? Are the conditions for granting or rejecting anonymity set for comparable circumstances?

☐ Can members access information directly or via dependable sources? Are there proper professional standards set for journalists, and is their compliance enforceable by law? Do members appreciate the difference between the output of recognised reporters and speculative stories or fake comments put out by others?

☐ Are the standards that members rely on undermined by practices that cross international borders? Do members find it difficult to deal with information that may be unreliable or deceptive when it comes from sources that cannot be readily scrutinised or regulated? Is enough being done to establish global oversight to curtail irresponsible communication emanating from other countries?

PART FOUR

How to achieve democratic power balance

NINE

Participatory decision making

Of the four classic governance strategies, none regards power balance as a challenge requiring ongoing adjustment. The hierarchical strategy assumes people will accept power differences as a fact of life, and not seek to usurp the order of things. The minimalist takes it that without a central authority amassing power, nobody else would either. The egalitarian believes the issue can be resolved once and for all with everyone having the same power, even though that can only be secured paradoxically by a very powerful authority. And the disciplinarian threatens severe punishment for anyone not submitting to the uneven distribution of power that will sustain the regime in control. The meta-strategy of democracy, however, seeks to respond to the dynamic changes of power relations by engaging the people themselves in adapting policies, personnel, and practices to maintain an overall equilibrium so that none can come to dominate others. In this chapter, we will look at why participatory decision making has a vital role to play in attaining democratic power balance, what superficial or counterproductive forms of participation should be avoided, and how participatory involvement in decision making can be improved.

Why decision making needs members' participation

Disillusionment breeds irrationality. When things go wrong, the proverbial baby is never far from making an untimely exit with the bathwater. Whenever some voting arrangements have, for example, led to outcomes that are detrimental to a large number of people, democracy is blamed.

The Brexit outcome of the UK's EU Referendum and Trump's win in the 2016 US presidential election have both raised questions for many observers about where opening up decision making to all may lead us. Meanwhile, authoritarian regimes cite the turmoil engendered to illustrate the pitfalls of allowing the public a say in matters that should be left to those in charge (Phillips, T., 2016). But as civic-communitarian critics have consistently warned, if the democratisation of our governance arrangements does not advance and continuously improve, dangerous fault lines may remain. Instead of dismissing democracy, we should be asking how it can be strengthened further to prevent its current weaknesses from being exploited.

Perhaps a reminder is in order as to why a turn towards participatory decision making is necessary in the first place. There are three main reasons. First, no one is infallible. Individuals or cliques who insist they alone know all they ever need to know for making any decision are the ones most likely to overlook relevant facts, ignore inconvenient evidence, and make fallacious arguments with no one else daring to correct them. Even highly intelligent despots cannot grasp the full range of issues that concern the governing of contemporary society, and to permanently exclude people whose expertise or experiences may cast vital light on assumptions on which decisions are to be made is to risk committing serial errors. As for authoritarians whose capacity for factual analysis and logical reasoning is severely limited, in the absence of amendments coming from elsewhere, costly mistakes will almost certainly recur.

Secondly, if decisions affecting people's lives can be made without those who will be affected taking part in making them, it opens the door to those with the decision-making power to form whatever view they wish of the impact their decisions will have on others. As the edicts drop on a powerless populace, a benign dictator can imagine that the people are deep down better off even if they seem unduly upset for now, while a callous tyrant will just grin without remorse.

Thirdly, as people keep having to live with the consequences of decisions made without any meaningful involvement from them, they become more and more alienated from the collective system under which they have to abide by the rules and commands decreed to be binding on all. If stability is maintained, and excesses are few, people may put up with their lot, though the prospect that they can achieve more together will be far from their minds since the system for collective action is not one they have any control over. If people's livelihood is threatened, and oppressive measures multiply, discontent will intensify, and the only unifying collective action to draw crowds will be the overthrow of the ruling regime.

It is to avoid these three problems that the meta-strategy of democracy has come into being. But democratisation is a process that requires ongoing learning, sustained improvement, and constant readjustment. A ballot box and a voting slip are symbolically important, but by themselves they are a long way from delivering effective governance. Indeed, any system that is 'democratic' in name but does not go far enough to establish a sound foundation in terms of togetherness of the people, objectivity of discourse, and robust power balance can end up suffering the same problems that are endemic to dictatorships. A partially democratic system may nonetheless hand power to people who will deny mutual respect to any group that they choose to scapegoat, brush aside facts and findings they prefer to ignore, and shift even more unaccountable power to their family and billionaire chums.

The culprit is not democracy, but inadequate democratisation. We have looked at how key elements relating to togetherness and objectivity need to be improved. In parallel with them, the ingredients for power balance – among which participatory decision making is vital – must also be strengthened.[1] We should begin by dispelling a particular misconception of political participation, namely the idea that it asks too much of us, and that it is premised on some kind of devotion to a higher social ideal that is either unattainable for most people or, worse, undesirable in itself.[2] In other words, ordinary folks cannot afford to spend too many evenings attending meetings about public policies, and

---

[1] We will consider the other two elements of power balance – civic parity and public accountability – in the next two chapters.

[2] This is sometimes associated with the notion of 'positive freedom' (Blau, 2004; Putterman, 2006).

the odd ones who obsess about getting involved at every turn have a misguided view of what life is about. Quentin Skinner has explained that it is a false dichotomy to suppose that people should aspire to be free either as individuals with no constraints from anyone else (including the state), or as activists who realise their true freedom by pursuing some higher purpose (embedded in their state, religious organisation, or some other institution).[3] From a civic-communitarian perspective, people become more free in so far as they shape their own governance, so that the laws and policies that set out what they should or should not do are formulated by themselves (Skinner, 1990).

As Skinner pointed out, there is no need to postulate any higher purpose. A shared mission is constituted by what people seek for themselves and in partnership with others. It does not entail any moral objective located in a different metaphysical order. At the same time, it follows that there is no need for citizens to be constantly absorbed in politics to advance democracy. How much time they should allocate to it would depend on how effective the established arrangements are for facilitating decision making at different levels.

To be effective, decision-making arrangements in a democratic society should enable citizens to develop an informed view of what they are deciding about, deliberate without undue interference as to what their preferred option would be, select an option by means of an agreed procedure, and review the outcome. Historically, because of the tendency of monarchic regimes in the 18th century to respond to the emergence of democratic demands by suppressing public discussions and censoring publications, there was from the beginning a burning concern with opposing any barrier to the flow of information. But once those regimes became political relics, the focus did not move on accordingly to examine whether the information needed for democratic decisions was actually flowing at all.

Advocates for deliberative democracy have pointed out that unless useful information is exchanged, without being distorted

---

[3] Hannah Arendt and Alasdair MacIntyre are among those who argue that people should make a moral commitment to a higher purpose beyond their individual preferences (Alexander, 2012).

by deceptive claims or drowned out by irrelevant materials, so that people can think through with one another what decision would make most sense for them under the circumstances, a mere majority vote for one option rather than another could be as arbitrary a decision as one made by an autocrat. Instead, they propose that lessons from cooperative problem solving be applied to democratic option selection (Tam, 1998; Fishkin & Laslett, 2003; Gutmann & Thompson, 2004).

This would involve facilitated sessions where the expectation of mutual respect is upheld and the safeguards for objectivity enforced. Participants will be made aware (like jurors) that they are to make up their mind only after they have given due consideration to what is put before them. Abuse, false evidence, threats, unsubstantiated claims, and anything that may derail proceedings will be ruled out.[4] The parameters will be explained so that those attending understand what is or what is not up for their decision. For example, there will be no discussion of the merits of a candidate who is not on the official ballot, or a policy option that would violate commitments to mutual respect. Those advocating specific options will be given time slots to make their case, but attempts to bring in misleading or irrelevant information will be halted so that the whole event does not lose its credibility. The facilitator will ensure reasonable questions are put to advocates and experts before the participants deliberate among themselves which option they favour.

Philosophically, thinkers from C. S. Peirce (1992) to Habermas (1986) have reflected on how under ideal conditions of undistorted information exchange and reasoned deliberations enquiring minds will converge on what best stands up to critical scrutiny and their emerging consensus will approximate ever more closely to the correct position.[5] But since in practice it is quite possible that not all the relevant information is

---

[4] Anyone who thinks such a setup is impossible may deem the rule of law as inherently implausible because it would require precisely this kind of impartial oversight.

[5] As we have seen in the earlier chapter on collaborative learning, such joint deliberative enquires are the only coherent way to resolve disputes about what is the correct claim, without invoking some transcendental notion that by its very non-empirical nature defies objective examination.

transparently communicated, or those taking part have not attained a sufficiently shared mission, we have to allow for the fact that people may not all come to the same conclusion, and those opting for contrasting choices may have good reasons for doing so. And in cases where a consensus is not forthcoming, going with the decision backed by a simple majority is not the only, and indeed not always the appropriate, option.

If we look at the simple majority route itself, it should be recognised that it can sometimes be a feasible method of resolving differences, but only if certain conditions are met. Provided the implementation of the decision in question can be kept under review, changed at a future date, and not have severe irreversible impact on the basic wellbeing of some people, it could supply a time-limited answer. But where the potential effects of the decision could be wide-ranging and the likely damage and benefits highly unpredictable, then other options should be considered.

For example, with the election of a large group of representatives to run a city or a country, the simple majority option could be particularly unhelpful. Should one political party take all the seats if they obtain a majority of the votes cast? Should every seat be given to a political party's candidate with a majority of the votes, or even just more votes than any other individual candidate? Or should the allocation of power to representatives be proportional to the extent to which the electors are convinced of the political platform they offer? Each party can be given the same proportion of seats as they have won votes across the city or country, and the order by which each party's candidates are ranked for the purpose of selection will be determined by the percentage of the votes they secured in their respective constituency. With such a system, highly respected and well-liked representatives with strong backing from their constituents will gain a seat without losing out from being placed low down on the party list for some other reason.[6]

---

[6] For example, a party with 38% of the votes will take 38% of the seats, and these X number of seats will go to the top X of candidates on that party's list which, unless it is ranked by percentage of votes won, could end up handing seats to the candidates with the least support in their constituencies.

The problem with superficial participation

Despite the warnings of civic-communitarians, all too many political leaders have taken the participatory structures of their countries for granted. It is as though once we have moved one step away from a single individual or an elite group making all the key decisions for everyone, we could assume no further improvement is necessary. But universal suffrage was reliant on two factors: one, voting was primarily directed at picking out candidates who stand on a relatively familiar political platform; and two, the custodians of those political platforms were relatively well-established political groups or parties.

With the onset of the 20th century, public policy challenges and dilemmas intensified both quantitatively and qualitatively. And as more and more voters came to sense that they had little influence over what was decided by those they elected (because they were in a minority in the legislature, or they did not do when in government what their voters thought they should do[7]), the political parties themselves increasingly became more remote from their supporters. Instead of providing a bridge for ordinary citizens to get their concerns into the political decision-making process, the parties increasingly became a vehicle for career politicians who preferred to anticipate the unreflected views of electors rather than engage with them in making informed assessments of what should be done in the public realm.

By the early 21st century, backers of the New Right agenda were saturating the media with the simple narrative that benefit claimants, immigrants, and 'foreign' institutions such as the European Union were culpable for the ills of society. When the banking sector caused the financial crisis in 2008, the Labour Party ended up not pushing for radical banking reforms, but declaring that it had not taken the 'problem' of immigration seriously enough up to that point. Similarly, Hillary Clinton decided to rely more on large donations to

---

[7] Prominent examples would include the failure of the Labour government to refrain from participating in the invasion of Iraq; the Liberal Democrats reneging once they got into power on their electoral promise to abolish tuition fees; and the Conservatives under Cameron promoting fracking instead of being a pro-environment government.

fund generic campaigns than to engage with voters on how to tackle the plutocratic causes of job insecurity and lagging pay. It left the door wide open for the unscrupulous to use the New Right's playbook to put the blame for economic uncertainty on immigrants and foreign competitors.[8]

The corrosive culture of anti-politics can only be countered with a thorough restructuring of decision-making arrangements to enable civil and informed discourse to underpin democratic choices. Before we look at some of the changes that should be brought in, we ought to consider why a variety of proposals to strengthen citizen participation have turned out to be superficial at best, and counterproductive at worst. One particularly dominant option is that of the consumerist model. The analogy is that as individual consumers can shape companies' decisions by their purchasing behaviour, citizens can shape public decisions if they are given opportunities to express their personal preferences to specific offers. So the breaking down of budgets into personal vouchers, individual allocations, or transfers to independent organisations are supposed to give people greater influence over the way public sector bodies behave. Externalising primarily 'delivery-focused' government institutions into contracting arms that can in turn lose money as a result of complaints or gain bonuses from higher signup of users is another device to enable citizens to have a direct impact on public decisions and priorities.

Unfortunately, if people make decisions without taking into account other people's needs and concerns, they could not only miss opportunities that would have served them better, but end up bringing about consequences that are undesirable for others, which in turn cause others to respond in a negative way to them. For example, if polluters act as they please to maximise their own profits, everyone else will be disincentivised to do anything to protect the environment, and there will be all round deterioration, unless collective limits are put in place. And if businesses cut jobs and pay, thinking they can increase their margins, they will be hit by long-term economic decline caused

---

[8] In the case of Trump, the tactics were pushed to such an extreme that the alliance between big business, the military establishment, religious fundamentalists, and organised bigotry became unstable.

by diminished purchasing power unless wealth is redistributed sufficiently to revive the economy. In these diverse cases, variants of the Prisoners' Dilemma are played out. People do not know how they could get better outcomes unless arrangements are put in place to help them enter into agreements for cooperation. Left on their own, each has far less leverage to challenge a bad deal, and many become more vulnerable to having their services downgraded or cut off.[9] In many cases, choices are illusory as the information needed to make any meaningful comparison is difficult to access or presented in a deliberately overcomplicated form.

While some decisions can be left to individuals to make, many require the shared understanding of those involved (Prior et al, 1995). Everyone in a neighbourhood complaining individually about what each of them is not getting from a local authority may aggregate to a set of contradictory demands that cannot be met. A neighbourhood council supported by deliberative meetings of representative sample groups of residents may, by contrast, bring out what the main priorities are, what misconceptions should be corrected, and how local people can help to ensure the proposed solutions are workable given their experience on the ground.

Besides consumerist techniques, there are participatory approaches that superficially engage people in groups, but do not in fact empower them to reflect on or shape any relevant policy decision affecting them. While some of these approaches are adopted by those who merely want to pay lip-service to citizen engagement, they are also taken up by political leaders and public officials who mean well but do not fully grasp what meaningful democratic participation should involve.

Typically, these approaches focus on reaching out to a large number of people and inviting them to take part in some publicly funded activities. At the most basic level, information is made available online or sent out in printed form. The contents may range from voluminous details about the operations of a

---

[9] Services such as water supply, broadband connections, and doctors' surgeries have become more precarious as the private sector's involvement expands, especially for those who are poor or live in remote areas. (For the impact of transferring the management of public services to for-profit enterprises, see Goodman & Loveman, 1991; Tam, 1994; Scott-Samuel et al, 2014.)

particular public service to short, skeletal outlines of the work and objectives of a large government department or a city-wide authority. Those who bother to read it are sometimes asked to give their views after digesting what they have perused. But without guidance or the opportunity to discuss with others what is set out, very few can comprehend all the details or deduce from the highly generalised statements what to agree or disagree with. The feedback is unlikely to be of much use in considering what would be in the public interest to maintain or change.

At this juncture, two suggestions appear at the fork of the superficial participation road. One points to engagement activities which use sports and cultural events to bring large numbers of targeted groups, particularly among younger people, to come together. Promoted, for example, as 'youth participation events', these will encourage those who normally do not engage with political figures or public service managers to take up offers from statutory bodies to play a sport or take part in a concert. While it is important in its own right to promote sports and arts, unless such events incorporate elements of deliberative discussions of certain public policy options that lead to reviews of how to select from those options in the future, they should not be regarded as anything other than sports and cultural initiatives.

The other suggestion at least takes engagement with participants over specific public policy options as central. So people are invited to come together at events where they meet with representatives from the relevant authority. But these can only work if they manage to steer clear of four common pitfalls. First, if the aim is to seek the views of a particular group of people (for example, residents in an area; people affected by a new medication rationing policy; an age/ethnic group), then, except where the entire group is small enough to meet in a single or a manageable number of sessions, random sampling procedures need to be applied to avoid just those who happen to be supportive or deeply hostile to what is proposed turning up. Furthermore, where sound sampling has taken place, the engagement with those who attend the event(s) should be communicated to others in the target group, so everyone knows that a representative sample of their peers was asked to give their considered views, and what these turn out to be.

Secondly, if those in charge give presentations that are either long and boring, or full of vague generalities without key details, and then expect those in attendance to fire back their thoughts, it is not likely to reflect what the participants think about the issues. And even if the information presented is clear and concise in conveying what the options up for consideration are, without a chance to discuss critically with others what the implications of those options are, there is a real risk that the participants will fall into the Prisoners' Dilemma trap of thinking only of what each regards as their own costs/benefits without forming any broader comprehension of what would improve conditions for their group, and ending up with something that makes life worse for all of them.

Thirdly, there is the situation where the need for deliberation is formally recognised, but the importance of having a skilled facilitator is overlooked. Without someone explaining the basic parameters, encouraging considered input, and securing mutual respect, a vocal minority might take over proceedings, disagreement could turn into disruptive rows, or participants just may interject without any coherent discussion moving forward. Some elected politicians and public officials have thought that their status would entitle them to 'direct' the event, but those who were not the most competent facilitators became liabilities themselves when they alienated those present by repeatedly pushing their own favoured option, or antagonised them with their seemingly arbitrary interventions in determining who should speak and who must stop speaking.

Fourthly, even with well-facilitated deliberations, there is still one last trap to avoid, namely the feedback-less 'black hole' phenomenon. It is not unheard of – indeed, it happens all too frequently – that people are brought together at a participatory event to give their views on a matter that affects their wellbeing. It may have a relatively focused topic (such as local access to emergency medical services) or a very wide remit (such as the main challenges facing the country), but the end point of the discussions is a 'thank you for your time and contributions', followed by silence thereafter. The premise of such events is often summed up in lines like 'let's have a conversation' or 'we want to listen to you'. Yet without any indication of what is being done with the thoughts shared, participants are left feeling that it is all for nothing. Soon these exercises are perceived as window-dressing events. Worst of all is when the reflected views converge overwhelmingly on one option, and those in charge subsequently, without any explanation, brush that option aside.

If the decisions that affect a whole group are not to be overwhelmingly determined by a powerful few, or arbitrarily shaped by people who have little idea what those decisions could lead to, then more participatory decision making must be built into our governance arrangements, and each approach should be continuously improved based on the experiences of its implementation.

How to advance participatory decision making

There are four main areas where participatory decision making should be supported more to ensure democratic engagement is informed and influential. These relate to:

- improving the quality of deliberative engagement;
- delegating decisions in line with subsidiarity;
- expanding opportunities for decision-making roles; and
- strengthening existing voting arrangements.

Let us first take a look at how we should improve the quality of deliberative engagement. An effective way to achieve this is through action learning where what organisers and participants learn from their engagement activities are constructively shared with others, who in turn apply those lessons and learn further ones to pass on through a process of continuous improvement.

For example, in the 2000s, the UK government developed the Together We Can programme[10] that invested in learning and advisory hubs across the country to help citizens, communities, and state bodies at all levels to shape public policies and practices (Tam, 2015b). Guide Neighbourhoods shared their experiences

---

[10] The Together We Can programme involved 12 government departments, coordinated by a central policy team. Its funding and policy coordination ended in 2010.

with other neighbourhoods as to how to engage local residents to work in partnership with statutory agencies in prioritising challenges and formulating responses. Civic Pioneers were local authorities committed to improving their co-designing of policies with local people and groups, and sharing the lessons learnt with other statutory organisations. The programme also pursued through regional umbrella groups the twin goals of raising awareness of the value of deliberative engagement, and promoting a culture of learning among citizens, activists, public officials, and elected politicians. One of these, the group in North West England, helped to advance effective practices through a wide range of case studies, including the setting up of a young people's centre in Barrow-in-Furness that, unlike previous youth initiatives, succeeded because of the involvement of young people in its planning and development; the reduction of crime figures and reversal of environmental degradation in Colne through a partnership that worked through 'walkabouts' during which residents and public representatives could point to problems in the targeted area and assess viable responses; and the cutting down of the carbon footprint in Tattenhall that was only achieved because local people were co-assessors and planners of what actions would be most appropriate (North West Together We Can, 2008).

The key to attaining continuous improvement in deliberative engagement is to go beyond the description of a technique, and develop an ongoing learning relationship with those who seek to apply and adapt that technique. The contrast between the Healthy Communities initiatives in the US and the experiment with the National Institute for Health and Care Excellence's Citizens Council in England, for example, shows that networked learning for improvement is vital. With the former, the movement began in 1988 with the aim of empowering interested members of diverse communities to engage fellow residents in collaborating with public health agencies to identify and tackle local priorities. By the 1990s it was having state-wide impact in South Carolina, California, Indiana, Colorado, and Massachusetts. In 1996 the Coalition for Healthier Cities and Communities was established, and thereafter training and support spread to more states and public health improvements were achieved which state officials acting alone previously had thought impossible (Sirianni & Friedland, 2001, pp 166-185).

The Citizens Council experiment, on the other hand, recruited 30 volunteers to deliberate on the social (but not 'technical') dimension of medical prescription policies, leaving patients' groups feeling that they were not given a say, while those serving on the Council lacked any real influence over the Institute's thinking on what drugs should be made available on the NHS. Detached from other exercises in deliberative engagement, it did not readily learn to adapt its approach, and a review of its operations concluded on a pessimistic note (Davies et al, 2006).

It may be argued that deliberative engagement is more suited to the subnational level, and many countrywide issues cannot be opened up to critical discussions except for a small number of people. This may be true of some national policy issues, but many decisions taken nationally ought to be left to people at a more local level.[11] This takes us to the second area for improvement, namely the need to have decisions taken in line with subsidiarity. The principle of subsidiarity serves as a reminder that pragmatically people should be left to work things out for themselves unless they encounter difficulties that can only be dealt with effectively through the involvement of others at a higher level of decision making. The onus thus falls on those who seek to centralise the organisation of otherwise independent groups and units to demonstrate that the advantages would outweigh the drawbacks, particularly in terms of the added remoteness of the decision makers.

Critics of centralisation have argued that democracy runs the risk of being unnecessarily diluted when decision-making powers are taken away from associations and federations (Hirst, 1994; Cohen & Rogers, 1995). They propose instead that more organisations, such as those dealing with housing, education, energy, and local amenities, should be left to manage themselves. Where they find it useful to join forces in a federated structure, they may do so, but powers are thus delegated up by the constituent groups, and can be withdrawn later on. It should be

---

[11] At the same time, some should be decided at a supranational level.

pointed out, however, that the presumption of favouring leaving decisions as close as possible to those affected by them must be qualified by the decision-making group being democratically inclusive (Fung & Wright, 2001). The praising of civil society organisations has often overlooked the fact that many of them operate on a top-down basis without much meaningful engagement of their members. Decentralisation of decision-making powers should be pointing to local agencies or NGOs that take deliberative engagement seriously.

Apart from groups with shared vocational or recreational interests, and community-based organisations, there are two types of body that have attracted particular attention in relation to the demands for more devolved decision making. These are local branches of political parties, many of which feel cut off from their national headquarters, and businesses which have sought greater autonomy from complex regulation. The key to empowering both to make more decisions is raising the deliberative engagement of these organisations, internally and externally. Political parties are meant to serve their members and the wider society (Taylor, 2001). Businesses should meet the needs of those who work for them and the public who pay for their services (Cole, 1917; Pateman, 1970). So if they are to be given a greater say in setting a policy agenda or determining how a certain business is to be run, that should happen on condition that they will actively and continuously involve their respective stakeholders in developing informed views on what they should do. Political parties will need to do more in working alongside local members and diverse communities in identifying and responding to everyday problems (Garland & Brett, 2014), and avoid becoming a mere conduit for individual protests. And businesses can learn from companies that have proven over time how to flourish by empowering workers to make decisions that matter to them (Semler, 1993), and apply lessons derived from systematic research on how to support participatory decision making at the workplace (Bernstein, 1980).

The third area for improvement concerns how far we can expand opportunities for decision-making roles. Many decisions have to be taken by an individual or a group because there is not sufficient time to involve others, especially in cases where even a basic level of understanding of the issues requires long experience or prior studies. There are also cases where the outcome of a group's deliberations is to assign the executive power for the type of decision in question to an individual, or in the absence of a consensus emerging, pass the decision to a designated executive.

There are many such decision-making roles in society; some are filled by elections, some by appointment from a list of applicants, and some are randomly selected as with a jury. The main barriers to running for elections are twofold: the insignificance of the roles on offer, and the inadequate support given to vie with others to take on those roles that are influential. While J. S. Mill suggested that local-level authorities could provide citizens with more opportunities to experience decision making on behalf of their communities (Mill, 2008), in recent decades in England it has become more difficult to find people to stand in parish council elections because the range and depth of powers are so limited. The difficulty of finding candidates surfaces for district, county, and unitary authorities too. Despite central government's rhetoric, the influence of local government has diminished. There is no question that the greater the difference a statutory body can make, the more interest there will be in becoming involved in it. When devolved powers were proposed for the creation of the Scottish Parliament, the Welsh Assembly, and the North East Regional Assembly, public support was strong for the first, with substantial powers proposed; moderate for the second, with a more modest package; and the last, with few significant concessions of devolved power, was rejected.

Parallel to giving public decision-making roles more tangible powers to attract candidates, more support should be given to raise awareness of these roles and develop people's confidence and skills in seeking them. The Take Part programme,[12] for example, combined outreach to underrepresented groups, familiarisation activities with statutory bodies, and development of deliberative and leadership skills in order to broaden the pool of citizens who are prepared to put themselves forward to contest public office positions (Mayo & Annette, 2010). Charitable foundations may

---

[12] For information on the Take Part Programme, see: www.takepart.org/manageContent.aspx?object.id=10229&mta_htm=home

find that one key way to tackle poverty and social exclusion is to fund the development of civic leaders from neglected and disadvantaged groups so they are more likely to secure long-term policy changes.

The appointment route faces similar challenges in terms of the need for mentoring and training to help people apply to join and thereafter seek promotion. But unfavourable reward and status could be a barrier. Before the 1980s, there was a broad consensus that the career of a public official would not be remunerated exceptionally well, but it would be adequate and come with a reasonable pension, and the work of serving the public good would carry general respect. However, as part of the New Right's strategy of undermining the public sector, public servants' pay would often be made to lag behind inflation, their pensions attacked and downgraded wherever possible, and though even junior staff have responsibility for important everyday decisions, they are branded as bureaucrats who, if only they had the drive and abilities, would work in the private sector instead (Stevenson, 2013). Alongside this corrosive undermining of the public service ethos, there is the equally damaging trend of selecting a few top positions where pay can escalate because they are designed to attract applicants from the private sector, who will gain useful government contacts and information before returning to their core career.

The random selection, or sortition, route is generally neglected. It is often assumed that with a large group covering a city or a country there will not be enough positions to rotate to give everyone a chance to take part. But the number of roles can be increased by creating more appropriate opportunities. Participatory Budgeting (PB), for example, brings together a random sample of those potentially affected by the utilisation of a designated budget, and enables them to deliberate over different options, review priorities, and vote on what the budget is to be spent on.[13] Contrary to suspicions that people will vote in line

---

[13] The Together We Can programme supported the development of the Participatory Budgeting Unit which promoted PB. The unit's successor body retains a range of online resources: https://pbnetwork.org.uk/resources/

with preconceived ideas or their own demographic profiles, PB events have often witnessed participants changing their minds after listening to others, and people casting their votes for services not directly beneficial to their own age or ethnic categories.

Not only can Participatory Budgeting be used far more extensively, but other approaches utilising randomly selected members to make public decisions should be considered too. Instead of hiring external inspectors to check on the work carried out by contractors relating to a defined area, residents can take turns by rotation or drawing lots to serve as Environmental Monitors. They will assess and decide what instructions to give to the contractors in terms of any substandard outcome, the awarding of bonuses for services beyond the call of duty, and any other feedback or variations on what is being done. Another role is that of members of an Arbitration Panel which can meet with fellow residents who are in dispute with one another, and facilitate a reconciliation or, if necessary, call in enforcement agencies. Training will be required, but just as some cities have promoted CPR (cardiopulmonary resuscitation) training for all their residents, it would not be a bad thing if citizens acquire mediation skills that can help to ease tension and resolve disagreement in their communities.[14]

Last but not least, existing voting arrangements should be strengthened. The lack of proportionality means that a party/candidate can win power with the support of a small minority of the electorate, and exercise that power regardless of what the majority of voters think. If vast numbers of voters are not to continue to have no realistic influence over the outcome of 'contests' in safe single-member first-past-the-post

---

[14] The arbitration technique known as Restorative Justice was adopted by schools in England and was found to be more effective than any other approach in solving disputes and ending disruptive behaviour. Some schools trained their pupils to run their panels and these proved so successful that they offered their arbitration support to other schools. For more on the technique, see: www.restorativejustice4schools.co.uk/

constituencies, we need to make sure that everyone's vote counts equally in determining the result.[15]

Other changes to be considered would include assessment of fitness for office, recall for breach of trust, and higher assent threshold for a vote on highly complex issues with serious risk of societal destabilisation. At present, the basic suitability of candidates to stand for public office is rarely assessed. The idea that 'they can learn on the job' would not be given a hearing in relation to any other organisation, and yet it has been embraced for state bodies with responsibility for vast resources and urgent demands, protecting the wellbeing of large numbers of people, and balancing competing expectations.

And while some people may initially be deemed fit for office, it is still possible that they or a policy they introduce will turn out to be extremely unreliable, and likely to cause serious damage. In such cases, waiting for the end of their term of office or for the policy to have run its course may be too long. Recall procedures should be in place to trigger a critical re-examination of whether their tenure should be terminated, or the policy in question suspended. If, for example, those with a minority of seats in the legislature do a deal with another group with a few seats, and come forward with a programme that is at odds with the vast majority of the country, the possibility of being recalled may help to bring about a rethink.[16]

Indeed, for some policies, because of the unprecedented disruption they may cause, or the threat they pose to vulnerable groups that cannot defend themselves, a higher threshold should be set when they are put to a deliberative referendum.[17] If a two-

---

[15] For more details on the alternatives, from the single transferrable vote, the list system, to two-round contests, and mixed member constituencies, see Farrell (2011). For a detailed argument for bringing in a proportional electoral system, see Richie and Hill (1999).

[16] For example, the Conservative-DUP deal that was struck after the June 2017 elections in the UK alienated many in the country.

[17] As noted in Chapter Four, the UK Conservative government declared that by law any trade union's call for strike action would only be legitimate if it had the backing of at least 40% of its registered members, but the call for the UK to leave the European Union (backed by only 37% of registered voters) was deemed to be 'the will of the people'.

thirds, or even three-quarters, majority cannot be obtained, it is better to settle for a suspended judgement with no ensuing action than to risk calamity when a significant number of people remain unconvinced.

The exact threshold for different types of issue or alteration to electoral arrangements is not to be decided in the abstract. Instead, constitutional conventions should be held so that the fundamental power allocation and decision-making procedures affecting a country can be deliberatively reviewed and reordered (White, 2015). In the meantime, we must urgently counter the attempts by those who, fearing that an inclusive electorate could make it too difficult for plutocratic interests to influence the outcome of elections, concoct voter registration procedures and identification arrangements to keep those most likely to object to them from casting their vote. False accusations of mass voter fraud need to be swept away and every hurdle designed to hamper poor, young, or transient voters from voting should be removed from electoral processes (Hardaway, 2008).

Consideration should also be given to building into voting arrangements the opportunities for voters to hear the views of others under deliberative conditions, when unsubstantiated claims can be kept at bay or readily exposed. John Gastil (2000) has suggested how random samples of electors can be invited to participate in deliberative sessions, and their findings shared with other voters. Bruce Ackerman and James S. Fishkin have proposed 'Deliberation Day' as a national holiday two weeks before major elections when all citizens will be paid a financial incentive to attend a deliberative event to consider the issues covered by the coming election, discuss them under the inclusive terms of the event, and cast their vote on election day (Smith, G., 2005, pp 52-55).

For voting that is directed at a single-issue referendum or citizens' initiative, there are techniques for consensus building that can be adapted to bring out what people can most agree on, rather than leaving uninformed opinions to be polarised by prejudices and propaganda. Such techniques include Planning for Real,[18] widely used to resolve conflicts over planning proposals since it was pioneered by Tony Gibson in 1977 (Gibson, 1998); and Sociocracy, an approach devised by Gerard Endenburg (1998) to attain unanimous decisions by encouraging reasoned objections and assessing mutual concessions. Access to information prior to deliberative events, and support with dissemination afterwards in cases where the reflections of sample groups need to be shared with the whole electorate, can be provided by dedicated civic institutions, provided they have cross-party support.[19]

[18] More on Planning for Real can be found here: www.planningforreal.org.uk/

[19] In Germany, the Federal Agency for Civic Education (Bundeszentrale für politische Bildung) provides impartial information in support of democratic participation: www.bpb.de/

Remedial checklist: participatory decision making

With reference to any group the governance of which you are concerned about, you can use the checklist below to identify what requires the most improvement in relation to the need for participatory decision making:

☐ Are current voting procedures adequate for all members to take part in decision-making processes? Do some members find it more difficult to participate because of deliberate or unintentional barriers? Is there a need for more deliberative elements to be integrated into the voting arrangements to reduce the extent to which people are making decisions as a result of ignorance or misleading information?

☐ Are the participatory opportunities backed by active learning and continuous improvement? How confident are most members about the quality of deliberative engagement on offer? Are there enough trained and experienced facilitators to ensure engagement events are conducted inclusively and effectively?

☐ How often are reviews carried out regarding the level at which decision making is situated? Should more decisions be left with members at a more local level, and should some be passed to a higher level? Are the options for delegation, centralisation, or federation considered in line with the principle of subsidiarity? And at each level, are there effective arrangements in place to support participatory decision making?

☐ Are most positions for elected representatives filled by the same, narrow range of people who tend to hold on to them? Can others be encouraged and supported to take on these roles? Can more be done to expand the range of decision-making roles by handing important responsibilities to additional positions?

TEN

Civic parity

Power imbalance is more likely to be prevented if no one is left to decide everyone else's fate. But creating opportunities for all to participate in the making of key decisions will not be enough unless people are rightly convinced that their views will count as much as others'. Democracy makes no demand on how similar or different people must be, except that as citizens, there should be no unbridgeable gulf between the influence they can bring to bear on the rules and practices that affect them all. In this chapter, we will look at why civic parity must be systematically pursued, what misconceptions of equality should be avoided, and how we can go about reducing the power gap.

Why democracy is dependent on civic parity

Against the backdrop of the Brexit vote, Trump's election, and the growing support for political parties on the far right across Europe in the early 21st century, commentators dwelled on people's desire to take back control of their countries, having become alienated by the relentless march of globalisation. But while it is true that many people have had enough of being disempowered in contemporary society, the focus should be on why so many of them were willing to embrace political options that would take even more power away from them.

Manipulative leaders convincing large numbers of people to back them against those who would really help them is not a new phenomenon. For example, citizens of the Roman Republic took great pride in rejecting monarchical rule and establishing by the 5th century BC a system whereby they periodically voted on laws and chose who would take up public offices. But over the next 300 years, wealthy Romans were able to accumulate vast resources that enabled them to command ever greater influence. Land was taken away from peasants, and soldiers returned from military campaigns to find a life of poverty awaiting them. Despite the attempts by Tiberius and Gaius Gracchus to redistribute land to displaced peasants and provide subsidised grain for the urban poor, the aristocratic elite deceived the people about the Gracchi brothers' intentions, bought the support of many who might otherwise have backed the reform agenda, and stirred a mob into killing the reformers. Within another two centuries, the Roman Republic collapsed altogether and an imperial dictatorship took its place.

The founding of the United States of America led many to hope that citizens' self-governance might prove to be a viable alternative after all. In de Tocqueville's famous assessment of democracy in the US, based on his stay in the country in the 1830s, it was observed that substantially lower inequalities of wealth and social status were key features of the democratic way of life (de Tocqueville, 1981). Fellow citizens were able to converse about public affairs on mutually respectful terms, because few were so poor that they had no time to consider broader issues in society, and none was so rich that they could buy their way to whatever they wanted regardless of what anyone else might think.

However, from the 1870s on a wealthy elite, skilled at extracting a hefty surplus from the revenue generated by the workers they hired, began to accelerate their capital acquisition so that soon they were existing on a different political plane where they could buy the laws and policies they favoured despite the negative consequences for others in the country. De Tocqueville had warned that under a democratic system lacking deep roots, citizens could be manipulated into accepting despotic rule. When in 1892 the overtly pro-business Republican Party lost control of the White House to Democrat Grover Cleveland, it was not long before the superrich of the day concluded that the levers of government would still be pulled in accordance with their wishes. Cleveland used every device at his disposal, including federal troops, to stop workers resorting to strikes to press for a living wage. The railway baron Jay Gould congratulated President Cleveland with the message, 'the vast business interests of the country will be entirely safe in your hands' (Derber, 2001, p 183).

From the closing of the 19th to the beginning of the 21st century, US citizens went through repeated cycles of anger, hope, and despair (Tam, 2015a, chapters 6-9). Agrarian protests rose and fell; corporate interests were consolidated by three successive Republican presidents in the 1920s;[1] the damage caused by the resultant Great Depression was repaired under Roosevelt's presidency; Lyndon Johnson sought to build on the New Deal with concerted policies to combat racism and poverty; but the rise of the New Right pushed the political agenda relentlessly in the plutocratic direction. By 2016, a combination of the rich voting to get even better deals, a sizeable number of the poor and insecure voting, with steadfast disregard of the evidence, for someone whose priority was the superrich, and 42% of registered voters not casting their vote[2] led to Trump obtaining sufficient electoral college votes to become US president.

Trump's political stance continued the New Right's tradition of conflating the freedom of corporate barons with the liberty of the people. So long as the public buy into the notion that those who have amassed a fortune should not be prevented in any way from doing as they please (because a lot of people might find such freedom subliminally appealing even if the prospect of any of them becoming superrich was remote), the slide towards billionaires' rule will only accelerate further.

Beyond the deceptive rhetoric of freedom, there are two counterarguments lying in wait to oppose any economic restructuring in support of civic parity. The first is that it is only petty jealousy that may turn wealth differentials into a political

---

[1] Aided by Republican Senator Boies Penrose using the financial connections of his corporate backers to secure the nomination of Warren Harding against Leonard Wood, who was committed to bringing in reforms to constrain business irresponsibility. Harding was followed by two more Republican presidents – Coolidge and Hoover – and their successive policies, which gave greater licence to big corporations, led to the Great Depression.

[2] That is roughly equivalent to 95 million people. See: www.telegraph.co.uk/ news/2016/11/14/us-election-2016-voter-turnout-fell-to-58-per-cent-this-year-est/

issue. So long as every adult has a vote, then whether some people are richer or poorer than others is of no consequence to how democracy works. This argument ignores the fact that widening resource gaps place those disadvantaged by them in an increasingly weakened position to exert any influence comparable to those who profit from the greater strength they have thereby gained. Such weaknesses cover poorer health, lower self-confidence, inadequate educational attainment, precarious work and housing conditions leading to pervasive insecurity, paltry financial power to back political parties, sense of alienation arising from the exclusivity generated by the wealthiest, and greater susceptibility to bribes and threats from those who can dramatically alter other people's lives with a single payment.

The serious health and social problems caused by high income inequalities has been widely documented (Wilkinson & Pickett, 2010; Stiglitz, 2013). Rich regions that concentrate their wealth at the top of their pyramid hierarchies leave those at the bottom with poorer health and shorter lifespans than their counterparts in areas that are not so divided in terms of individual earnings and possessions. The average death rates among men 25-64 years old are lower in US states and Canadian provinces in which the proportion of total income received by the poorest half of the population is higher (Ross et al, 2000). In the North East of England, where economic inequalities have been widening, the mortality rates among those with a low-paid routine manual job are almost 3.5 times higher than those with high managerial/professional positions[3] (Marmot Review, 2010, p 11). The aggravated sense of marginalisation also leads to a shorter emotional fuse and greater propensity to violence. Over 40 published studies of data from 39 countries (from different continents) have confirmed that homicide rates are higher in countries where income inequalities are greater (Fainzylber et al, 2002).

Daily reminders of one's relative insignificance in a world defined by purchasing power and material possessions affect how those on the lower rungs are disposed to interact with others.

---

[3] The difference is between around 700/100,000 and 200/100,000 deaths per year.

Racial prejudice levels have been found to be higher in states in the US with greater income inequality (Kennedy et al, 1997). International research discovered that in countries with greater income inequality as measured by the Gini Coefficient, fewer people agree with the statement, 'most people can be trusted' (Uslaner, 2002). In studies carried out across regions in Italy and states in the US, a similar pattern emerged of lower participation in community activities where income differentials were higher (Putnam et al, 1993; Putnam, 2011).

Since the reduction in wealth inequalities was halted in the US and UK following the rise of the New Right in the 1980s, the trends have worsened overall. A detailed study conducted in 2010 found that economic inequalities in the UK were high compared with other industrialised countries (except the US), and their large increase since the 1980s have not been reversed (Centre for Analysis of Social Exclusion, 2010).

In the absence of a sustained political programme to counter the erosion of civic parity, economic equalities have continued to grow around the world (Milanovich, 2012; Piketty, 2014). According to research by Oxfam, in 2017 '[e]ight men own the same wealth as the 3.6 billion people who make up the poorest half of humanity'; and '[s]even out of 10 people live in a country that has seen a rise in inequality in the last 30 years'.[4]

But this is where the second counterargument to resource redistribution pops up. It will hold that, however bad the consequences of civic disparity are, any departure from the prevailing approach to 'market-based' distribution would be much worse, and should be avoided at all costs. Its proponents would regard the marginalisation of some people from having any democratic influence (which, based on voter non-registration and non-turnout, could be between a third and a half of the entire adult population) as a small price to pay for sustaining what they consider to be an indispensable economic system. The problem with this line of argument is that it grossly

[4]   Oxfam press release: www.oxfam.org/en/pressroom/ pressreleases/2017-01-16/just-8-men-own-same-wealth-half-world. Oxfam's report, 'An Economy for the 99%' can be found at: www.oxfam. org/en/research/economy-99

underestimates the damage caused by the unrestrained capitalist system favoured by the New Right, and totally overlooks other options that offer better social and economic outcomes.

The 'free' market tirelessly advanced by the New Right is in fact rigged. It is structured to maximise the freedom of the corporate elite to act as they see fit by imposing detailed restrictions on what workers, communities, and smaller businesses can do (Harvey, 2007). This unbalanced structure enables the unscrupulous to amass greater wealth and power by exploiting the inability of others to challenge their self-serving actions. Increasingly over the last four decades, protection for workers and the power of the trade unions have been eroded so that ever more people fear they will not receive sufficient pay or attain any job security;[5] environmental degradation has spread through local pollution and global climate change;[6] transnational financial systems have continued to channel investment towards rich corporations regardless of the damage done to local communities (Karliner, 1997); medicine is developed with vast public subsidies but sold at prices unaffordable for most individuals and many public health institutions (Farmer, 2005); and addictive consumerism has relentlessly driven people on to borrow money to spend on things they can well do without (Klein, 2001). Above all, myopic deregulation at every turn makes the system highly susceptible to credit bubbles, asset swings, and financial crashes (Reich, 2009; Stiglitz, 2010; Frydman & Goldberg, 2011).

As for the claim that there is no viable alternative – usually accompanied by a supposedly triumphant reference to the collapse of Soviet communism – it simply ignores the facts. Social democratic practices have long given workers better

[5] The effects of the widening power gap between corporate bosses and workers can be seen in the case of the education publisher, Pearson, which in 2016 cut 4,000 jobs worldwide to generate £350 million of savings, and rewarded its senior executives with £55 million in bonus payments – even though under their watch, the company had ended up with pre-tax losses of £2.6 billion that year (Sweney, 2017).

[6] In 2016, Theresa May as UK prime minister abolished the Department of Energy and Climate Change; in 2017 Donald Trump as US president put a known climate change denier in charge of the Environmental Protection Agency.

pay and job security across northern Europe, and provided the citizens of Scandinavian countries with good standards of living underpinned by high-quality public services. Cooperative enterprises under the umbrella of Mondragon in Spain have consistently delivered stable employment, decent pay, and immunity from corporate whims. The post-war consensus in the UK in support of worker rights, public investment, and the development of the welfare state led to security for families and growing prosperity for the country, until those policies came to be reversed following the ascendency of the New Right from the 1980s on. In the US, even a small shift in fiscal policies was found to have a dramatic impact.

From 1995 to 2000, when productivity in the US grew by 13% overall, median family income rose by 11%, and significantly, among the bottom 20% of earners, income went up by 23.4%. But from 2001 to 2007, after George W. Bush took over the presidency from Bill Clinton, and brought in tax changes that were directed at benefiting the rich most of all, even though productivity kept improving by 2.5% per year, the income of the average working family fell during that time by 3.7%. The rich simply paid themselves more, their workers less, and pocketed generous tax cuts.[7] If the national income of the US was distributed in 2004 (at the end of Bush's first term) as it had been in 1981 (just before the New Right dominance arrived with Ronald Reagan becoming president), the top 1% would have had $640 billion less, while the bottom 80% would have had $637 billion more (Sperling, 2009).

It is hardly surprising that those who want to structure market conditions to help them amass wealth and power irrespective of the concerns of others would claim that those conditions embody the ideal of the free market, towards which society must move ever closer. But the deep flaws of allowing this to happen have been widely exposed. The challenge now is to change course and improve the way in which resources are distributed. Before we consider a number of recommendations, we should deal

---

[7] One reason why tax cuts for the poor can lead to no improvement for them is that their employers believe they can then cut their wages to leave them with the same take-home pay as before (Hartmann, 2017).

with a number of common, yet misconceived, approaches that are put forward to deal with power inequalities.

The problem with misconceiving equality

The more a group or society is organised in such a way that some members can accumulate substantially more resources that will enable them to attain better conditions in terms of health, confidence, and efficacy than others, the less likely it is that its members can govern themselves democratically. As a corrective, the equality of citizenship must in practice be backed by responsive resource distribution that will counter any serious disequilibrium. But this pursuit of civic parity can be misinterpreted as a quest for some form of 'equality' that is irrelevant or even undesirable. To pre-empt efforts from being diverted down the wrong paths, let us examine five approaches that may consume much political energy but not get us any closer to where we need to be. Indeed, despite their appeal in certain quarters, they may turn out to be counterproductive if taken forward.

One of the most common misconceptions is that political equality must involve the material equalisation of all money, land and possessions. For some, this means that it is the last thing anyone should pursue, since it will eliminate all prospect of being rewarded for efforts, skills, or talent, and threaten to take away the fruits of past achievements. In the 17th century, opponents of the Levellers deployed this notion as a scare tactic to rally people against reformists who were merely seeking an equal vote.[8] But there are those who believe this is precisely what is needed. Thinking that the Soviet regime had merely carried out the communist plan ineffectively, and pining for a radical alternative to the grip of plutocracy, they contemplate absolute material equality as the true goal to be brought about by protest, confrontation, and, if necessary, a full-scale revolution.

They fail to remember that the imposition of such equalisation would require handing vast power to an authority which

---

[8]   Indeed, they came up with the name 'Levellers' to insinuate that the reformists were aiming to level everything – income and property alike.

could then trample on the wishes of individuals. If resource redistribution is not guided by collaborative learning and participatory decision making then someone vested with unchallengeable power will be left to declare what it should be and enforce it regardless of the discontent it provokes. Furthermore, forced equalisation can be as debilitating as a widening chasm of inequality. It is demoralising when others get away with siphoning off wealth for themselves. But it is just as demotivating to get no recognition or benefit at all despite the greater contributions one makes. And one of the most important issues any group will want to consider is precisely how the power gap between fellow members can be reduced without hindering the group from achieving its shared mission. Instead of ruling out all discussions by imposing one single answer, there should be ongoing opportunities for critical re-examination of what adjustments may work better.

Another misguided route takes us away from resource distribution altogether. Instead of recognising the divergence in the economic powers of citizens as a major barrier to effective political participation, the New Right has sought to frame this sense of disempowerment in terms of the disconnection from some construct they posit, usually the country in a glorified, pure, traditional form. People are divided, on this interpretation, not by the vastly different levels of resources they and others have, but by the existence of 'aliens', 'deviants', 'foreigners', or even 'women who do not know their place'. These 'others' and the support they get from the 'cosmopolitan elite' and 'liberal establishment' are blamed for many people (the 'true Brits', the 'real Americans') feeling they have lost control over their country.

For them, people can only feel united if the 'others' who have disturbed the balance are put back where they belong – foreigners deported (or assimilated without a trace of cultural difference), those with the 'wrong' faith converted to the 'right' one, homosexuals reversing the process of coming out, and women heading back to their domestic duties and nothing else. This pseudo-cure for disempowerment comes with a prescription for resentful antagonism towards the selected scapegoats. By constantly presenting them as threats, social cohesion will somehow be better protected.

Equality is thus to be extracted through demands for conformity and the routine denigration of diversity. As we have earlier explored, both the pursuit of shared missions and the maintenance of coherent membership are essential to the development of collective self-governance. A common language to underpin communications, a commitment to mutual respect, a recognition of the broad moral consensus and acceptance of the rule of law are elements that should be promoted and safeguarded. However, to go beyond them to castigate (or even punish) people for speaking their own language when they are talking among themselves, practising their harmless customs, and professing their own religious faith or secular belief is simply to dress up oppressive acts as attempts to defend a distorted 'common' identity. Significantly, apart from being inherently obnoxious, such acts do nothing to facilitate political participation. In practice, they merely serve to divert anger and frustration to scapegoats and deflect attention from the self-serving agendas of the political demagogues who resort to this technique.

Thirdly, we have the approach of utopian egalitarianism.[9] This urges everyone to abandon the mechanism which stirs up divisive comparisons and contrasts between people – namely competition. It traces the differentials in resource acquisition to competitive sifting of human beings on a wide range of factors. For example, those who happen to have the ability to think quickly, a talent to trick others, the appearance or demeanour to appeal to most, or a propensity to work hard will be branded 'successes' and given more than they can fully utilise, while others will be labelled 'failures' and be deprived of what they need.

The problem with eliminating competition completely is that it neglects its useful dimension, and creates an artificial uniformity that is as stultifying as that championed by racial or religious purists. Competition, structured constructively and fairly, with proportionate rewards, can be (and often is) a healthy means of engaging people to apply themselves more to produce what they may otherwise not have bothered to even attempt

---

[9]   Thinkers from William Godwin to Pyotr Kropotkin are among those who have influenced this outlook.

to bring about. The key is not to load it so that a few will win everything and others are left with little. The best way to achieve this is not to have no competition at all, but have a wide range of competitions so that people with different talents, interests, and inclinations can have an overall balanced experience of losing some and winning some.

Psychologically, the idea that people will be content with not competing over anything has no more evidential basis than the supposition that people will thrive through relentless competition in every dimension of life. This implies that if seriously pursued, this goal of no competition will necessitate the suppression of comparative advantages. In Kurt Vonnegut's story 'Harrison Bergeron', the US has passed constitutional amendments to ensure no one has any competitive advantage over others, and the protagonist, for example, has a gadget implanted in his head to disrupt him thinking more effectively with his higher IQ. And in L. P. Hartley's novel *Facial Justice*, the UK (after the traumatic experience of the Third World War) does not tolerate any personal qualities that may help to secure benefits in life, and those who may otherwise be deemed attractive have to have an average looking face transplanted onto them to maintain equality. These satirical tales highlight the danger of assuming that we should render everyone the same rather than focus on curbing the excesses of competitive rewards.

The fourth misconceived approach regards the key issue as the provision of equal opportunity to everyone. The underlying assumption is that if people have the same opportunity as everyone else to try to obtain whatever they may seek, then they are likely to accept the outcomes even when these involve distributing what is sought quite differently among them. So, in theory, if all those interested in a job are given a chance to attend an interview for a job, and are questioned on a similar basis, they cannot complain that the job goes to the chosen candidate and not the rest.

The difficulty with claiming that equal opportunity can ignore inequality of outcomes is that the latter affects the former.[10] If one has not got a particular job that will help with obtaining promotion to a better position down the line, one is not going to have the same opportunities as others with such a job. And when we push the question of why certain candidates did not get a particular job, it could lead to previous incidents when, for example, a series of examinations at school marked them with lower grades. That might in turn be down to the relative lack of parental support or family resources to invest in additional tutoring. At no point can we say that everyone has been guaranteed the same starting position which renders all the divergent outcomes thereafter negligible. Unless everyone's home upbringing and school experience are equally supportive, the relative strengths and weaknesses one carries on graduation day (for those who get that far) will already be so varied as to make it highly likely that some will secure more advantages in life than others.

This is not to say that structuring equal opportunity for participation in education, accessing services, or applying for jobs is not important. It is vital on mutual respect grounds alone that it should be instituted in every sphere of life. But it is not sufficient for civic parity. To insist that giving people an equal opportunity to succeed or fail means we can ignore how wide the gaps are between the rewards and penalties for those deemed successful or to have failed is to brush aside the widespread problems caused by systems which callously (and in many cases deliberately) promote these gaps to widen the distance between the wealthy elite in control and those who are trapped in desperation to make ends meet.

Before we go on to consider what can be done to improve on the current situation, we should look at one last approach to equality which should be handled with care. This is what may be termed the 'spiritual' diversion. Organised religions, New Age

---

[10] For an insightful examination of how the British Left contested the notions of 'equal opportunity' and 'equality of outcomes', see Jackson (2007). For a dystopian satire on the dangers of meritocracy arising from its legitimisation by equal opportunity, see Young (1994).

devotees, and cults of every shade all offer a deity or some cosmic force, communion with which would make all other differences insignificant. For the rich, this is comforting reassurance that however wide the gap between them and the seriously disadvantaged may be, it is nothing compared with the same blessing they will receive in an afterlife or some transcendental realm. For the poor, this was throughout the Middle Ages one of the most potent tools in getting them to accept their lot in the hope that all would be balanced out 'later on'; and in these anti-Enlightenment times it is proving popular again.

Far from dismissing this diversion as hollow, it has to be addressed in partnership with religious advocates who take their moral responsibility in the here and now seriously. There are leading national/international figures and local practitioners of all faiths who connect their spirituality to rectifying the injustice and suffering in this world. For them, it is deceptive to use religious language and theological claims to turn people's attention away from the exploitative regime polarising the have-lots and have-nots. They see it as their duty to open people's eyes and lead a challenge to these arrangements so that they can be displaced by more inclusive arrangements that will bring people closer together.

The aim is not to make everyone identical in abilities or circumstances, and certainly not to allow those who invoke religious texts, economic dogmas, or outmoded traditions to justify the marginalisation, or even subjugation, of vast numbers of people, but to improve on resource distribution and power relations.

How to counter the causes of civic disparity

People have different dispositions and abilities, and that is vital for the development of the personal identity of each as well as the deepening of the collective wellbeing of all. Because we have different things to offer, are capable of entertaining diverse perspectives, can come up with new ideas others have not thought of, that is why humanity is infused with fresh experiences and the prospects of improvement. What individuals contribute to their work group, local community, or society more generally may accordingly merit different rewards. But if the allocation of resources as rewards were set arbitrarily, or structured to serve some at the expense of others, that would undermine interpersonal relationships and hamper political cooperation.

What is put forward below are a number of recommendations to curb resource distribution that has dubious foundations and objectionable consequences. They cover five areas:

- supporting the development of multi-stakeholder cooperative enterprise;
- redirecting the public source of money to the common good;
- guaranteeing a decent level of income and public support for all citizens;
- setting parameters for differentials in pay and for services dealing with adversarial interactions; and
- curtailing private wealth's power to shape the public agenda.

Let us begin with actions to support the development of multi-stakeholder cooperative enterprise. Cooperatives that share their decision making and surplus with their members when these include workers and customers, and engage suppliers and local communities in their strategic planning, are in a stronger position to withstand unfavourable circumstances and find ways to improve their performance. Between 2008 and 2011, when the UK was hit by a double-dip recession, the number of cooperatives grew by 23% to nearly 6,000, while individual members grew by 19.7% to 13.5 million. During that period, as the UK economy shrank by 1.7%, the turnover of the cooperative sector expanded by 19.6% to £35.6 billion.[11] Furthermore, consumer research found that cooperatives are among the top third of ethical performers in 80% of the markets surveyed in the UK, while in 23% of the markets they are the top performers (Mayo, E., 2016).

In worker-owned enterprises, the positive outcomes in terms of revenue and job satisfaction (and their effects on better health)

[11] Details from Co-operatives UK: www.uk.coop/performance-co-operative-economy

are shared out more fairly in line with the deliberations of those involved in the business (Lewis & Conaty, 2012). But many businesses do not adopt the cooperative model, and among those that do, some have not embraced their own workers as members. In order to have more opportunities for people to work in an inclusive, cooperative structure, we need to put in place a cooperativist development agency (Tam, 2015c) to channel investment and advice in support of the setting up and consolidation of multi-stakeholder enterprises.[12] Such an agency will be tasked with ensuring that the recipients of its support have a sustainable strategy to empower their workers to shape their future, anticipate and plan for wider societal concerns, and minimise the risk of future demutualisation by applying asset locks to capital acquired through the investment provided.[13]

While not all businesses may be ready to convert to a fully cooperative form, those who work in them should be given the option to seek the advice of the cooperativist development agency and, where appropriate, request an internal referendum to decide if their organisation should change its structure accordingly. This can be left to businesses to take on board on a voluntary basis in the short term, but if they prove to be persistently unresponsive, regulatory measures should be devised to require any firm that ignores workers' requests to consider and vote on ownership/participation options to be subject to compulsory referrals to an independent arbitration service in relation to any disputed arrangements being imposed on its workers. These contested arrangements may cover, for example, unreasonable shift demands, intrusive monitoring of workers, zero-hour contracts, externalising of workers as contractors, wage cuts, plant closures, and automation-led redundancies.

---

[12] While many enterprises with self-governing members who work in them, such as the highly successful Buurtzorg in the Netherlands, are widely praised, without investment and advice, the spread of the approach remains slow and limited.

[13] In the past, provided a majority of members are prepared to sell, the assets built up by all can be irreversibly taken over by corporations with no interest in cooperative working. It is vital that investment made available to create multi-stakeholder cooperatives is properly protected.

Our next recommendation is aimed at redirecting the public source of money to the common good. Contrary to popular conceptions of money as something 'created' by people who manage to pocket the monetary difference between what they acquire and what they sell, money today originates from credit derived from the guarantee given by a country's central bank (Ingham, 2014). The central bank gives selected institutions permission to borrow 'its' money, and these institutions then lend out more money in line with the prevailing leverage ratio to whoever they decide to lend money to. If people keep paying back enough money (which they have made in the public or private sector) to maintain the flow of money around the system, nobody asks any awkward questions. But if large amounts are not paid back then a credit gap opens up, confidence in the system plummets, and the government has to step in to rescue the situation.

The causes of the crashes that commenced in 1929 and 2008 were linked to banks lending to firms that would not pay their employees a sufficient wage, as well as to those individuals who had to borrow unsustainably to get by. It was a foolhardy recipe to prop up businesses by supplying them with debt-laden consumers whose debt would be called in at some point, leaving banks and other businesses short of money to cover their debt in turn. Instead of repeating the same catastrophic mistake, central banks should be steered to direct their primary lending – the source of money for the economy – to institutions that will help people engage in sustainable businesses, and earn enough to acquire what they need to lead a fulfilling life.

There are increasingly effective ways developed outside the City of London and Wall Street to channel investment into activities that generate healthy social and economic outcomes. Community development finance, ethical lenders, and public banks are leading the way to identify and invest in enterprises and projects that, far from polarising people into those who hoard money in offshore accounts and those plagued by debt-ridden insecurity, will provide valuable infrastructure, essential services, innovative products, universally affordable renewable energy and recycled materials, and decent pay to enable all citizens to work and live to a good standard. Instead of perpetuating the deeply flawed no-strings-attached approach in handing over billions to banks so they can continue with their irresponsible lending, central banks should set priorities for supporting socially minded institutions[14] (Brown, E., 2013; Bollier, 2016).

Our third recommendation concerns the guaranteeing of a decent level of income and public support for all citizens. Between the polarised ideas of totally replacing prevailing market arrangements with a flawless system and deregulating those arrangements even more to suit the powerful, there is the option of testing out redistributive reforms backed by a safety net that will protect everyone. Even for those who have amassed so much wealth for themselves that they are convinced no ill fortune could possibly befall them and their families, they cannot escape the reality that if others were cast aside without hope, they too would eventually be caught up in the social upheaval.

An effective safety net that does not stigmatise or degrade citizens must be a universal provision that genuinely delivers a quality of life that no one would consider intolerable if they had to rely on it (Culpitt, 1992). Not having means testing would guarantee accessibility, cut bureaucracy, and maximise efficiency. The components of public support should include a basic income;[15] provision of decent education, housing, childcare, and protection under the law; and adequate assistance for anyone with particular physical or mental health needs.

The focus cannot be on a basic income alone since what level it should be set at depends on how adequate other support in the form of free public services is going to be. Any weakening of the established infrastructure for delivering public services can mean that a much higher level of basic income will be required to compensate for the costs of having to resort to fee-charging services. A basic income cannot by itself secure citizens a decent level of wellbeing and protect them from precarious work, and it may even be presented as a catch-all alternative by some who just want to cut welfare provisions overall. However, that does

---

[14] Including investment bodies like the proposed cooperativist development agency.

[15] A universal basic income is being explored in Finland as a countermeasure to low wages and automation-led reduction in jobs (Sodha, 2017).

not alter the fact that developed as an integrated component of a proper package of support for citizens, a universal basic income can help to eliminate the anxiety and insecurity that have pushed millions of people to the margins of society (Huws, 2016).

Some of the public support can be provided through regulation without ongoing funding requirements, such as limits on the level of rent being charged, standards for occupancy, and restrictions on 'gentrification' changes to residential properties that would make them unaffordable to the majority of people. In Germany, some cities have been implementing *Milieuschutz* (social environment protection) laws for over 40 years, to stop people buying up properties to convert into large luxury units or split into small but expensive holiday homes (Connolly, 2016). But other support will need funding streams, and these can be drawn from existing as well as new fiscal mechanisms such as the Tobin Tax on financial transactions; land value levies; enforced penalties on tax evasion; a luxury tax (Yamamura, 2017); and a societal profit-sharing scheme that transfers a percentage of the additional profit generated through the replacement of workers by automation technology to a public fund[16] (Aronoff, 2017).

Fourth on our list of recommendations is the setting of parameters for differentials in pay at one's workplace and for fees relating to services dealing with adversarial interactions. People who work in the same organisation would not find the valuation of their contributions diverging so radically if they had a say in the process themselves. Research has shown that worker cooperatives are not only on average more productive and offer more stable employment, but they also have lower pay differentials (Pérotin, 2016). Workers as members recognise that it makes sense to reward some among them with higher pay, but the extent to which that is agreed is grounded on a shared assessment of how much greater the contributions from those colleagues are, and not simply on the power of those at the top

---

[16] As automation, particularly Artificial Intelligence, advances with the support of directly accessed renewable energy, the substantial displacement of workers could also lead to a drastic reduction in purchasing power that would leave fewer people to buy the products made almost entirely by the machines. At some point, a completely different model may be needed to manage the cycle of production and consumption.

to pay themselves substantially more. Even with firms that decide against going down a worker cooperative route, it should be a mandated practice for all workers to engage in participatory decision making to set their own pay differentials.

The same principle applies to the differentials in the fees charged by different professionals engaged in resolving potentially adversarial disputes. Just as people can be marginalised as citizens because they are deprived of their share of the proceeds they generate along with others, their influence in society can be further diminished by the hypersensitivity to wealth when contested assessments are made in relation to issues of critical interest to them. For example, lawyers engaged on either side of a criminal or civil case; accountants involved in establishing or denying financial anomalies; or scientific experts commissioned to scrutinise or defend the safety of a new brand of medicine or food.

In all such cases, if there is a vast gulf between the fees demanded at the lower and upper ends, then firms with fees at the upper end will on the whole be able to tempt and recruit more of the most impressive performers, and they will offer clients who can afford to pay their exclusive fees the unmatched calibre of their recruits in winning the disputes in question. However, if the professional bodies concerned are required to bring their members together to set limits on their fee differentials, then all the relevant firms may fall into a more affordable range, and can compete against each other on a more level playing field.[17] Consequently, citizens in general will be less likely to be disadvantaged by decisions that will favour the wealthy few at the expense of the interests of the wider public or particular less well-off individuals.

Finally, we direct our attention to curtailing private wealth's power to shape the public agenda. Money's role in securing public office and determining public policies has continued to expand, leaving most citizens feeling they have little real influence over their governance. In the US presidential election of 2012, the executives of the top 10 publicly listed companies

---

[17] But not to the extent of becoming a cartel with all of them charging the same fees.

alone spent $102 million on political donations (Reeves, 2016). Overall spending on federal campaigns in that one year was over $6.2 billion, and 68% of that money came from just 0.26% of the population. Among the biggest contributors were those determined to minimise regulatory constraints that might otherwise serve the public interest (for example, casinos, banking, fossil fuel, private healthcare providers). And in case anyone seriously doubts that money has anything to do with electoral outcomes, between 2004 and 2012, in each of the five biannual contests in the House of Representatives, over 80% of the candidates who spent more than their rivals won (Prokop, 2014).

In between elections, superrich firms and individuals can also use their financial power to get rid of policy proposals they dislike,[18] and undermine candidates critical of their outlook with orchestrated social media attacks, false accusations, and a steady flow of distorted stories.[19] Attempts at limiting campaign finance have not had much success, especially when groups purportedly separate from political candidates can raise and spend money without any serious restriction (Mutch, 2014; Post, 2014).

We need a two-pronged approach that will, on the one hand, outlaw as an act of bribery any direct payment, indirect payment in kind (for example, provision of office space, communications support), or promise of favours to political candidates or those who have won office; and, on the other hand, allow funding to be given to political parties or other organisations engaged in supporting or lobbying those parties, provided the funders duly register the amounts they give, and a transparent audit trail can be established with the understanding that the information will be made public and any falsification will be punishable by law. The former will prevent any form of personal indebtedness

---

[18] In Australia, proposed reform of the poker machine business was dropped by the Labor government after the gaming industry, which donated money to Labor, started to donate even more money to their rivals (the Liberal Party). When the Liberals came out against the proposals, Labor dropped them despite public support for the reform (Smith, W., 2014).

[19] For information on how billionaire Robert Mercer funded Breitbart and offered the resources of Cambridge Analytica to support those, such as Trump and Farage, who shared his political aims, see Cadwalladr (2017).

developing between individual politicians and paymasters outside their own political parties. They can rely on financial support from their parties, but nothing offered to them externally, including promises of lucrative assignments or enviable sinecures, will be acceptable.[20] The latter will require political parties and large funders to be fully open in accounting for who is funding whom at a time when particular policy issues are being considered. The information can then be made accessible to aid scrutiny and promote awareness of the wealthy players who are pulling the policy strings. The penalties for giving false information can include confiscation of the money given to a party, a fine amounting to a set multiple of what was actually spent by the funder, or even, in some cases, imprisonment.

With more systematic exposure of the undue influence exerted by individuals and corporations, the public will be more ready to judge political parties unfavourably for the financial support they get from those with interests at odds with the public, and the plutocratic value of political funding will correspondingly diminish.

---

[20] For example, if any individual or group seeks to pay for campaign advertising that would help a particular candidate, that would be a form of personal bribery, making that candidate indebted to those who will settle the bill. On the other hand, the individual or group can make a contribution to the relevant political party which can then fund any promotional campaign it can be held accountable for. The transparent listing of who/what company gives how much to each party will then readily show whose resources are backing which party and its policy stance.

Remedial checklist: civic parity

With reference to any group the governance of which you are concerned about, you can use the checklist below to identify what requires the most improvement in relation to the need for civic parity:

☐ Is members' ability to influence decisions that affect them all sharply varied because of the substantially different resources they possess? Do they have meaningful opportunities to work in and with multi-stakeholder organisations that will enable them to have more control over their socioeconomic positions? Can they have pay differentials limited by parameters they themselves agree to?

☐ Are credit and investment channelled to those with neither a track record nor a serious commitment to supporting the common wellbeing of all members? Is the monetary system sufficiently directed at prioritising support for those who are more likely to produce fair and sustainable outcomes?

☐ Can members count on a decent level of income and public support so that they are not at risk of being so marginalised that they are incapable of having any influence on decisions which they are supposed to have an equal share in making? Does everyone understand the need to contribute to the provision of public support to protect each of them from exclusionary threats?

☐ Do members feel that the wealthiest few can buy more favourable (though not necessarily justifiable) outcomes in political contests and other disputes that affect them? Is there any mechanism ordinary members can readily turn to in order to curtail the power of money to shape the public agenda and secure a more level playing field for everyone?

ELEVEN

Public accountability

Democratic self-governance protects those under its jurisdiction from the arbitrary exercise of power, by either those who would otherwise be able to dictate terms to others, or those who might abuse the authority entrusted to them. It requires a distribution of power that will enable any given group to hold to account anyone in that group whose actions impact on the lives of others. In this chapter, we will look at why a democratic balance of power needs to be sustained by an effective system of public accountability, what problems can arise from responsibility being misplaced, and how the prevailing approach to accountability can be enhanced.

Why we need public accountability

When people can carry out a relatively straightforward assessment of how particular cases of cooperation will help them, and they can easily see that everyone is doing what they have agreed to do, they will most likely be confident about working together. However, when the arrangements are at the level of a vast organisation (not to mention a country or an international body), it is much more difficult to pinpoint exactly who should do what, keep an eye on whether agreed roles are being properly fulfilled, or if the hoped-for benefits are achieved and properly shared out.

One way to maintain collaborative working arrangements is to assign clear responsibilities to individuals and put in place a system for checking and adjudicating to ensure that we can rely on them in carrying out their duties. So long as people are confident that those with the relevant power can be held to account for their judgements and actions, they will be more disposed to trust them to act in accordance with public expectations.

Unfortunately, vigilance can all too easily subside. Since the 1980s, a combination of complacency about how much democratisation has already helped to achieve, and the advancement of the plutocratic agenda for governments to serve the wealthy elite (Mayer, 2017), has led to the exponential rise in cynicism about the accountability of public institutions.

As the connections between citizens and those in government at all levels weakened, the New Right advocates began to exploit the accountability gap. They champion the smaller state, and further dismantle accountability arrangements in the name of cutting down bureaucracy, while insisting that they uniquely can be trusted to serve the public without such arrangements.[1] And they increasingly use their power to relieve large corporations of their accountability to the public, which in turn further incentivises antisocial businesses to provide financial and other in-kind support to them in gaining and holding on to political power.[2]

Against this backdrop, attempts to strengthen public accountability have to constantly resist being misrepresented as bureaucratic interference that gets in the way of whatever 'needs to be done'. To counter the subversion of civic responsibility, citizens need to be reminded of the preventable harm that comes from people acting without having to comply with fair and enforceable rules.

Let us begin by looking at the corrosion of public accountability in the epistemological structure of society. In all civilisations, the

---

[1] David Cameron used the 'Big Society' rhetoric as cover for shrinking the British public sector (Tam, 2011b), while Donald Trump ignored the conflict of interest involving his business empire and his role as US president (Mindock, 2017).

[2] Antisocial businesses are those that engage in activities which are damaging to society because of their negative impact on people's physical, psychological, or environmental health. Casinos, irresponsible lenders, and polluters are among the biggest donors to political parties, especially those on the Right, and they benefit when regulation is loosened to suit them. For more on the growing influence of corporate finance in politics, see Clements (2014).

emergence of a powerful ruling regime has almost always been accompanied by a supportive priestly/scholastic group whose members interpret key texts, phenomena, and events, and make pronouncements that on the whole validate the position and actions of the ruling elite.[3] Occasionally, some of them may venture to control the rulers or even take power directly for themselves. By and large, such usurpation does not last long, and in any case most of them prefer to accept their subordinate role in return for the backing of the rulers that shields them from having to justify their claims to 'lay' people.

All this changed after the Enlightenment movement of the 18th century subjected, without exception, all knowledge claims to the demands of logical consistency and empirical examination. Those with ruling power began to discover that any 'expert' willing to be co-opted by the dominant regime to state only what was helpful to them would cease to have any credibility with the wider network of experts. Governments which pressed ahead with actions that did more harm than good soon found they could not invoke the blessing of some invisible deity or the obscure interpretation of ancient texts to defend themselves. Objective evidence could no longer be easily dismissed, or at least not until the late 20th century when the rapidly growing complexity of scientific and technical investigations transformed experts into an increasingly remote 'sect' whose exposition appeared no less esoteric than the priestly class of old.

Although scientists and other technical experts can defend the veracity of their claims with reference to evidential procedures and cross-checking arrangements, they have fallen short of publicising or explaining these well enough to the wider public. The door thus came to be opened for political charlatans to revive the pre-Enlightenment technique of dismissing as unfounded any findings not welcome to the powerful. Irrespective of what experts who have studied the relevant subjects may say, they are brushed aside as biased or befuddled. Fabrications could be propagated against the protest of denigrated experts; while inconvenient truths would be thrown aside as fake.

---

[3] Priests, theologians, Confucian scholars, and public servants, have all in the past performed this role in their respective cultures.

Not surprisingly, this has heralded a return of the autocratic breed of politicians who had previously been sidelined by the risk of being exposed as liars. Nixon's Watergate folly probably deterred a few would-be crooks from seeking high political office. But once the gap between what empirical investigation may establish and what people may come to believe can again be substantially widened, people with few qualms about playing the pied piper in politics are ready once more to push themselves forward into the electoral limelight, especially when they are aided by the revival of geopolitical paranoia.

The ending of the Cold War had suggested in some quarters that secret surveillance by the state along with questionable use of force might no longer be so readily shielded from public scrutiny. But then came 9/11, and suddenly Islamophobia was heightened and repackaged as patriotic vigilance. In the US and UK, demands for holding the government to account for any action taken in the name of countering terrorism were castigated for making it more difficult to protect one's country. Surveillance powers and covert operations quickly went beyond what was attempted even during the darkest days of the Cold War.[4]

With secrecy shrouding responsibility, some have hoped that whistle-blowing can expose dubious activities that might otherwise have remained hidden. But unless whistle-blowing subscribes to some form of accountability system itself, its lack of transparency may in certain cases make it even less clear who has really acted irresponsibly, and where the most serious blame may lie. For example, amid allegations that Russia sought to help Trump get elected president of the US, WikiLeaks released hacked information that undermined Trump's opponent, Hillary Clinton, and information discrediting the CIA (which officially suspected Russia of having played an illegitimate role in trying to influence the US presidential elections), but nothing against Russia or Trump. Without any means of checking what strategy or arrangements were behind these leaks, we are left with more

---

[4]   The radical expansion of executive powers in the name of national security echoes the tendency Arthur Schlesinger ascribed to the 'Imperial Presidency' (Schlesinger, 1974), and is summarised in Schwarz and Huq (2007).

uncertainty over who was trying to undermine the democratic processes of a country.

The water is further muddied by the many diversionary tactics money can buy. As the wealth gap continues to expand, the lack of effective means to restrain financial influence over public decisions and policies inevitably result in a downward spiral towards blame-denying behaviour. The rich can already deploy the most expensive lawyers, public relations consultants, accountants, and lobbyists to minimise their chances of being held responsible for damage they cause to others. As Trump showed with the appointment of his billionaire cabinet, they are now so confident that they openly take direct control of governmental powers at the highest level, dismantle regulatory bodies and environmental protection that get in the way of their profit making, cut social safety nets so workers become even more vulnerable and compliant as their potential employees, and pocket more tax benefits and government subsidies (Thompson, D., 2017).

Indeed, Trump's presidency took plutocracy to a whole new level when he and his family members would use his profile and power as US president to benefit his commercial holdings (Venook, 2017). The unprecedented refusal to disclose his tax returns made it clear that transparency over his financial links and how these might affect his actions would not be permitted.[5] The checks and balances that were supposed to constrain questionable use of power would fall away as Republican control of the Senate and the House of Representatives enabled Trump to consolidate the Republican-leaning majority on the Supreme Court.

It is no coincidence that Trump and Brexit advocates regard a non-compliant judicial system as an objectionable barrier to their plans. Like the voting system itself, if the outcomes were on their side, it would be deemed legitimate; but otherwise it

---

[5] Given Trump's out-of-court settlement with Deutsche Bank after he was sued for not paying off his $640 million loan, and a subsequent new loan amounting to $300 million from the same bank, which was under federal investigation (Kirchgaessner, 2017), it is remarkable that there is no requirement for him to disclose his financial backers in securing the new loan from Deutsche Bank, or that he could be left to appoint the top official who would oversee the federal investigation of that bank.

would be dismissed as flawed. When judges ruled against the UK government's attempt to trigger Article 50 to commence the process of leaving the EU without putting the vote to Parliament, right-wing media such as the *Daily Mail* condemned those judges as 'enemies of the people', and government ministers said nothing in defence of the independence of the judiciary and spoke repeatedly of the right of the media to attack whomever they chose. When judges in the US ruled against Trump's executive order to ban people from Muslim-majority countries which had never been the home of anyone responsible for any fatal terrorist attack in the US, he dismissed them as 'so-called judges'.[6]

The tactical show of disrespect for highly qualified and experienced judges undermines trust in the judiciary; makes it easier for corrupt, misguided, and deceptive practices to be perpetrated by those with executive power; and quickens the slide from democratic cooperation to 'each for oneself' insularism.

The problem of misplaced responsibility

In order to underpin democracy with a robust system of accountability, we have to ensure that the people covered by that system understand who should be held responsible for what under different circumstances. The blurring of responsibility in social discourse has led to considerable misapprehension about where blame (or praise, for that matter) should be assigned.

In practice, the basis for determining what behaviour for which a person can be held responsible consists of the conjunction of three elements: the person in question is a causal factor in bringing about an effect; that person is aware of their causal role

---

[6] Trump, notably, did not seek to impose the ban on Muslim-majority countries which had in fact been the home of terrorists responsible for causing deaths on US soil, but unlike the countries targeted by the ban, these all had substantial commercial dealings with Trump's businesses (Roberts, 2017b).

under a relevant description in bringing about that effect;[7] and it is the exercising of that person's own volitional capacity (and not a result of an external force) that led to them becoming a causal factor of the effect.[8]

It should be further pointed out that being responsible for any given outcome does not necessarily mean that one is blameworthy. The outcome may be neutral in its impact, or it may be helpful to others, which makes the one responsible praiseworthy. And even where the outcome is bad for some, there may be legitimate excuses, or wider considerations concerning more people that may serve as an overall justification. Establishing who is responsible for what is simply the precondition for holding the right people accountable for any given outcome.

The three elements outlined above for ascribing responsibility provide us with a clear set of criteria to expose attempts to misplace it. The requirement that a responsible agent must be a causal factor rules out devious arguments that try to cast aspersions by irrelevant association. People who have played no causal role whatsoever in a terrorist attack, for example, cannot be painted as somehow responsible just because they have a similar skin colour to the actual perpetrators, have read one or more of the same books, or were born in the same country. On the other hand, people who own or manage powerful businesses cannot distance themselves from the impact of those companies just by saying they are not involved in the day-to-day activities when they have an undeniable causal role in determining what key decisions and commands are made by their subordinates.

The awareness element is incontrovertible insofar as no one can be responsible for what they are ignorant about. For example, if someone has wired the light switch of my living room to an explosive device that will go off in a house two blocks away, and

---

[7] If unbeknown to a pharmacist, deadly poison had been injected into the medication they are handing over to a patient, then they can be said to be aware of their action under the description 'handing over the prescribed medication', but not under the description 'handing over deadly poison'.

[8] There is a long civic-communitarian tradition that connects the notions of responsibility and intention to the structure of personal interactions. (For more on the basis of responsibility ascription, see Downie & Telfer, 1971; Duff, 1990; Tam, 1990; Rachels, 1997).

I have without any such knowledge or remote warning flicked the switch on, my accidental role in causing the explosion means that I am not answerable for this unfortunate event. However, what is foreseeable is critical in establishing what may fall within the net of accountability. Suppose a man embarks on a drinking binge by driving to a succession of pubs and getting increasingly drunk, and eventually he loses control of his car and kills a pedestrian. He may have lost consciousness just before the fatal crash and is genuinely not aware of his own behaviour at that point. But since he was aware of his behaviour when he drank heavily and then got into his car, he knew he was engaging in a life-endangering activity, and he callously continued. In such a case, there is no escape from his responsibility. Similarly, if a politician orders an airstrike having been informed that there is a high risk of civilian casualties, or introduces a policy of welfare cuts that may increase the number of preventable deaths among vulnerable people, even though the politician cannot be said to know that it would definitely bring about the deaths of the victims, there would certainly be an awareness of the likely outcome of the actions. Of course whether the politician should be blamed or excused[9] depends on the specific circumstances of the case. But whatever those circumstances may turn out to be, there is a case to answer for.

As for the element of exercising one's volitional capacity without external force, it places a requirement for possessing and exercising the necessary efficacy at the relevant time. If a police officer is thinking about hurting a fugitive and just then the latter is hit by a tree blown over unexpectedly by strong wind, the officer cannot be held responsible for that injury. If a tourist is pushed hard into the tour guide, who tragically falls over a cliff, the one to be interrogated is not the tourist but the person who gave the violent push.

But the relationship between one's volitional capacity and what may act on one as an external force can get more complicated.

---

[9]   In the case of military action to risk the death of civilian hostages to save many more innocent lives, it is conceivable that some orders may even merit praise when there is no alternative. The critical point is that accountability cannot be brushed aside just because the one who gave the order was only aware of the probable outcomes of that order.

For example, duress is certainly a form of external pressure to make a person act in a manner they would not otherwise even contemplate, but so long as the pressure does not reach the level of an irresistible force that no one can possibly withstand, to respond to it one way or another is to engage in a deliberate action for which one is responsible. We can compare two kinds of pressure to illustrate this. In one case, a man burns down a building that stores evidence vital to prosecuting criminal cases after he has been blackmailed by criminals over an affair he had with his boss's spouse (which, if exposed, could end his career and marriage). In the other case, a man burns down the same building because criminals threaten to kill his family if he refuses. In both cases, the man is in control of his own will power in deciding what he is going to do, and that leads to him setting the building on fire. Most people will probably find him excusable in the second case though not the first, but he is no less responsible in either case. The weighing of an action's consequences against the extenuating circumstances only comes into play if the person is responsible. Otherwise, however bad the burning down of the building may be, a person who is not responsible would not have to give any explanation for an event that has nothing to do with them.[10]

We can now consider why certain approaches tend to misplace responsibility and thus undermine efforts to reinforce public accountability. One of the most damaging, even if it had good intentions to begin with, is that of total responsibility denial. This approach was initially deployed by trial lawyers to secure the acquittal of those charged with even the most serious crimes, by convincing juries that if the accused could not be held responsible for the circumstances that led to them becoming someone who would commit those crimes (for example, the type of family they were born into, their genetic inheritance, their upbringing, the disadvantages confronting them from birth),

[10] While psychological pressures such as duress cannot be considered an external force which acts on people without their own volitional capacity being exercised at all, in some cases of mental illness there is a discernible force that operates within an individual's own brain but is sincerely regarded as external/alien and thus actively resisted, though not necessarily with success (see Tam, 1990, chapter 5).

then they could not be held responsible for those crimes either.[11] Tactically, they conflated the case for giving consideration to possible extenuating circumstances with a generic dismissal of responsibility. They ignored the fact that their argument, if correct, would equally sustain the claim that no one is ever responsible for anything, since no one can be held responsible for the factors that started to shape their character development before their volitional capacity even existed. But the argument is fallacious because to hold people responsible for what they do at a specific time does not imply we hold them responsible for anything that may have happened to them before that time.

Of course, factors such as how kind or cruel their parents were, or what support or neglect came their way, may rightly influence whether we want to treat them more leniently, give them a second chance, or pick a certain type of rehabilitation programme. But as we noted before, the weighing of such options only becomes relevant if responsibility is already established. Responsibility is about acknowledging that one is the person with the awareness and volitional role to have brought about the event in question, and therefore one is required to account for why one caused it to happen. While different accounts may lead us to apportion varying degrees of blame, excuse, or even praise to the responsible person, the responsibility cannot be denied provided the three aforementioned elements are present.

Unfortunately, where fallacious arguments misplacing the basis of responsibility grow in circulation, they cast doubt on the prospect of securing accountability beyond one's family and friends. Upon hearing repeatedly that people cannot reasonably be held responsible for their behaviour, or that attempts at attributing responsibility are ultimately arbitrary, many people buy into the outlook that outside a relatively small group of like-minded individuals, they cannot trust anyone to take on and fulfil important obligations. When they are told that worker unions, public services, local or central government, or transnational public institutions are set up to help them pool their resources to achieve more for them than they could on their own, they doubt that those running such organisations or other members involved

---

[11]   Clarence Darrow being one of the best remembered.

in them can be trusted to play their part. Their propensity to believe that responsibility can never be coherently ascribed to these people if they let others down reinforces their reluctance to support these loci for collective action.

As confidence in collective arrangements dwindles along with diminished trust in the prospect of holding others responsible for their actions, people look for alternative means to cope with the challenges they face in an increasingly complex society. From the 1980s on, three strands of the New Right offered 'solutions' that would bypass the accountability constriction. The first is to shrink the state at every level. The smaller government institutions are, the less likely they can cause problems for citizens, and there is less to worry about holding these unaccountable bodies responsible for their actions. In this utopian vision of a proto-anarchic world, a minimalist government does a few things which it can just about be trusted to do, but by and large people can manage on their own (Nozick, 1977).

Secondly, the private sector is presented as the saviour. Their sector's focus on profit making is celebrated as a unique virtue because there is no need for any distracting talk of responsibility in this realm. Instead, businesses that give their customers what they want will prosper, and those that let them down will suffer losses or even bankruptcies. Furthermore, the less they are tied up by regulatory requirements to account for their behaviour, the more freedom they will have in serving the people. So if there is still residual reluctance to shrink the government's range of functions, at least ensure more of those functions are handed over to private businesses to deliver. The drive towards privatisation and deregulation since the 1980s shows that it is a political mantra that has long met with relatively little effective resistance.[12]

Thirdly, far from being considered a warning on community fragmentation, the splintering of society into insular groups is welcomed as a sign of the healthy pursuit of freedom. Anything that drains support away from a national or transnational structure that has been built on the foundation of shared responsibilities

---

[12] The tragic inferno that broke out at Grenfell Tower in 2017 led many critics to rally against decades of attacks on regulation (Heathcote, 2017).

for the common good is encouraged on the grounds that 'others' cannot be trusted to take on their share of responsibilities. So people who reject civic values prefer to have their children taught where they will not have to mix with those who are not of the same faith or ethnicity, want to set up their own quasi-militia to defend their distinct way of life, or are determined to prepare for survival through a looming apocalypse that no one else can see are praised in the name of liberty.

For the New Right, such diminution of trust in sharing responsibility through state institutions means that it is likely to have fewer united forces to contend with as it seeks to take political power. But even as it chalks up more electoral and policy victories than its opponents, the discontent it stokes is turning out to be more difficult to control than expected. Apart from the wealthiest, people who have backed the shrinking of the state start to find that the meagre 'gains' they get from tax cuts are nowhere near enough to compensate for the loss of support for their children's education, their elderly parents' care, their own health and welfare, and countless other forms of deficit, from lowering environmental standards to underfunded criminal justice services. Without effective regulation, too many private firms, including those that have taken over previously publicly run services, have shown how their focus on profit maximisation is not always good for the life chances of others involved – escalating charges, below-subsistence pay for workers, and reduced responsiveness or even cutting off of vital services for the poorest users (Drakeford, 2014; Hermann, 2015; Meek, 2015).

As discontent simmered in the 2010s among those who have bought into the New Right's agenda of 'one for one, and none for all', conservative-minded political leaders had a choice. They could steer away from using divisiveness as a tool, and move towards what in the UK is often termed 'one nation conservatism', or in the US 'compassionate conservatism'. It would have meant that they would reach out to all citizens, and make it clear that everyone could be, and should be, held responsible for their actions in serving their common needs. Instead, they moved even further to the 'right', where extreme divisiveness is not a tool, but an end in itself. The responsibility of the rich, powerful, and privileged stays out of the picture, and the spotlight is directed exclusively at scapegoats – benefit claimants should get a well-paid job and not rely on the state, immigrants and asylum seekers should stay away and not 'use up' limited resources, and people with the wrong or no religion should acquire the correct faith or be treated with suspicion.

It would be a mistake to reject the talk of responsibility and insist on discussing the rights of those targeted with criticisms. The focus should be on people's responsibility without exception, be they rich or poor, whatever their gender or ethnicity, so that there is real understanding of what they need to account for. With the claiming of benefits, we should distinguish those who have worked hard without getting adequate pay, or those who are too ill or disabled to get paid work, from the very small minority who try to bend the rules.[13] With people who have arrived from a foreign country, we should separate out the vast majority who do valuable work and contribute economically and culturally, and those who seek sanctuary from persecution, from the few who try to exploit the system. And above all, with those who run powerful public or private sector organisations, we should differentiate between those who do what they can to help the people who rely on their policies and services, and those who have little compunction in advancing their own interests at the expense of others.

How to enhance public accountability

With the help of a coherent conception of responsibility ascription, we can review accountability arrangements to establish where democratic cooperation may be undermined by irresponsible behaviour going undetected. Variations of the Prisoners' Dilemma have consistently shown that the vast majority of people will back each other in achieving the optimal outcome for all, provided they are convinced that others will not backslide from fulfilling their side of the bargain. To give

[13] According to 2011/2012 figures, fraudulent benefit claims in Britain amounted to less than 0.9% of the benefits budget, and were six times smaller than the amount the government failed to pay over to those in need but who had either under-claimed or not known how to claim (Joint Public Issues Team, 2013).

citizens the confidence that cheats and free-riders, especially those with the greatest wealth and power to shield them from scrutiny, will be held to account for their acts and omissions, there are four aspects of accountability reinforcement that ought to be considered:

- reviving the conditional licence to act model;
- strengthening community channels to press for compliance;
- developing a cross-sector accountability support service; and
- extending global arrangements for securing cross-border accountability.

The conditional licence to act model originated from the sovereign power setting out the terms for private actors to make gains for themselves in return for benefits rendered to the public realm. In England, the practice could be traced back to Henry VIII, who would grant individuals a licence (or charter) to form a company to carry out certain activities (from trade to exploration) that would enable them to take advantage of conditions made possible by past or future actions of the state. The licence was conditional upon the company in question serving the interests of the country, and could expire when its time limit had been reached or be revoked if in practice it led to damage to the common good. After the 1688 revolution, the model was applied to the British monarchy itself, with the Bill of Rights setting out what the head of state could or could not do, and the conditions that must be met if the power to rule was to be maintained.

In the US, after independence from Britain was obtained, individual states adopted a similar approach to the granting of corporate charters to individuals wishing to set up companies that would give them protection while carrying out transactions with others. These charters set clear conditions for what the companies in question were permitted to do. Typically, they forbade activities that would go beyond what was necessary to fulfil their chartered purpose, made explicit that the permission granted would be revoked if the companies abused their power or caused public harm, and would not allow them to spend money to influence legislation. By the late 19th century, however, large companies were able to use their growing influence to undermine the model. Following the Supreme Court case of *Santa Clara County v Southern Pacific Railroad* (1886), which ruled that corporations should be treated no differently from individual citizens, state power to make corporations publicly accountable began to wane (Grossman & Adams, 1993).

It is time to revive the use of conditional licences for those with corporate and governmental powers precisely because they can do so much that can affect the lives of others, and their actions cannot be adequately held in check by the general rules that apply to all individuals. Corporations have amassed immense powers that allow them to write down their tax liabilities, liquidate their debts, reshape legislation, or destroy the environment on which others depend. The British government has taken over the use of the Royal Prerogative and with its command of a majority in the House of Commons could ignore the constraints that were meant to be in place to limit executive overreach. The lack of oversight to prevent the US president from systemic conflicts of interest has been shown up by the Trump family's seamless links between activities in the White House and the Trump business empire.

Legislatures must begin to draw up licences to act that will set specific conditions with which elected politicians, senior government officials, and large corporations must comply if they are to continue to wield the powers they have. These should include restrictions on the seeking and use of emergency powers, which must be predicated on time limits and independent adjudication of when those powers shall cease.[14] Any failure to fulfil any of the conditions set out in the relevant licence should lead to clear-cut penalties, including, in the case of serious violations, the complete revocation of the licence. Major tax evasion, for example, should not be followed by behind the scenes bargaining over how much to pay back, but the full unpaid amount must be handed over plus a penalty that is equivalent to, for example, twice or three times what is owed so it is a genuine

---

[14] For example, any attempt to seek significant new powers to deal with imminent threats should have conditions for the termination of those powers built in.

deterrent. Threats to proceed with environmental degradation should be met with an immediate suspension of any previously granted right to operate in the threatened area.

There are many other instances where it would be better late than never for such licences to be drawn up to halt further abuse of power. For example, membership of the European Parliament must surely be made conditional on an individual not committing fraud against the institution, or, even more glaringly obvious, on that person upholding its values in private and public. As J. S. Mill and others have pointed out, it is not undemocratic to protect democratic institutions from their avowed enemies. It is absurd, for example, for the European Parliament to allow people to join it with the explicit purpose of undermining and dismantling it. The UK Parliament too needs to rethink and set out more exact conditions for its members. Following the 2015 general elections, concerns were raised about some Conservative candidates breaking electoral laws to get themselves elected. In 2017, 12 police forces completed their investigation and handed files to the Crown Prosecution Service, but nobody knew what prosecution and conviction might lead to. As there were 20 Conservative MPs who were investigated, and the Tory Party had a working majority of under 20 at the time, a guilty verdict could have had serious constitutional implications – would just those MPs have to resign, would the Conservative Party be held responsible collectively, or would the penalty be as trivial as the £70,000 fine handed down by the Electoral Commission for the transgression (Elgot, 2017)?

The second aspect of accountability enhancement to consider relates to the strengthening of community channels to press for compliance. It is often said that cynicism, apathy, and misinformation are so prevalent that there will be neither enough interest nor trust in any attempt to improve accountability arrangements. But this goes against the experience of those who have studied or worked with activists in communities that routinely engage in flagging up issues which should get the attention of others in the locality.

Having reviewed this matter in *The Public and Its Problems*, John Dewey concluded:

> [T]hat expansion and reinforcement of personal understanding and judgment by the cumulative and transmitted intellectual wealth of the community which may render nugatory the indictment of democracy drawn on the basis of the ignorance, bias and levity of the masses, can be fulfilled only in the relations of personal intercourse in the local community. (Dewey, 1991, p 218)

It is direct encounters between people that build up understanding and trust, and when these are connected to actions that rectify wrongs against the public, they deepen the foundation for holding future wrongdoers to account.

Local government has a key role to play in developing effective community channels to raise accountability issues. It should recognise that there is not a single mechanism that has all the answers, and should give its support to as many groups and networks as possible that are not tied to commercial interests. These may include community organising, where activists rally local people to look at specific problems they need to tackle, and help them organise themselves to press those with the relevant responsibility to act differently (Alinsky, 2013); community development, which can through regular outreach bring local people and public sector bodies together to build long-term working relations, and develop shared strategies to address people's concerns (Gilchrist & Taylor, 2011); community-based alliance, which is set up by residents' groups to form partnerships with other local organisations to enter into a dialogue with public agencies in setting future priorities.

More should also be done by local authorities to ensure their elected members and appointed officials are given the skills and opportunities to listen and respond to citizens regarding problems they are concerned about.[15] Research has found that most people know little about what councillors do, but those who have met with their local elected representatives tend to

---

[15] One of the often neglected aspects of communication training for public servants is how to engage the emotional side of people's concerns, and not just discuss facts and statistics (see, for example, Westen, 2007).

value what they do (Councillors Commission, 2007). Therefore, far from minimising contact between councillors and their constituents, more should be done to promote the convening of problem-solving meetings, where accountabilities can be clarified, complaints addressed, and improvements reviewed (Gardiner, 2010).

Instead of striving to conform to a misguided notion of efficiency by becoming as faceless and literally robotic as possible, councils should prioritise interactions with local people as key to building trust in collective endeavours. People should be encouraged to visit council facilities to discuss problems with officers who act on their behalf. Visits to community venues and schools should be conducted regularly to enable representatives of the council to facilitate reviews of problems and what is to be done about them (Baker et al, 2000).

None of the aforementioned community channels will by itself transform scepticism about public accountability into a trusting partnership. But nurturing community relations through diverse contacts over time will have a significant impact on people's belief that there are people who take seriously their role in helping them hold to account not just those who should serve them responsibly in the locality, but also those whose base of operations may be some distance away at their national or international headquarters.

Turning to the third aspect of accountability reinforcement, we should develop a cross-sector accountability support service that will be dedicated to helping citizens raise concerns about any public agency or private corporation suspected of breaching its duties. At the moment, for the vast majority of people, if the breach is relatively minor, it is not worth going through the cumbersome procedures to get it investigated; if it is serious, the complex and remote arrangements do not inspire confidence that those responsible will be held to account.

A cross-sector support service will provide a single point of contact for complainants and whistle-blowers to raise their concerns. It will guide them through the process and provide them each with a case worker who will see it through. Whether the issue is the underhanded practice of a bank, a cover-up by a police force, or deception perpetrated by an energy supplier, the support agency will monitor how the investigation is being handled by the lead investigatory body. If, in its opinion, the matter has not been given sufficient attention, it can arrange for a critical review. If it is satisfied that a thorough investigation has taken place, it will provide assurance to the original complainant as an independent third party.

Those who work for the agency will be required to have their earnings placed in one transparent account,[16] and they will not be permanently assigned to one particular sector, so as to minimise the chance that they become too familiar and relaxed in their working with the main organisations in that sector. However, where their particular expertise is needed in any special case, operational flexibility should permit them to return to work in areas they were previously assigned to.

A key function of such a support service is to cut through the layers of bureaucracy that tend to make the public feel that they can never hold anyone to account. By giving people a chance to speak to a person live, find out straightaway what steps to take next, and, most importantly of all, follow up with that same person (and not be transferred to some other section in cyberspace) if the outcome is not satisfactory will substantially boost confidence in the accountability system. Furthermore, as the agency delivering this service is completely independent from those carrying out the investigations, it can give a fully impartial view as to whether any given case should be closed or further examined.

Finally, let us look at the need to extend global arrangements for securing cross-border accountability. Since the closing decades of the 20th century, plutocratic resistance to public accountability has been greatly aided by the growth of transnational corporations, and the rapid advancement of information technology. Rich and powerful organisations can easily move their resources and operations around the world and defy attempts by national governments to hold them to account for the damage they cause. Where nations join forces through institutions such as the UN or the EU, the political

---

[16] This would make any attempt to bribe the agency's staff more easily detectable and thus much less likely.

wing of global plutocracy dons the mask of nationalism and relentlessly attacks them for weakening state autonomy, when in fact their role is to help countries achieve what they can no longer manage on their own.

Instead of conceding to the spread of false nationalism, we should invoke true nationalism in setting out why the power of a country to protect its own people has to be strengthened by joining forces with others globally. Fraudulent financial deals, environmental degradation, cybercrime, conflicts fuelled by irresponsible arms sales, people trafficking, and child labour exploitation are just some of the problems no country can deal with on its own when the culprits can stay out of the reach of its jurisdiction.

There is no doubt that existing UN institutions need to be strengthened, and new global regulatory bodies established to combat worldwide threats. The development of a better system for making and enforcing global laws is already receiving increased attention (Tetalman & Belitsos, 2005). While such efforts may take time and face opposition from countries run by plutocratic cliques, progressive NGOs like Oxfam, Save the Children, Greenpeace, Amnesty International, and others can build on the global networks they have created, and exert greater influence over policies and practices that can help to counter cross-border threats (Diehl, 1997; Cerny, 2013).

Researchers have found that NGOs can, through adjusting the terms of joint action when planning operational collaboration, proposing new conditions during in-depth policy dialogue, and promoting global campaigns through the formation of large-scale coalitions, bring considerable pressure to bear on issues ranging from international protection of children's rights to the World Bank's lending priorities (Covey, 2000; Lent & Trivedy, 2001). Government and business organisations can be persuaded to accept and rectify their errors if there are sufficiently well coordinated efforts to draw public attention to them.

There are three particular issues global coalitions should address to maximise their efficacy in holding transnational groups to account. First, they must set down organising principles and operational rules so that they have a shared understanding of their respective responsibilities (Brown & Fox, 2000). Secondly, like any self-governing cooperative body, it is essential for them to have an arbitration mechanism to settle infractions of the rules in a just manner; to uphold and if necessary enforce penalties and restitution; and to protect all involved from the violation of the overall agreement by any member (Bernstein, 1980, pp 83–89). Lastly, they need to develop communication practices that take on board the cultural diversity of different countries, particularly in relation to how people with distinct national backgrounds may relate to what Geert Hofstede termed the 'power distance' measure, which differentiates along a continuum of national dispositions that, at one end, tend to expect authority to be exercised by those high up in a command chain without being questioned by those below; and, at the other end, incline towards scrutinising decisions from above unless these are made closer to those affected by them and with their involvement (Hofstede et al, 2010, pp 53–134).[17] Different techniques will be needed to take into account these contrasting dispositions across the world to engage people in considering the responsibilities of transnational actors.

---

[17] Countries closest to the 'authoritarian' end include Slovakia, Russia, Serbia, Malaysia, Saudi Arabia, the Philippines; those found nearest to the 'participatory' end include Finland, Norway, Sweden, Ireland, New Zealand, and Denmark. Those around the mid-point cluster include Poland, Belgium, Chile, and Thailand.

Remedial checklist: public accountability

With reference to any group the governance of which you are concerned about, you can use the checklist below to identify what requires the most improvement in relation to the need for public accountability:

☐ Are members aware of their respective responsibilities, and what should they do if there is reason to believe that someone is not fulfilling their obligations? How easy is it to detect unjustifiable actions and call for investigation and impartial judgement? Is there a need for reminding or informing members through direct contact why and how they should help to hold to account those who violate the trust of others?

☐ Is there general confidence that most people are acting responsibly? Or is there widespread concern that too many are betraying the trust of others and getting away with it? Are better rules and clearer specification of what is required needed to set out where further infringement would be duly penalised?

☐ Do members know where to turn for support if they want to draw attention to acts against the public interest or complain about irresponsible behaviour by those in powerful positions? Is the support available sufficient to help them find redress and protect them, if necessary, from intimidation?

☐ Beyond the accountabilities within your own group, are there adequate arrangements for members to hold those outside the group, in other parts of the country or the world, to account for their actions which impact on the wellbeing of your group? How effectively are you working with other groups to develop networks and coalitions that can curb the irresponsible or erroneous activities emanating from elsewhere?

Conclusion:
Learning to govern ourselves

In 1988, a well-travelled documentary film maker, Patrick Watson, remarked, "I have been repeatedly struck by the fact that some of the most corrosive cynicism about democracy and some of the most leaden indifference towards it are expressed by people who live comfortably in prosperous democratic countries" (Watson & Barber, 1990, p x). Alas, now the cynicism is commonplace among those living comfortably or precariously alike.

It should never have come as a surprise to anyone that trying to govern ourselves is not easy. When things go well, some become complacent and slacken in their support. When times are hard, many get frustrated and blame the system. Between those who turn their apathy into a badge of honour, and those who fall for the tricks of political con-merchants, the ones seeking to make democracy work are squeezed with ever less room to manoeuvre.

But no one can pretend there is a better governance strategy available. The four classic strategies may each be suited to one fleeting set of circumstances, yet none of them is inherently adaptable to changing conditions, or capable of responding to complaints or suggestions to alter the course they have set. The hierarchical strategy would lock everyone into rigid roles and inflexible relations. The egalitarian would demand that every valuable difference be surrendered, or resort to an unequalled force to impose an inescapable sameness. The minimalist would rely on individuals dealing with all serious problems by themselves, and take no concerted action even if they cannot fend off predators. The disciplinarian would insist that everything is working out for the best just because everyone is forbidden to question any command that has been handed down. As for leaving the deployment of these strategies to a single individual or group that will change policies without taking into account the thoughts or concerns of anyone else, history is full of unmitigated disasters engendered by arbitrary rule.

If anyone today is tempted to jettison democratic governance, it can only be because they have closed their mind to the chaos of lawlessness and the prospect of brutal oppression. They complain about democratic rule, even as they ignore the fact that if they were to be complaining under any other form of governance, they might never get to do it again. They bemoan having to reach collective decisions, while they overlook how individuals acting without restraint can callously ruin the lives of others.

Undeniably, for democracy to work we have to learn to govern ourselves more effectively. Civic-communitarian reformists have been putting forward ideas for improvement for over a century, and the ebb and flow of effective democratic rule has reflected the extent to which those ideas were neglected or embraced at different times. We can now see that backing away from democracy to let an unaccountable few seize power is not an option; and neither is hoping that its shortcomings can be cured simply by getting more people to vote. Unless we continuously work on developing the relations, institutions, and practices that will enable us to work out what common challenges we face, and cooperate in devising collective responses, our governance could end up being hijacked by deft manipulators.

Past attempts at improving a society's governance have tended to focus on developing the skills and attitudes of leaders, the civic knowledge and dispositions of citizens, or the rules and processes of decision-making systems. By now it should be clear that we need to cover all these aspects. What is more, we should recognise that there is no end point at which it can be claimed that sufficient improvement has been achieved. Continuous learning and adaptation are essential to guide us towards aiding citizens, political leaders, and the reforming of governance arrangements to deal with ongoing challenges.

In this book, we have looked beyond mere electoral machinery and voter inclinations, and reviewed the extent to which democratic governance is functioning to meet the three core requirements of sustaining togetherness among the people;

underpinning objectivity in their joint deliberations on what should be done; and achieving sufficient power balance so that any agreement on what should be done will be honoured by all, with none being strong enough to ride roughshod over others. Under each of these, we in turn identified key factors that are necessary for bringing any democratic system closer to fulfilling those requirements. After explaining why each of these nine key factors is needed, and clarifying what implications should or should not be derived from them, we explored a number of recommendations that would aid their realisation. In summary, the 40 recommendations are listed below:

Togetherness

- Shared mission:
    - ➤ develop familiarisation arrangements;
    - ➤ ensure planning processes are structured for co-designing;
    - ➤ give collective endeavours a clarity of purpose;
    - ➤ build in sustained engagement;
    - ➤ strengthen support through mission-forming intermediaries.

- Mutual respect:
    - ➤ tackle misunderstanding with reflective awareness-raising;
    - ➤ expose hidden discrimination with procedural consistency and transparency;
    - ➤ provide rapid adjudication and correction;
    - ➤ make better use of reconciliatory exploration.

- Coherent membership:
    - ➤ provide comprehensive induction for all members;
    - ➤ subject disputes to a civic compatibility test;
    - ➤ commit to member-led revisions of terms and conditions;
    - ➤ improve processes for the suspension and restoration of membership.

Objectivity

- Collaborative learning:
  - ➤ establish a collaborative network for giving practical guidance;
  - ➤ provide training for teaching collaborative learning approaches;
  - ➤ remove institutional barriers to collaboration;
  - ➤ place sufficient investment in collaborative research;
  - ➤ promote understanding of scientific enquiry.

- Critical re-examination:
  - ➤ embed responsive trigger mechanisms for requesting re-examination;
  - ➤ develop sufficient capability for re-examination;
  - ➤ nurture the cultural readiness to challenge assumptions;
  - ➤ organise the strategic re-examination of re-examination processes.

- Responsible communication:
  - ➤ rationalise the law on responsible communication;
  - ➤ develop media arbitration services;
  - ➤ set legally recognised professional standards in journalism;
  - ➤ recalibrate the conditions for anonymity;
  - ➤ advance global oversight of communications.

Power balance

- Participatory decision making:
  - ➤ improve the quality of deliberative engagement;
  - ➤ delegate decisions in line with subsidiarity;
  - ➤ expand opportunities for decision-making roles;
  - ➤ strengthen existing voting arrangements.

- Civic parity:
  - ➤ support the development of multi-stakeholder cooperative enterprise;

- ➤ redirect the public source of money to the common good;
- ➤ guarantee a decent level of income and public support for all citizens;
- ➤ set parameters for differentials in pay and for services dealing with adversarial interactions;
- ➤ curtail private wealth's power to shape the public agenda.

- Public accountability:
  - ➤ revive the conditional licence to act model;
  - ➤ strengthen community channels to press for compliance;
  - ➤ develop a cross-sector accountability support service;
  - ➤ extend global arrangements for securing cross-border accountability.

For each of these recommendations, we considered what they might involve and how they could impact on democratic cooperation where they are taken forward. There is no doubt that relevant expertise is needed to develop and deploy them, and the extent and quality of their implementation would affect their influence on the collective behaviour of those who are involved in governing themselves. Although no single organisation or country can claim to have fully acted on all these recommendations, those that have done better on more of them tend to perform better than others which have not.[1]

At the organisational level, worker-run enterprises and multistakeholder cooperatives around the world generally deliver fairer rewards, more stability, and higher job satisfaction for their members. Countries that have done more to meet the requirements of democratic governance give their citizens a better quality of life, and provide them with greater freedom and security compared with other parts of the world. And while transnational institutions face the greatest challenge, the ones that are relatively more democratic in how they operate, such as

---

[1] The recommendations point to approaches involving continuous improvement, so not surprisingly, no form of human association can be said to have done all it needs to do in following them. There is always room for improvement, and the key to democratic health is to strive to identify and overcome shortcomings as an ongoing commitment.

the UN and the EU, are substantially more effective than others in maintaining peace, addressing humanitarian concerns, and facilitating cross-border cooperation.

But demutualisation can dismantle member-owned businesses; xenophobia can threaten the stability of hitherto inclusive societies; and small-minded jingoism can destroy the most precious transnational collaboration. To counter the threats against democracy, a comprehensive programme addressing all the key issues outlined must be taken forward. It will undoubtedly be resisted by those who prefer to amass power for themselves, and some may even suspect that such opposition to reforms cannot be overcome.

One enduring lesson remains from past struggles against oppression and exploitation. While success is hard to secure, considerable progress can be made, provided appropriate reform ideas are formulated, and carried out by astute and determined strategists (Grayling, 2007; Lux, 2009; Tam, 2015a). The soundness of the ideas that have been put forward in this book can be judged and further improved by its readers. As to their advancement by those with the necessary strategic skills and commitment, much will depend on development in four areas.

First, will those responsible for education in the broadest sense help to raise public understanding of why and how democracy should be improved? Will they be so afraid of being accused of showing 'political bias' that they stay silent, or will they find ways to get more people of all ages to become interested and informed in what may get better or worse in their lives as a result of the way they are governed? People with educational roles are not just to be found in schools and universities, they are involved in lifelong learning, the arts, and news reporting. Many of them are liable to be castigated for not being 'impartial' whenever they present anything not to the liking of certain politicians or their backers. It will take courage and skill to navigate through their obstructions.

Secondly, as many of the improvements that are necessary to strengthen democracy can only be secured by people with the relevant aptitudes, will there be concerted efforts to provide the appropriate training in an accessible and affordable manner? The skills for, say, promoting empathy, exploring reconciliation, or facilitating deliberative engagement are often neglected or assumed to be something anyone can summon up at a moment's notice. There needs to be systematic and well-funded provisions to equip those who have to carry out the delicate interface functions with the know-how and support to do it sufficiently well.

Thirdly, will those currently in charge of or who may one day be taking control of organisations in any sector at the local, national, or global level be prepared to introduce the recommended approaches into their respective institutions, and ensure they are taken forward with sensitivity and determination? It is not just a challenge for government bodies, because the culture of democracy is woven into the fabric of human interactions across society. The more people get to experience and value mutually supportive relations, the more likely they are to seek and sustain democratic arrangements. The biggest stumbling block is going to be the 'short-term priorities win all' syndrome. Although the proposed changes to the governing processes and requirements will enhance adaptability and help to secure outcomes that are in the long run more satisfactory for all, there will always be pressure to push them further down the line until the more 'urgent' matters have been dealt with.

The fourth and final area is where the lack of progress in the previous three will have to be addressed. If those with educational roles do not help to raise understanding of democracy, effective training for vital democratic practices is not provided or sufficiently taken up, or institutional reforms keep slipping to the back of the queue, who will step in to steer the necessary changes forward? Political parties, as we have seen, used to provide a platform for citizens to rally behind a distinct policy programme, but have in recent decades become far less effective in fulfilling this role. Some of them have become the political wing of corporate interests that are ever ready to subordinate public wellbeing to private gains. Some have become vehicles for discontent that is channelled towards either right-wing anti-immigrant agendas or left-wing anti-capitalist rhetoric. Others commit themselves exclusively to campaigning for one or another single issue. And some are at a loss as to what they really stand for beyond their latest opportunist positioning.

Nonetheless, organised political parties remain necessary to connect citizens to the levers of statutory power. Even the superrich have to work through party machinery, while ordinary individuals stand little chance of exerting any influence at all if they act alone without any party structure.[2] So what kind of political party can reach out to citizens and engage them in improving their lives through more effective self-governance? It will have to take on board the suggested remedies for the malaise affecting contemporary democratic politics. The development of togetherness among its own members, objectivity in their deliberations, and power balance across the party will have to be pursued consistently. Furthermore, it will only succeed if it applies the recommended approaches to its interactions with potential supporters outside as well as those inside the party.

For example, a political party that aims to enable citizens to govern themselves on the basis of what is objectively most supportive of their common good, and without discrimination against any individuals, will build ongoing relations with people at all levels, and not contact them just when their votes or donations are sought. It will develop partnerships with community groups, cooperative enterprises, NGOs, responsible businesses, and diverse associations so that, far from keeping them at arm's length for fear of tainting them with partisanship, it can collaborate with them as fellow participants of a civic alliance. Members of the party will actively work with those in the partner organisations, and many ought to be members of one or more of those organisations as well. Through everyday service, support, and conversation, people's trust and understanding deepen, and the party thus increases its ability to win electoral support and enact the changes required to secure better life chances for citizens.

There is of course no guarantee that any political party will develop itself in that direction and offer people a focal point for

---

[2] The rich have found that buying their way into dominance within an established party, or funding a new one, gives them more leverage than acting alone. For the poor and disenchanted, protests in the absence of an organised party to secure the necessary political power to change things, or at least pressure the governing party to alter course, mean they will most likely go on protesting in vain.

democratic renewal. But once this gap is identified, instead of turning away and giving up on all parties, the response should be to explore more urgently if one of the existing parties is willing to change course accordingly, or, as a last resort, support the establishment of a new one.[3] Whether it is called a political party or not, an organised association dedicated to formulating, advocating, and winning electoral power to implement policies for the public good is indispensable for democratic politics. While people may in the short term turn their attention to local administration, single-issue campaigns, or their own self-managed commons, it will dawn on them eventually that in the absence of a truly pro-democracy party nationally and transnationally, the organised enemies of democratisation will continue to hold power at the highest levels. Whatever anarchic utopian dreams may be conjured up, the reality is that there will always be the powerful few who want to exploit the vulnerabilities of others to gratify their own reckless ambitions. And without a well-organised rival to champion the cause of the public against them, they will win.

Democracy, as a meta-strategy for governance, is the only thing that can hold back the devious and unscrupulous from dictating terms to the rest of us. It enables us to work out in an informed and unintimidated way what we should agree to secure or forbid for our own wellbeing. The flawed conviction that we have more important priorities to deal with than democracy is precisely why democracy has been left in a debilitated state, thus allowing ill-conceived and manipulated views to be promoted in aid of political advocates who are not the least bit concerned with the public interest. Indeed, for them, there is no 'public' interest as such, just their own private agenda that must take precedence over what other people seek.

If might, of the monetary or military variety, is not to settle what is right, then the concerns and aspirations of different people must be taken into account inclusively when decisions

---

[3]   For example, the Association for the Renewal of Politics, better known as *En Marche!*, was set up by Emmanuel Macron in 2016 to organise political campaigns. Despite its successes in the 2017 presidential and parliamentary elections in France, it remains to be seen if it will develop deeper, long-term relations with its supporters and the wider public.

are made that will be applied to everyone. Democracy is not a secondary issue, but the prime device for us to give due consideration to a wide range of critical matters. From threats such as wage poverty, human trafficking and abuse, planetary degradation, cyber infringement, and vile extremism to opportunities for advancing renewable energy, global peace and security, a commons approach to technological innovation, better health protection, and economic safety nets, we need decisions that reflect our shared concerns. To rescue us from decisions that favour the powerful few to the detriment of everyone else, we must first save democracy itself.

References

Adams, R. (2014) 'Rise in number of unqualified teachers at state-funded schools in England', *The Guardian*: www.theguardian.com/education/2014/apr/10/rise-number-unqualified-teachers-state-funded-schools-england

Addams, J. (1960) *A Centennial Reader*, New York: The Macmillan Company.

Alexander, J. (2012) 'Three rival views of tradition (Arendt, Oakeshott and MacIntyre)', *Journal of the Philosophy of History*, 6(1): 20–43.

Alinsky, S. (2013) *Rules for Radicals*, New York: Vintage Books.

Allen, A. (2013) 'Gender and power', in Clegg and Haugaard (2013), pp 293-309.

Alleyne, M. D. (1997) *News Revolution: political and economic decisions about global information*, New York: St Martin's Press.

Amadeo, K. (2017), 'Deficit by president: what budget deficits hide', *The Balance*: www.thebalance.com/deficit-by-president-what-budget-deficits-hide-3306151

Anderson, B. (2006) *Imagined Communities: reflections on the origins and spread of nationalism*, London: Verso.

Arendt, H. (1979) *The Origins of Totalitarianism*, Orlando: Harcourt Brace & Co.

Aronoff, K. (2017) 'How to share the wealth if the robots start doing the work', *Alternet*: www.alternet.org/labor/robots-automatation-and-redistribution

Axelrod, R. (1984) *The Evolution of Co-operation*, New York: Basic Books.

Ayo, I. S. C. (2016) 'Mondragon's third way: reply to Sharryn Kasmir', *Global Dialogue* 6(3): http://isa-global-dialogue.net/mondragons-third-way-reply-to-sharryn-kasmir/

Baker, K., Sillett, J. and Neary, S. (2000) *Citizenship: challenges for councils*, London: LGIU.

Barber, B. R. (1984) *Strong Democracy: participatory politics for a new age*, Berkeley and Los Angeles: University of California Press.

Barber, B. R. (1995) *Jihad vs. McWorld: how the planet is both falling apart and coming together and what this means for democracy*, New York: Times Books.

Barber, B. R. (2001) 'The need for more democracy', in Tam (2001a), pp 193–200.

Barber, B. R. (2013) *If Mayors Ruled the World*, London: Yale University Press.

Bellah, R. N., Madsen, R., Sullivan, W. M., Swidler, A. and Tipton, S. M. (1992) *The Good Society*, New York: Vintage Books.

Bellah, R. N., Madsen, R., Sullivan, W. M., Swidler, A. and Tipton, S. M. (1996) *Habits of the Heart: individualism and commitment in American life*, Berkeley and Los Angeles: University of California Press.

Bellah, R. N. and Sullivan, W. M. (2001), 'Cultural resources for a progressive alternative', in Tam (2001a), pp 21–35.

Berman, R. (2017) 'CBO analysis endangers GOP health-care bill', *The Atlantic*: www.theatlantic.com/politics/archive/2017/06/cbo-senate-republican-bill-22-million/531663/

Bernstein, P. (1980) *Workplace Democratization*, New Brunswick: Transaction Books.

Bew, J. (2016) *Citizen Clem: a biography of Attlee*, London: riverrun.

Blau, A. (2004) 'Against positive and negative freedom', *Political Theory*, 32(4): 547–553.

Bleicher, J. (1980) *Contemporary Hermeneutics*, London: Routledge & Kegan Paul.

Bock, G., Skinner, Q. and Viroli, M. (eds) (1990) *Machiavelli and Republicanism*, Cambridge: Cambridge University Press.

Bollier, D. (2016) 'Democratic money and capital for the commons', The Commons Strategies Group: http://commonsstrategies.org/democratic-money-and-capital-for-the-commons/#comment-191

Bollier, D. and Helfrich, S. (eds) (2015) *Patterns of Commoning*, Amherst, MA: The Commons Strategies Group.

Boswell, J. (1994) *Community and the Economy: the theory of public cooperation*, London: Routledge.

Bourgeois, L. (1902) *Solidarity* (3rd ed), Paris: Colin.

Bowles, M. (2008) *Democracy: the contribution of community development to local governance and democracy*, London: Community Development Foundation.

Bowles, S. and Gintis, H. (2011) *A Cooperative Species: human reciprocity and its evolution*, Princeton: Princeton University Press.

Boyle, D. and Harris, M. (2009) *The Challenge of Co-production: how equal partnerships between professionals and the public are crucial to improving public services*, London: NESTA.

Boyte, H., Barber, B. R. and Marshall, W. (1994) *Civic Declaration*, Dayton: Kettering Foundation.

Brandom, R. B. (2000) *Rorty and His Critics*, Oxford: Blackwell Publishers.

Brennan, T., John, P. and Stoker, G. (eds) (2007) *Re-energising Citizenship: strategies for civil renewal*, Basingstoke: Palgrave Macmillan.

Breslin, B. (2004) *The Communitarian Constitution*, Baltimore: The Johns Hopkins University Press.

British Humanist Association (2016) 'New evidence shows Government proposal to allow 100% religious selection in schools will lead to increased segregation': https://humanism. org.uk/2016/09/30/new-evidence-shows-government-proposal-to-allow-100-religious-selection-in-schools-will-lead-to-increased-segregation/

Bromley, C., Curtice, J. and Seyd, B. (2004) *Is Britain Facing a Crisis of Democracy?*, London: The Constitution Unit, UCL.

Bronner, S. E. (2004) *Reclaiming the Enlightenment*, New York: Columbia University Press.

Brown, E. (2013) *The Public Bank Solution*, Baton Rouge: Third Millennium Press.

Brown. J. (2010) *The Community Shares Programme: one year on*, Manchester: Co-operatives UK.

Brown, L. D. and Fox, J. A. (2000) 'Accountability within transnational coalitions', in Fox and Brown (2000), pp 439–483.

Brown, S. C. (ed) (1984) *Objectivity and Cultural Divergence*, Cambridge: Cambridge University Press.

Brown, W. (1993) 'Research chiefs fearful as privatisation looms', *New Scientist*: www.newscientist.com/article/mg13818771-800-research-chiefs-fearful-as-privatisation-looms/

Burdekin, K. (1985) *Swastika Night*, New York: Feminist Press.

Burke, T. E. (1983) *The Philosophy of Popper*, Manchester: Manchester University Press.

Bush, S. (2017) 'Jeremy Corbyn's policies aren't that different from Ed Miliband's or even New Labour. So why is he being attacked?', *New Statesman*: www.newstatesman.com/politics/welfare/2017/04/jeremy-corbyns-policies-arent-different-ed-milibands-or-even-new-labour-so

Cadwalladr, C. (2017) 'Robert Mercer: the big data billionaire waging war on mainstream media', *The Observer*: www.theguardian.com/politics/2017/feb/26/robert-mercer-breitbart-war-on-media-steve-bannon-donald-trump-nigel-farage

Cairncross, F. and McRae, H. (1975) *The Second Great Crash*, London: Methuen Paperback.

Camden, B. (2016) 'Troops to teachers scheme questioned as figures show just a fifth of trainees qualified', *Schools Week*: http://schoolsweek.co.uk/troops-to-teachers-scheme-questioned-as-figures-show-just-a-fifth-of-trainees-qualified/

Campbell, J. (1995) *Understanding John Dewey*, Chicago: Open Court Publishing.

Canovan, M. (1992) *Hannah Arendt: a reinterpretation of her political thought*, Cambridge: Cambridge University Press.

Carlo, S. (2016) 'The Snooper's Charter passed into law this week', *Independent*: www.independent.co.uk/voices/snoopers-charter-theresa-may-online-privacy-investigatory-powers-act-a7426461.html

Carrington, D. (2014) 'Fracking trespass law changes move forward despite huge public opposition', *The Guardian*: www.theguardian.com/environment/2014/sep/26/fracking-trespass-law-changes-move-forward-despite-huge-public-opposition

Centre for Analysis of Social Exclusion (2010) *An Anatomy of Economic Inequality in the UK*, London: Government Equalities Office.

Cerny, P. G. (2013) 'Reconfiguring power in a globalizing world', in Clegg and Haugaard (2013), pp 383-399.

Cesarani, D. and Fulbrook, M. (eds) (1996) *Citizenship, Nationality and Migration in Europe*, London: Routledge.

Chan, W. T. (1963) *A Source Book in Chinese Philosophy*, Princeton: Princeton University Press.

Chapman, A. R. and Van Der Merwe, H. (2008) *Truth and Reconciliation in South Africa*, Philadelphia: University of Pennsylvania Press.

Claassen, R. L. (2015) *Godless Democrats and Pious Republicans? Party activists, party capture and the 'god gap'*, New York: Cambridge University Press.

Cladis, M. S. (1992) *A Communitarian Defense of Liberalism: Emile Durkheim and contemporary social theory*, Stanford: Stanford University Press.

Claeys, G. (1989) *Citizens and Saints: politics and anti-politics in early British socialism*, Cambridge: Cambridge University Press.

Clarke, M. and Stewart, J. (1999) *Community Governance, Community Leadership and the New Local Government*, London: Joseph Rowntree Foundation.

Cleary, T. (1993) *The Essential Tao*, London: Bravo Ltd.

Clegg, S. R. and Haugaard, M. (eds) (2013) *The Sage Handbook of Power*, London: Sage Publications.

Clements, J. D. (2014) *Corporations are not People: reclaiming democracy from big money and global corporations*, Oakland: Berrett-Koehler Publishers.

Cohen, J. and Rogers, J. (1995) 'Secondary association and democratic governance', in Wright (1995), pp 7-98.

Cohen, L. J. (1977) *The Probable and the Provable*, Oxford: Oxford University Press.

Cole, G. D. H. (1917) *Self-Government in Industry*, London: G. Bell.

Cole, G. D. H. (1920) *Guild Socialism Re-Stated*, London: Leonard Parsons.

Connolly, K. (2016) '"No bling in the hood": does Berlin's anti-gentrification law really work?', *The Guardian*: www.theguardian.com/cities/2016/oct/04/does-berlin-anti-gentrification-law-really-work-neukolln

Co-operatives UK (2008) *Starting a Co-operative: a guide to setting up a democratically controlled business*, Manchester: Cooperatives UK.

Councillors Commission (2007) *Representing the Future*, London: Department for Communities and Local Government.

Covey, J. G. (2000) 'Is critical cooperation possible? Influencing the World Bank through operational collaboration and policy dialogue', in Fox and Brown (2000), pp 81-119.

Cramme, O. and Diamond, P. (eds) (2009) *Social Justice in the Global Age*, Cambridge: Polity Press.

Crick, B. (ed) (2001) *Citizens: towards a citizenship culture*, Oxford: Blackwell Publishers.

Crick, B. and Lockyer, A. (eds) (2010) *Active Citizenship: what could it achieve and how?*, Edinburgh: Edinburgh University Press.

Croly, H. (1998) *Progressive Democracy*, New York: Transaction Publishers.

Crosland, P. and Liebmann, M. (eds) (2003) *40 Cases: restorative justice and victim–offender mediation*, Bristol: Mediation UK.

Culpitt, I. (1992) *Welfare and Citizenship*, London: Sage Publications.

Curtis, M. (1998) *The Great Deception*, London: Pluto Press.

Dahl, R. A. (1989) *Democracy and Its Critics*, New Haven: Yale University Press.

Daniels, N. (ed) (1975) *Reading Rawls: critical studies of A Theory of Justice*, Oxford: Basil Blackwell.

Davies, C., Wetherell, M. and Barnett, E. (2006) *Citizens at the Centre: deliberative participation in healthcare decisions*, Bristol: Policy Press.

Davies, Z. and McMahon, W. (eds) (2007) *Debating Youth Justice: from punishment to problem solving*, London: Centre for Crime and Justice Studies.

De Tocqueville, A. (1981) *Democracy in America*, New York: Random House.

Dearden, L. (2016) 'The Sun and Daily Mail accused of "fuelling prejudice" in report on rising racist violence and hate speech in UK', *Independent*: www.independent.co.uk/news/media/press/the-sun-and-daily-mail-fuelling-prejudice-racist-violence-hate-crime-speech-uk-ecri-report-a7351856.html

Deckman, M. M. (2004) *School Board Battles: the Christian Right in local politics*, Washington, DC: Georgetown University Press.

Derber, C. (1998) *Corporation Nation: how corporations are taking over our lives and what we can do about it*, New York: St. Martin's Press.

Derber, C. (2001) 'Corporate Power in the New Gilded Age', in Tam (2001a), pp 182-192.

Devlin, H. (2016) 'Cut-throat academia leads to "natural selection of bad science", claims study', *The Guardian*: www.theguardian.com/science/2016/sep/21/cut-throat-academia-leads-to-natural-selection-of-bad-science-claims-study

Dewey, J. (1921) *Reconstruction in Philosophy*, London: University of London Press.

Dewey, J. (1930) *The Quest for Certainty*, London: George Allen & Unwin Ltd.

Dewey, J. (1944) *Democracy and Education*, New York: The Free Press.

Dewey, J. (1962) *A Common Faith*, New Haven: Yale University Press.

Dewey, J. (1973) *Lectures in China, 1919–1920*, Honolulu: The University Press of Hawaii.

Dewey, J. (1991) *The Public and Its Problems*, Athens: Ohio University Press.

Diamond, L. and Plattner, M. F. (eds) (2015) *Democracy in Decline?*, Baltimore: Johns Hopkins University Press.

Dickinson, T. (2013) 'How Republicans rig the game', *Rolling Stone*: www.rollingstone.com/politics/news/how-republicans-rig-the-game-20131111

Diehl, P. F. (ed) (1997) *The Politics of Global Governance*, Boulder: Lynne Rienner Publishers.

Dodds, L. and Akkoc, R. (2015) 'Mapped: where is Ukip's support strongest? Where there are no immigrants', *Telegraph*: www.telegraph.co.uk/news/politics/ukip/11539388/Mapped-where-is-Ukips-support-strongest-Where-there-are-no-immigrants.html

Dorling, D. (2013) *Unequal Health: the scandal of our times*, Bristol: Policy Press.

Downie, R. S. and Telfer, E. (1971) *Respect for Persons*, London: George Allen & Unwin.

Downs, J. (2012) 'Focus on exams and get the curriculum right first, says CBI', *Local Schools Network*: www.localschoolsnetwork.org.uk/2012/11/focus-on-exams-at-18-and-get-the-curriculum-right-first-says-cbi

Drakeford, M. (2014) *Social Policy and Privatisation*, London: Routledge.

Dreyfus, H. and Rabinow, P. (1982) *Michel Foucault: beyond structuralism and hermeneutics*, Brighton: The Harvester Press.

Drury, S. (2005) *The Political Ideas of Leo Strauss*, Basingstoke: Palgrave Macmillan.

Duff, R. A. (1990) *Intention, Agency and Criminal Liability*, Oxford: Blackwell.

Duffy, S. J. (2016) *Citizenship and the Welfare State*, Centre for Welfare Reform: www.centreforwelfarereform.org/uploads/attachment/487/citizenship-and-the-welfare-state.pdf

Durkheim, E. (1984) *The Division of Labour in Society*, Basingstoke: Macmillan.

Eagleton, T. (2002) 'Humanity and other animals', *The Guardian*: www.theguardian.com/books/2002/sep/07/highereducation.news2

Easlea, B. (1980) *Witch Hunting, Magic and the New Philosophy: an introduction to the debates of the scientific revolution 1450–1750*, Brighton: The Harvester Press.

Eaton, G. (2013) 'Why is Nigel Farage on Question Time so often?', *New Statesman*: www.newstatesman.com/politics/2013/06/why-nigel-farage-question-time-so-often

Economist Briefing (2016) 'The post-truth world: Yes, I'd lie to you', *Economist*: www.economist.com/news/briefing/21706498-dishonesty-politics-nothing-new-manner-which-some-politicians-now-lie-and

Economist Intelligence Unit (2016) 'Democracy in an age of anxiety': www.eiumedia.com/index.php/latest-press-releases/item/2127-democracy-in-an-age-of-anxiety

Edwards, M. and Gaventa, J. (eds) (2001) *Global Citizen Action*, Boulder: Lynne Rienner Publishers.

Ekins, P. (1992) *A New World Order: grassroots movements for global change*, London: Routledge.

Elgot, J. (2016) 'Philip Hammond defends "doom and gloom" Brexit forecast', *The Guardian*: www.theguardian.com/uk-news/2016/nov/24/philip-hammond-defends-doom-and-gloom-brexit-forecast

Elgot, J. (2017) 'Conservatives fined record £70,000 for campaign spending failures', *The Guardian*: www.theguardian.com/politics/2017/mar/16/conservatives-fined-70000-for-campaign-spending-failures

Endenburg, G. (1998) *Sociocracy: the organization of decision-making*, Delft: Eburon.

Etzioni, A. (1997) *The New Golden Rule: community and morality in a democratic society*, New York: Basic Books.

Evers, W. M. (1998) 'How progressive education gets it wrong', *Hoover Digest*: www.hoover.org/research/how-progressive-education-gets-it-wrong

Fainzylber, P., Lederman, D. and Loayza, N. (2002) 'Inequality and violent crime', *Journal of Law and Economics*, 45(1): 1-40.

Farmer, P. (2005) *Pathologies of Power*, Berkeley and Los Angeles: University of California Press.

Farrell, D. M. (2011) *Electoral Systems: a comparative introduction*, Basingstoke: Palgrave.

Faulkner, R. K. (1993) *Francis Bacon and the Project of Progress*, Lanham: Rowman & Littlefield.

Feyerabend, P. (1975) 'How to defend society against science', in Hacking (1981), pp 156-167.

Feyerabend, P. (2010) *Against Method*, New York: Verso.

Fielding, M. (2011) 'Schools for democracy', in Lawson and Spours (2011), pp 34-39.

Fishkin, J. and Laslett, P. (eds) (2003) *Debating Deliberative Democracy*, Oxford: Blackwell.

Fitzgerald, R. (2010) 'Active citizenship: gender equality and democracy', in Crick and Lockyer (2010), pp 71-84.

Foucault, M. (1991) *Discipline and Punish: the birth of the prison*, London: Penguin.

Foley, D. (2008) *Adam's Fallacy: a guide to economic theology*, Cambridge, MA: Harvard University Press.

Follett, M. P. (1998) *The New State*, University Park: Pennsylvania State University Press.

Forster, K. (2016) 'Hate crimes soared by 41% after Brexit vote, official figures reveal', *Independent*: www.independent.co.uk/news/uk/crime/brexit-hate-crimes-racism-eu-referendum-vote-attacks-increase-police-figures-official-a7358866.html

Fox, J. A. and Brown, L. D. (eds) (2000) *The Struggle for Accountability*, Cambridge, MA: MIT Press.

Frank, T. (2006) *What's the Matter with America: the resistible rise of the American Right*, London: Vintage Books.

Freeland, C. (2012) *Plutocrats: the rise of the new global super-rich and the fall of everyone else*, London: Penguin Publishing.

Freire, P. (1996) *Pedagogy of the Oppressed*, London: Penguin.

Frydman, R. and Goldberg, M. D. (2011) *Beyond Mechanical Markets: asset price swings, risk and the role of the state*, Princeton: Princeton University Press.

Fukuyama, F. (1992) *The End of History and the Last Man*, London: Hamish Hamilton.

Fulbrook, M. (1996) 'Germany for the Germans?', in Cesarani and Fulbrook (1996), pp 88–105.

Fung, A. and Wright, E. O. (2001) 'Deepening democracy: innovations in empowered participatory governance', *Politics & Society*, 29(1): 5–41.

Gardiner, T. (2010) *Community Engagement and Empowerment: a guide for councillors*, London: Improvement & Development Agency.

Garland, J. and Brett, W. (2014) *Open Up: the future of the political party*, London: Electoral Reform Society.

Gastil, J. (2000) *By Popular Demand: revitalizing representative democracy through deliberative elections*, Berkeley: University of California Press.

Gay, P. (1973) *The Enlightenment: an interpretation – vol 1, The rise of modern paganism*, London: Wildwood House.

Gellner, E. (2009) *Nations and Nationalism*, Ithaca: Cornell University Press.

Gibson, T. (1998) *The doer's guide to planning for real*, Telford: Neighbourhood Initiatives Foundation.

Gilchrist, A., and Taylor, M. (2011) *A Short Guide to Community Development*, Bristol: Policy Press.

Gilpin, R. (2000) *The Challenge of Global Capitalism: the world economy in the 21st century*, Princeton: Princeton University Press.

Goldberg, D. J. (1999) *Discontented America: the United States in the 1920s*, Baltimore: Johns Hopkins University Press.

Goldstein, R. N. (2015) 'Don't overthink it: are Enlightenment ideas messing with your head? Only if you don't understand them', *The Atlantic*: www.theatlantic.com/magazine/archive/2015/05/dont-overthink-it/389519/

Goodman, J. B. and Loveman, G. W. (1991) 'Does privatization serve the public interest?', *Harvard Business Review*: https://hbr.org/1991/11/does-privatization-serve-the-public-interest

Gore, W. (2016) 'In a post-truth world, here's how to spot politicians fact dodging', *Independent*: www.independent.co.uk/voices/post-truth-donald-trump-how-to-spot-the-lies-a7430221.html

Goss, S. (2007) 'How far have we travelled towards a collaborative state?', in Parker and Gallagher (2007), pp 38-47.

Gray, J. (2002) *Straw Dogs: thoughts on humans and other animals*, London: Granta Books.

Gray, J. (2012) 'The violent visions of Slavoj Žižek', *The New York Review of Books*: www.nybooks.com/articles/2012/07/12/violent-visions-slavoj-zizek/

Grayling, A. C. (2007) *Towards the Light: the story of the struggles for liberty and rights*, London: Bloomsbury.

Green, D. P. and Shapiro, I. (2012) *Pathologies of Rational Choice Theory*, New Haven: Yale University Press.

Griswold, C. L. (1999) *Adam Smith and the Virtues of Enlightenment*, Cambridge: Cambridge University Press.

Gross, D. (2008) 'Subprime suspects: the right blames the credit crisis on poor minority homeowners', *Slate*: www.slate.com/articles/business/moneybox/2008/10/subprime_suspects.html

Grossa, S. R., O'Brien, B., Hu, C. and Kennedy, E. H. (2014) 'Rate of false conviction of criminal defendants who are sentenced to death', *Proceedings of the National Academy of Sciences of the United States of America*, 111(20): 7230-7235.

Grossman, R. and Adams, F. (1993) *Taking Care of Business: citizenship and the charter of incorporation*, South Yarmouth, MA: Program on Corporations, Law & Democracy.

Gutmann, A. and Thompson, D. (2004) *Why Deliberative Democracy?*, Princeton: Princeton University Press.

Gvosdev, N. K. (2016) *Communitarian Foreign Policy*, New Brunswick: Transaction Publishers.

Habermas, J. (1986) *Theory of Communicative Action Vol. 1: Reason and the rationalization of society*, Cambridge: Polity.

Habermas, J. (1992) *Autonomy and Solidarity* (ed by P. Dews), London: Verso.

Hacking, I. (ed) (1981) *Scientific Revolutions*, Oxford: Oxford University Press.

Halbrooks, G. (2016) 'Does the media have a liberal bias?', *The Balance*: www.thebalance.com/is-the-media-liberal-2315202

Halsey, A., Lauder, H., Brown, P. and Wells, A. S. (eds) (1996) *Education: culture, economy, society*, Oxford: Oxford University Press.

Hanagan, M. and Tilly, C. (eds) (1999) *Extending Citizenship, Reconfiguring States*, Lanham: Rowman & Littlefield.

Hardaway, R. (2008) *Crisis at the Polls*, Santa Barbara: Greenwood.

Harrison, J. F. C. (2010) *Robert Owen and the Owenites in Britain and America: the quest for the new moral world*, Abingdon: Routledge.

Hartmann, T. (2017) 'The perennial GOP tax scam', *Alternet*: www.alternet.org/right-wing/perennial-gop-tax-scam

Harvey, D. (2007) *A Brief History of Neoliberalism*, Oxford: Oxford University Press.

Hayden, J. (2016) 'Trump is blaming a "rigged election" and his supporters pivot to discussion of "violent rebellion"', *Daily Kos*: www.dailykos.com/story/2016/10/15/1581936/-Trump-is-blaming-a-rigged-election-and-his-supporters-pivot-to-discussion-of-violent-rebellion

Heathcote, E. (2017) 'Grenfell Tower blaze shows we tinker with rules at our peril', *Financial Times*: www.ft.com/content/80c884d4-51af-11e7-a1f2-db19572361bb

Held, D. and McGrew, A. (2002) *Globalization/Anti-Globalization*, Cambridge: Polity Press.

Helm, T. (2017) 'Osborne's huge tax giveaway starts for rich – as the poor are hit', *The Guardian*: www.theguardian.com/politics/2017/apr/01/huge-tax-giveaway-for-rich-as-poor-are-hit-george-osborne-tax-benefit-budget-changes

Hermann, C. (ed) (2015) *Privatization of Public Services*, London: Routledge.

Hertz, N. (2001) *The Silent Takeover: global capitalism and the death of democracy*, London: William Heinemann.

Hirst, P. (1994) *Associative Democracy: new forms of economic and social governance*, Cambridge: Polity Press.

Hobhouse, L. T. (1994) *Liberalism and Other Writings* (ed by J. Meadowcroft), Cambridge: Cambridge University Press.

Hobson, J. (1996) *The Social Problem*, Bristol: Thoemmes Press.

Hofstede, G., Hofstede, G. J. and Minkov, M. (2010) *Cultures and Civilizations*, New York: McGraw-Hill.

Howard, E. (2010) *To-Morrow: a peaceful path to real reform*, Cambridge: Cambridge University Press.

Hunter, J. D. (1991) *Culture War: the struggle to define America*, New York: Basic Books.

Huntington, S. P. (2002) *The Clash of Civilizations and the Remaking of World Order*, London: The Free Press.

Hutner, G. and Mohamed, F. G. (2013) 'The real humanities crisis is happening at public universities', *New Republic*: https://newrepublic.com/article/114616/public-universities-hurt-humanities-crisis

Huws, U. (2016) 'The key criticisms of basic income, and how to overcome them', *Open Democracy*: www.opendemocracy.net/neweconomics/the-key-criticisms-of-basic-income-and-how-to-overcome-them/

Ingham, G. (2014) 'Whose money is it?', *Open Democracy UK*: www.opendemocracy.net/ourkingdom/geoffrey-ingham/whose-money-is-it

Irvin G. (2008) *Super Rich: the rise of inequality in Britain and the United States*, Cambridge: Polity Press.

Jackson, B. (2007) *Equality and the British Left*, Manchester: Manchester University Press.

James, H. (2016) 'The Brexit mentality goes global', Centre for International Governance Innovation: www.cigionline.org/articles/brexit-mentality-goes-global

Jayanetti, C. (2016) 'Government "hid" report revealing full impact of cuts to Sure Start children's centres', *Independent*: www.independent.co.uk/news/uk/politics/government-hid-report-revealing-full-impact-of-cuts-to-sure-start-childrens-centres-a6808321.html

Jenkins, S. P. (2015) 'The income distribution in the UK: a picture of advantage and disadvantage', ISER (Institute for Social & Economic Research) Working Paper Series (No 2015-01): www.iser.essex.ac.uk/research/publications/working-papers/iser/2015-01.pdf

Johnston, I. (2016) 'Fracking allowed in Lancashire in landmark Government ruling', *Independent*: www.independent.co.uk/news/uk/home-news/fracking-lancashire-cuadrilla-sajid-javid-planning-permission-overturned-a7347576.html

Joint Public Issues Team (on behalf of the Baptist Union of Great Britain, Methodist Church, Church of Scotland, and the United Reformed Church) (2013) *The Lies We Tell Ourselves: ending comfortable myths about poverty*, London: Methodist Publishing.

Jones, G. and Stewart, J. (1985) *The Case for Local Government*, London: George Allen and Unwin.

Jones, J. M. (2016) 'Democratic, Republican identification near historical lows', Gallup: www.newstatesman.com/politics/2014/06/rage-against-machine-rise-anti-politics-across-europe

Jones, S. and Roberts, C. (2007) 'Involvement in community involvement: referral order volunteers', in Brennan et al (2007), pp 41-62.

Kagan, R. A., Krygier, M. and Winston, K. (eds) (2002) *Legality and Community: on the intellectual legacy of Philip Selznick*, New York: Rowman & Littlefield.

Karliner, J. (1997) *The Corporate Planet*, San Francisco: Sierra Club Books.

Kasmir, S. (2016) 'The Mondragon Cooperatives: successes and challenges', *Global Dialogue*, 6(1): http://isa-global-dialogue.net/the-mondragon-cooperatives-successes-and-challenges/

Katwala, S., Ballinger, S. and Rhodes, M. (2014) *How to Talk About Immigration*, London: British Future.

Keen, R. and Audickas, L. (2016) *Membership of UK Political Parties*, London: House of Commons Library (SN05125).

Kennedy, B. P., Kawachi, I., Lochner, K., Jones, C. P. and Prothrow-Stith, D. (1997) '(Dis)respect and black mortality', *Ethnicity and Disease*, 7: 207–214.

Kessler, G. (2016) 'The biggest Pinocchios of election 2016', *Washington Post*: www.washingtonpost.com/news/fact-checker/wp/2016/11/04/the-biggest-pinocchios-of-election-2016/

King, D. S. (1987) *The New Right: politics, markets and citizenship*, Basingstoke: Macmillan.

Kinsky, F. (2001) 'Federalism and the personalist tradition', in Tam (2001a), pp 54–65.

Kintz, L. (1997) *Between Jesus and the Market: the emotions that matter in right-wing America*, Durham: Duke University Press.

Kirchgaessner, S. (2017) 'Democrats question Trump "conflict of interest" with Deutsche Bank', *The Guardian*: www.theguardian.com/business/2017/mar/11/democrats-question-trump-conflict-of-interest-deutsche-bank-investigation-money-laundering

Klein, N. (2001) *No Logo*, London: Flamingo.

Klein, N. (2007) *The Shock Doctrine*, London: Penguin Books.

Konnikova, M. (2017) 'Trump's lies vs. your brain', *Politico*: www.politico.com/magazine/story/2017/01/donald-trump-lies-liar-effect-brain-214658

Koven, S. G. (2008) *Responsible Governance: a case study approach*, New York: M. E. Sharpe.

Kuhn, D. P. (2012) 'The incredible polarization and politicization of the Supreme Court', *The Atlantic*: www.theatlantic.com/politics/archive/2012/06/the-incredible-polarization-and-politicization-of-the-supreme-court/259155/

Kuhn, T. (1970) *The Structure of Scientific Revolutions*, Chicago: University of Chicago Press.

Kuhne, J. (2015) 'Notable urban commons around the world', in Bollier and Helfrich (2015), pp 92–99.

Kumar, K. (1996) 'The post-modern condition', in Halsey et al (1996), pp 96–112.

Kurtz, P. and Dondeyne, A. (eds) (1972) *A Catholic/Humanist Dialogue: humanists and Roman Catholics in a common world*, London: Pemberton Books.

Lakatos, I. and Musgrave, A. (eds) (1970) *Criticism and the Growth of Knowledge*, Cambridge: Cambridge University Press.

Laudan, L. (1981) 'A problem-solving approach to scientific progress', in Hacking (1981), pp 144-155.

Lawson, N. (2013) 'The failure of politics won't be solved by single-issue campaigners', *The Guardian*: www.theguardian.com/commentisfree/2013/jun/17/build-good-society-formal-informal-politics

Lawson, N. and Spours, K. (eds) (2011) *Education for the Good Society*, London: Compass.

Layton, L. (2016) 'GOP-led states increasingly taking control from local school boards', *The Washington Post*: www.washingtonpost.com/local/education/gop-led-states-increasingly-taking-control-from-local-school-boards/2016/02/01/c01a8e4e-bad3-11e5-b682-4bb4dd403c7d_story.html

Lees, L. (2013) 'Regeneration in London has pushed poor families out', *The Guardian*: www.theguardian.com/local-government-network/2013/aug/29/mixed-communities-plan-government-regeneration

Lent, T. and Trivedy, R. (2001) 'National coalitions and global campaigns: the international children's rights movement', in Edwards and Gaventa (2001), pp 163-174.

Leonard, M. (2014) 'Rage against the machine: the rise of anti-politics across Europe', *New Statesman*: www.newstatesman.com/politics/2014/06/rage-against-machine-rise-anti-politics-across-europe

Levi, I. (1984) *Decisions and Revisions*, Cambridge: Cambridge University Press.

Lewis, M. and Conaty, P. (2012) *The Resilience Imperative: cooperative transitions to a steady-state economy*, Gabriola Island: New Society Publishers.

Lewis, S. (2005) *It Can't Happen Here*, New York: Signet Classics.

Lowles, N. (2015) 'The sham of voter registration in the UK', *Open Democracy*: www.opendemocracy.net/ourkingdom/nick-lowles/sham-of-voter-registration-in-uk

Lowndes, J. E. (2008) *From the New Deal to the New Right*, New Haven: Yale University Press.

Lukes, S. (1973) *Emile Durkheim: his life and work*, Harmondsworth: Penguin Books.

Lusher, A. (2016) 'EU immigrants help create jobs, not take them, study claims', *Independent*: www.independent.co.uk/news/uk/politics/eu-referendum-immigration-immigrants-jobs-brexit-remain-what-happens-unemployment-a7091566.html

Lux, M. (2009) *The Progressive Revolution*, Hoboken: John Wiley & Sons.

Lynd, S. (1975) 'Brandenburg v. Ohio: a speech test for all seasons?', *University of Chicago Law Review*, 43(1), Article 10: 151-191.

MacLean, N. (2017) *Democracy in Chains: the deep history of the radical right's stealth plan for America*, New York: Viking Press.

Macmurray, J. (1995) *Persons in Relation*, London: Faber & Faber.

Mandeville, B. (1970) *The Fable of the Bees*, London: Penguin Books.

Maris, C. W., (1995) 'Franglais: on liberalism, nationalism, and multiculturalism', in Van Willigenburg et al (1995), pp 57-98.

Marmot Review (2010) *Fair Society, Healthy Lives*, London: The Marmot Review.

Marquand, D. (2004) *Decline of the Public*, Cambridge: Polity Press.

Martinson, J. and Mason, R. (2016) 'Theresa May had private meeting with Rupert Murdoch', *The Guardian*: www.theguardian.com/media/2016/sep/29/theresa-may-meeting-rupert-murdoch-times-sun

Mathews, M. and Soon, D. (2016) 'Cultivating in new citizens a heart for Singapore', *The Straits Times*: www.straitstimes.com/opinion/cultivating-in-new-citizens-a-heart-for-singapore

Matthews, D. (2013) 'What "Dallas Buyers Club" got wrong about the AIDS crisis', *Washington Post*: www.washingtonpost.com/news/wonk/wp/2013/12/10/what-dallas-buyers-club-got-wrong-about-the-aids-crisis/

Mattson, K. (1998) *Creating a Democratic Public*, University Park: Pennsylvania State University Press.

Mayer, J. (2017) *Dark Money: the hidden history of the billionaires behind the rise of the radical right*, New York: Anchor Books.

Mayo, E. (2016) *Values: how to bring values to life in your business*, Shipley: Greenleaf Publishing.

Mayo, M. and Annette, J. (eds) (2010) *Taking Part: active learning for active citizenship, and beyond*, Leicester: National Institute of Adult Continuing Education.

Mayo, M., Mediwelso-Bendek, Z. and Packham, C. (eds) (2013) *Community Research for Community Development*, Basingstoke: Palgrave Macmillan.

McCabe, A., Chilton, L., Purdue, D., Evans, L., Wilson, M. and Ardon, R. (2007) *Learning to Change Neighbourhoods: lessons from the Guide Neighbourhoods programme*, London: Department for Communities and Local Government.

McCarthy, T. (1981) *The Critical Theory of Jurgen Habermas*, Cambridge, MA: MIT Press.

McClain, L. C. (2001) 'The domain of civic virtue in a good society: families, schools and sex equality', *Fordham Law Review*, 69(5): 1617-1666.

McGirr, L. (2002) *Suburban Warriors: the origins of the New American Right*, Princeton: Princeton University Press.

McGregor, J. (2005) *Students as Researchers*, Cranfield: National College of School Leadership.

McMahon, D. M. (2001) *Enemies of the Enlightenment: the French counter-enlightenment and the making of modernity*, Oxford: Oxford University Press.

Meek, J. (2015) *Private Island: why Britain now belongs to someone else*, London: Verso.

Mei, Y.P. (1929) *The Ethical and Political Works of Motse*, London: Arthur Probsthain.

Meleady, R., Seger, C. R. & Vermue, M. (2017) 'Examining the role of positive and negative intergroup contact and anti-immigrant prejudice in Brexit', *British Journal of Social Psychology*: http://onlinelibrary.wiley.com/doi/10.1111/bjso.12203/full

Meyer-Bisch, P. (1995) *Culture of Democracy: a challenge for schools*, Paris: UNESCO.

Milam, G. (2017) 'Hate crime surges in America since Trump presidency', *Sky News*: http://news.sky.com/story/hate-crime-surges-in-america-since-trump-presidency-10876580

Milanovich, B. (2012) *The Haves and the Have-Nots*, New York: Basic Books.

Mill, J. S., (1993) *Auguste Comte and Positivism*, Bristol: Thoemmes Press.

Mill, J. S. (2008) *Considerations on Representative Government*, Rockville: Serenity Publishers.

Miller, R. W. (1987) *Fact and Method: explanation, confirmation and reality in the natural and the social sciences*, Princeton: Princeton University Press.

Milne, S. (2014) 'Who's to blame for the crisis, bankers or benefit claimants?', *The Guardian*: www.theguardian.com/commentisfree/2014/jan/16/crisis-bankers-benefit-claimants-class

Mindock, C. (2017) 'Donald Trump sued over business ties as attorneys general allege "unprecedented constitutional violations"', *Independent*: www.independent.co.uk/news/world/americas/us-politics/trump-sued-hotel-payments-conflicts-interest-emoluments-attorney-general-washington-maryland-a7786441.html

Monbiot, G. (2010) 'This state-hating free marketeer ignores his own failed experiment', *The Guardian*, 1 June 2010.

Morozov, E. (2011) *The Net Delusion*, London: Penguin Books.

Mullineux, A. (2014) 'The big bang: how demutualisation of building societies failed', *Co-operative News*: www.thenews.coop/85589/news/general/big-bang-demutualisation-building-societies-failed/

Mutch, R. E. (2014) *Buying the Vote: a history of campaign finance reform*, Oxford: Oxford University Press.

Nisen, M. (2013) 'They finally tested the "Prisoner's Dilemma" on actual prisoners – and the results were not what you would expect', *Business Insider*: http://uk.businessinsider.com/prisoners-dilemma-in-real-life-2013-7

North West Together We Can (2008) *Routes to Empowerment*, Stockport: North West Together We Can.

Nozick, R. (1977) *Anarchy, State, and Utopia*, New York: Basic Books.

O'Connor, S. and Warrell, H. (2017) 'Net migration falls by a quarter as EU citizens leave UK', *Financial Times*: www.ft.com/content/81b25aa0-4129-11e7-9d56-25f963e998b2

O'Donoghue, G. (2016) 'US election 2016: voter ID laws threaten lifelong voters', BBC News: www.bbc.co.uk/news/election-us-2016-37569855

Office for National Statistics (2017) 'Electoral statistics for UK: 2016': www.ons.gov.uk/peoplepopulationandcommunity/elections/electoralregistration/bulletins/electoralstatisticsforuk/2016#total-number-of-uk-parliamentary-electors-increases

Onion, R. (2013) 'Take the impossible "literacy" test Louisiana gave black voters in the 1960s', *Slate*: www.slate.com/blogs/the_vault/2013/06/28/voting_rights_and_the_supreme_court_the_impossible_literacy_test_louisiana.html

Orlin, B. (2013) 'When memorization gets in the way of learning', *The Atlantic*: www.theatlantic.com/education/archive/2013/09/when-memorization-gets-in-the-way-of-learning/279425/

Ostrom, E. (2015) 'Eight design principles for successful commons', in Bollier and Helfrich (2015), pp 47-49.

Pagden, A. (2013) *The Enlightenment and why it still matters*, Oxford, Oxford University Press.

Parker, S. and Gallagher, N. (eds) (2007) *The Collaborative State*, London: Demos.

Parry, M. (2011) 'Raymond Tallis takes out the "Neurotrash"', *The Chronicle of Higher Education*: www.chronicle.com/article/Raymond-Tallis-Takes-Out-the/129279/

Pateman, C. (1970) *Participation and Democratic Theory*, Cambridge: Cambridge University Press.

Pearce, F. (2011) *Peoplequake: mass migration, ageing nations, and the coming population crash*, London: Eden Project Books.

Peirce, C. S. (1992) *Reasoning and the Logic of Things*, Cambridge, MA: Harvard University Press.

Pérotin, V. (2016) *What Do We Really Know About Worker Co-operatives?* Manchester: Co-operatives UK.

Peterson, R. T. (1996) *Democratic Philosophy and the Politics of Knowledge*, University Park: Pennsylvania State University Press.

Phillips, C. (2007) 'Ethnicity, identity and community cohesion in prison', in Wetherell et al (2007), pp 75-86.

Phillips, T. (2016) 'Democracy is a joke, says China – just look at Donald Trump', *The Guardian*: www.theguardian.com/us-news/2016/mar/17/democracy-is-a-joke-says-china-just-look-at-donald-trump

Piketty, T. (2014) *Capital in the Twenty-First Century*, Cambridge, MA: Harvard University Press.

Ponsford, D. (2017) 'Daily Mail and Sun launch front-page attacks on Corbyn as Fleet Street lines up behind Theresa May', *Press Gazette*: www.pressgazette.co.uk/daily-mail-and-sun-launch-front-page-attacks-on-corbyn-as-fleet-street-lines-up-behind-theresa-may/

Popper, K. (1966) *The Open Society and its Enemies*, London: Routledge & Kegan Paul.

Post, R. C. (2014) *Citizens Divided: campaign finance reform and the Constitution*, Cambridge, MA: Harvard University Press.

Postel, D. (2003) 'Gray's Anatomy', *The Nation*: www.thenation.com/article/grays-anatomy/

Preston, A. (2015) 'The war against humanities at Britain's universities', *The Guardian*: www.theguardian.com/education/2015/mar/29/war-against-humanities-at-britains-universities

Preston, P. (2017) 'Nothing can stop the mighty Ofcom: except, perhaps, the BBC', *The Guardian*: www.theguardian.com/media/2017/jan/08/ofcom-nothing-can-stop-except-perhaps-bbc-regulation

Pring, J. (2016) 'Government set to slash equality watchdog's budget … again', *Disability News Service*: www.disabilitynewsservice.com/government-set-to-slash-equality-watchdogs-budget-again/

Prior, D., Stewart, J. and Walsh, K. (1995) *Citizenship: rights, community and participation*, London: Pitman Publishing.

Prokop, A. (2014) '40 charts that explain money in politics', *Vox*: www.vox.com/2014/7/30/5949581/money-in-politics-charts-explain

Putnam, R. D., Leonardi, R. and Nenetti, R. Y. (1993) *Making Democracy Work: civic traditions in modern Italy*, Princeton: Princeton University Press.

Putnam, R. D. (2011) *Bowling Alone: the collapse and revival of American community*, New York: Simon & Schuster.

Putnam, R. D. (2015) *Our Kids: the American dream in crisis*, New York: Simon & Schuster.

Putterman, T. L. (2006) 'Berlin's two concepts of liberty: a reassessment and revision', *Polity*, 38(3): 416–446.

Quirk, B. (2011) *Re-imagining Government: public leadership and management in challenging times*, Basingstoke: Palgrave Macmillan.

Rachels, J. (1997) *Can Ethics Provide Answers?*, Lanham: Rowman & Littlefield.

Ramesh, R. (2012) 'Equality and Human Rights Commission has workforce halved', *The Guardian*: www.theguardian.com/society/2012/may/15/equality-human-rights-commission-cuts

Ranson, S. and Stewart, J. (1994) *Managing for the Public Domain: enabling the learning society*, Basingstoke: Macmillan Press.

Rapport, N., (2013) 'Power and identity', in Clegg and Haugaard (2013), pp 194–209.

Rawls, J. (1973) *A Theory of Justice*, Oxford: Oxford University Press.

Rawls, J. (2005) *Political Liberalism*, New York: Columbia University Press.

Reeves, J. (2016) 'Top 10 list of corporate donors to political parties reads like a most-hated-companies ranking', *MarketWatch*: www.marketwatch.com/story/these-10-companies-could-influence-the-presidential-election-again-2016-06-16

Regan, M. D. (2016) 'What does voter turnout tell us about the 2016 election?', *PBS*: www.pbs.org/newshour/updates/voter-turnout-2016-elections/

Reich, R. (2009) *Supercapitalism: the battle for democracy in the age of big business*, London: Icon Books.

Reich, W. (1970) *The Mass Psychology of Fascism*, Harmondsworth: Penguin Books.

Rethinking Crime & Punishment (2004): *Rethinking Crime & Punishment: the report*, London: Esmée Fairbairn Foundation.

Richardson, H. (2014) *To Make Men Free: a history of the Republican Party*, New York: Basic Books.

Richie, R. and Hill, S. (1999) *Reflecting All of Us: the case for proportional representation*, Boston: Beacon Press.

Ridley, M. (1996) *The Origins of Virtue*, New York: Viking.

Roberts, R. (2017a) 'Immigration raids in at least six states following Donald Trump's order to deport illegal immigrants', *Independent*: www.independent.co.uk/news/world/americas/immigration-raids-us-donald-trump-crackdown-illegal-immigrants-order-deportation-a7574796.html

Roberts, R. (2017b) 'Muslim-majority countries where Donald Trump does business left untouched by travel ban', *Independent*: www.independent.co.uk/news/world/americas/muslim-majority-countries-donald-trump-travel-ban-immigration-entry-visa-three-main-countries-exempt-a7552526.html

Rodgers, D. T. (1998) *Atlantic Crossing: social politics in a progressive age*, Cambridge, MA: Belknap Press of Harvard University Press.

Rodriguez, L. (2016) 'The troubling partisanship of the Supreme Court', *Stanford Political Journal*: https://stanfordpolitics.com/the-troubling-partisanship-of-the-supreme-court-da9fd5a900ac

Rorty, R. (1990) 'On Heidegger's nazism', in Rorty (1999), pp 190-197.

Rorty, R. (1998) *Truth and Progress*, Cambridge: Cambridge University Press.

Rorty, R. (1999) *Philosophy and Social Hope*, London: Penguin Books.

Ross, N. A., Wolfson, M. C., Dunn, J. R., Berthelot, J. M., Kaplan, G. A. and Lynch, J. W. (2000) 'Relation between income inequality and mortality in Canada and in the US', *British Medical Journal*, 320: 898-902.

Rumbaugh, A. (2012) 'In Florida, 1 in 4 blacks of voting age cannot vote because of felony conviction', *NBC News*: http://investigations.nbcnews.com/_news/2012/09/11/13806293-in-florida-1-in-4-blacks-of-voting-age-cannot-vote-because-of-felony-conviction

Sandel, M. (1996) *Democracy's Discontent: America in search of a public philosophy*, Cambridge, MA: Harvard University Press.

Sanders, B. (2017) 'How corporate media threatens our democracy', *In These Times*: http://inthesetimes.com/features/bernie-sanders-corporate-media-threatens-our-democracy.html

Schlesinger, A. M., (1974) *The Imperial Presidency*, New York: Popular Library.

Schmidt, J. (ed) (1996) *What is Enlightenment*, Berkeley: University of California Press.

Schumpeter, J. (1976) *Capitalism, Socialism and Democracy*, London: George Allen & Unwin.

Schwarcz, V. (1986) *The Chinese Enlightenment: intellectuals and the legacy of the May Fourth Movement of 1919*, Oakland: University of California Press.

Schwarz, A. O. and Huq, A. Z. (2007) *Unchecked and Unbalanced: presidential power in a time of terror*, New York: New Press.

Scott-Samuel, A., Bambra, C., Collins, C., Hunter, D. J., McCartney, G. and Smith, K. (2014) 'The impact of Thatcherism on health and well-being in Britain', *International Journal of Health Services*, 44(1): 53–71.

Seeley, T. D. (2010) *Honeybee Democracy*, Princeton: Princeton University Press.

Selznick, P. (1992) *The Moral Commonwealth: social theory and the promise of community*, Berkeley and Los Angeles: University of California Press.

Semler, R. (1993) *Maverick! The success story behind the world's most unusual workplace*, London: Arrow.

Sennett, R. (2003) *Respect: the formation of character in an age of inequality*, London: Penguin Books.

Shanahan, S. (1999) 'Scripted debates: twentieth-century immigration and citizenship policy in Great Britain, Ireland, and the United States', in Hanagan and Tilly (1999), pp 67-96.

Sheppard, K. (2011) 'The Koch Brothers' vast right-wing media conspiracy', *Mother Jones*: www.motherjones.com/environment/2011/02/koch-brothers-media-beck-greenpeace

Simmons, A. M. (2017) 'Russia's meddling in other nations' elections is nothing new. Just ask the Europeans', *Los Angeles Times*: www.latimes.com/world/europe/la-fg-russia-election-meddling-20170330-story.html

Sims, A. (2016) 'Tory austerity has "gravely and systematically" violated disabled people's rights, UN says', *Independent*: www.independent.co.uk/news/tory-austerity-has-gravely-and-systematically-violated-disabled-peoples-rights-un-says-a7405786.html

Sirianni, C. and Friedland, L. (2001) *Civic Innovations in America: community empowerment, public policy and the movement for civic renewal*, Berkeley and Los Angeles: University of California Press.

Skinner, Q. (1990) 'The republican ideal of political liberty', in Bock et al (1990), pp 293-309.

Smith, A. (1976) *An Inquiry into the Nature and Causes of the Wealth of Nations*, Oxford: Oxford University Press.

Smith, A. D. (2010) *Nationalism*, Cambridge: Polity Press.

Smith, G. (2005) *Beyond the Ballot*, London: The Power Inquiry.

Smith, W. (2014) 'Political donations corrupt democracy in ways you might not realise', *The Guardian*: www.theguardian.com/commentisfree/2014/sep/11/political-donations-corrupt-democracy-in-ways-you-might-not-realise

Sodha, S. (2017) 'Is Finland's basic universal income a solution to automation, fewer jobs and lower wages?', *The Guardian*: www.theguardian.com/society/2017/feb/19/basic-income-finland-low-wages-fewer-jobs

Sperling, G. (2009) 'The progressive challenge: shared prosperity', in Cramme and Diamond (2009), pp 239-258.

Standing, G. (2014) *The Precariat; the new dangerous class*, London: Bloomsbury Academic.

Stevenson, A. (2013) 'The dangerous denigration of public sector management', *Policy Network*: www.policy-network.net/pno_detail.aspx?ID=4506&title=The+dangerous+denigration+of+public+sector+management

Stewart, D. (2016) 'Future post-truth', *America*: www.americamagazine.org/content/dispatches/future-post-truth

Stiglitz, J. (2010) *Freefall: free markets and the sinking of the global economy*, London: Penguin Books.

Stiglitz, J. (2013) *The Price of Inequality*, London: Penguin Books.

Strang, H. and Braithwaite, J. (eds) (2001) *Restorative Justice and Civil Society*, Cambridge: Cambridge University Press.

Sweney, M. (2017) 'Education publisher Pearson reports biggest loss in its history', *The Guardian*: www.theguardian.com/business/2017/feb/24/education-publisher-pearson-loss-us-penguin-random-house

Taibbi, M. (2014) *The Divide: American injustice in the age of the wealth gap*, New York: Spiegel & Grau.

Tallis, R. (1999) *Enemies of Hope: a critique of contemporary pessimism*, Basingstoke: Macmillan Press.

Tallis, R. (2011) *Aping Mankind – neuromania, Darwinitis and the misrepresentation of humanity*, London: Routledge.

Tam, H. (1990) *A Philosophical Study of the Criteria for Responsibility Ascriptions: responsibility and personal interactions*, Lampeter: Edwin Mellen Press.

Tam, H. (ed) (1994) *Marketing, Competition and the Public Sector*, Harlow: Longman.

Tam, H. (1998), *Communitarianism: a new agenda for politics and citizenship*, Basingstoke: Macmillan.

Tam, H. (ed) (2001a) *Progressive Politics in the Global Age*, Cambridge: Polity Press.

Tam, H. (2001b) 'What is *the* Third Way?', *Responsive Communities*, 11(2): 71-75.

Tam, H. (2007a) 'The case for progressive solidarity', in Wetherell et al (2007), pp 17-23.

Tam, H. (2007b) 'Overcoming the hidden barriers', in Parker and Gallagher (2007), pp 142-152).

Tam, H. (2011a) 'Some like it thick: what does it really take for us to live together', *Ethnicities*, 11(3): 355-359.

Tam, H. (2011b) 'The big con: reframing the state-society debate', *PPR Journal*, 18(1): 30-40.

Tam, H. (2013) 'Cooperative problem-solving and education', *Forum for Promoting 3-19 Comprehensive Education*, 55(2): 185-201.

Tam, H. (2014) 'Quincentenary of the 1514 watershed', *Question the Powerful*: http://henry-tam.blogspot.co.uk/2014/01/question-powerful-quincentenary-of-1514.html

Tam, H. (2015a) *Against Power Inequalities* (2nd ed), London: Birkbeck.

Tam, H. (2015b) 'Find out more about Together We Can': http://hbtam.blogspot.co.uk/2015/05/find-out-more-about-together-we-can.html

Tam, H. (2015c) 'Towards an open cooperativist development agency', P2P Foundation: https://blog.p2pfoundation.net/towards-an-open-cooperativist-development-agency-henry-tam/2015/03/04

Tam, H. (ed) (forthcoming) *Whose Government is it? The renewal of state-citizen cooperation*, Bristol: Policy Press.

Taub, A. (2016) 'How stable are democracies?', *New York Times*: www.nytimes.com/2016/11/29/world/americas/western-liberal-democracy.html

Taylor, M. (2001) 'Party democracy and civic renewal', in Crick (2001), pp 18-26.

Tetalman, J. and Belitsos, B. (2005) *One World Democracy: a progressive vision for enforcing global law*, San Rafael: Origin Press.

Thomas, M. (2009) *Think Community: intergenerational practice and informal adult learning*, Leicester: NIACE.

Thompson, D. (2017) 'Trump's budget is a cruel con', *The Atlantic*: www.theatlantic.com/business/archive/2017/05/trump-budget-proposal-con/527667/

Thompson, M. J. (ed) (2007) *Confronting the New Conservatism*, New York: New York University Press.

Timmins, N. (1996) *The Five Giants: a biography of the welfare state*, London: Fontana Press.

Tomasello, M. (2009) *Why We Cooperate*, Cambridge, MA: MIT Press.

Trudo, H. (2016) 'Trump escalates attack on "Mexican" judge', *Politico*: www.politico.com/story/2016/06/donald-trump-judge-gonzalo-curiel-223849

Urbach, P. (1987) *Francis Bacon's Philosophy of Science*, La Salle: Open Court Publishing.

Uslaner, E. (2002) *The Moral Foundation of Trust*, New York: Cambridge University Press.

Van Biezen, I., Mair, P. and Poguntke, T. (2011) 'Going, going, ... gone? The decline of party membership in contemporary Europe', *European Journal of Political Research*, 51(1): 24-56.

Van Willigenburg, T., Heeger, F. R. and van der Burg, W. (eds) (1995) *Nation, State and the Coexistence of Different Communities*, Kampen: Kok Pharos Publishing House.

Venook, J. (2017) 'Trump's interests vs. America's, Russian trademarks edition', *The Atlantic*: www.theatlantic.com/business/archive/2017/06/donald-trump-conflicts-of-interests/508382/

Walby, S. (2009) *Globalization and Inequalities*, London: Sage.

Waldman, M. (2014) *The Second Amendment: a biography*, New York: Simon & Schuster.

Wales, J. (2017) 'With the power of online transparency, together we can beat fake news', *The Guardian*: www.theguardian.com/commentisfree/2017/feb/03/online-transparency-fake-news-internet

Walker, A. (2013) 'Why teach cooperative problem-solving in adult education?', *Forum for Promoting 3–19 Comprehensive Education*, 55(2): 217-225.

Walker, P. (2017) 'More than 2.3m people have registered to vote since election was called', *The Guardian*: www.theguardian.com/politics/2017/may/22/more-than-23m-people-have-registered-to-vote-since-election-was-called

Walzer, M. (1993) *Interpretation and Social Criticism*, Cambridge, MA: Harvard University Press.

Walzer, M. (1994) *Thick and Thin*, Notre Dame: University of Notre Dame Press.

Wasserman, H. (2016) 'Clinton on track to win the most votes. Abolish the electoral college', *The Progressive*: www.progressive.org/news/2016/11/189051/clinton-track-win-most-votes-abolish-electoral-college

Watson, B. (1996) *Han Fei Tzu: basic writings*, New York: Columbia University Press.

Watson, P. and Barber, B. (1990) *The Struggle for Democracy*, London: W. H. Allen.

Watson, T. and Hickman, M. (2012) *Dial M for Murdoch: News Corporation and the corruption of Britain*, London: Penguin.

Weil, P. (1996) 'Nationalities and citizenships', in Cesarani and Fulbrook (1996), pp 74-87.

Westen, D. (2007) *The Political Brain*, New York: Public Affairs.

Wetherell, M., Lafleche, M. and Berkeley, R. (eds) (2007) *Identity, Ethnic Diversity and Community Cohesion*, London: Sage Publications.

White, S. (2015) 'Will a constitutional convention democratically refound the British state?', *Open Democracy*: www.opendemocracy.net/ourkingdom/stuart-white/will-constitutional-convention-democratically-refound-british-state

White, S. and Leighton, D. (eds) (2008) *Building a Citizen Society: the emerging politics of republican democracy*, London: Lawrence & Wishart.

Wilkinson, R. and Pickett, K. (2010) *The Spirit Level: why equality is better for everyone*, London: Penguin Books.

Wilson, R. (2016) 'GOP platform calls for tough voter ID laws', *The Hill*: http://thehill.com/blogs/ballot-box/288302-gop-platform-calls-for-tough-voter-id-laws

Winkler, A. (2011) 'Did the Wild West have more gun control than we do today?', *Huffington Post*: www.huffingtonpost.com/adam-winkler/did-the-wild-west-have-mo_b_956035.html

Wright, E. O. (ed) (1995) *Associations and Democracy*, London: Verso.

Yamamura, K. (2017) *Too Much Stuff: capitalism in crisis*, Bristol: Policy Press.

Yao, X. (2000) *An Introduction to Confucianism*, Cambridge: Cambridge University Press.

YouGov Poll Report (2016) 'How Britain voted': https://yougov.co.uk/news/2016/06/27/how-britain-voted/

Young, M. (1994) *The Rise of the Meritocracy*, Piscataway: Transaction Publishers.

Žižek, S. (2011) *Living in the End Times*, New York: Verso.

Index